VOGUE® KNITTING

STITCHIONARY™ 2

The Ultimate Stitch Dictionary from the Editors of Vogue® Knitting Magazine

volume two
cables

VOGUE KNITTING
STITCHIONARY™ 2

The Ultimate Stitch Dictionary from the Editors of Vogue® Knitting Magazine

volume two
cables

Sixth&Spring Books
233 Spring Street
New York, New York 10013

Editorial Director
Trisha Malcolm

Book Editor
Carla Scott

Art Director
Chi Ling Moy

Graphic Designer
Sheena T. Paul

Project Coordinator
Eve Ng

Instructions Editors
Lisa Buccellato
Sandi Prosser

Technical Illustrations
Jane Fay
Uli Monch

Yarn Editors
Tanis Gray
Veronica Manno

Book Division Manager
Erica Smith

Production Manager
David Joinnides

President and Publisher, Sixth&Spring Books
Art Joinnides

1   3   5   7   9   10   8   6   4   2
Manufactured in China

Library of Congress Control Number: 2005934993
ISBN: 1-931543-89-5
ISBN-13: 978-1-931543-89-7

Photo Credits:
Jack Deutsch (Front cover, back cover, and all swatches)
Tom Wool (p. 9, 77)
Paul Amato (pp. 33, 85, 163)

contents

This second volume of the *Vogue Knitting Stitchionary* is on a subject near and dear to my heart—cables. Or rather, for the purpose of this book, it's "cables, cables and more cables!" I find the technique of making cables truly enjoyable—not only does it create a beautifully textured fabric, but it keeps your mind engaged in a unique way.

Where did cables originate? It is not known for sure, but they seem to have their origins in Celtic tradition, such as the Book of Kells with its incredible intertwining symbols. (This book, which is some 1200 years old, may even have an illustration of a cable-knit sweater!) On the Aran Islands off the west coast of Ireland, fishermen wear pullovers with a combination of cables that is unique to each person—hence the name Aran or Fisherman sweater. (Unfortunately, the one-of-a-kind pattern was said to identify a sailor if he washed up on shore.)

At *Vogue Knitting* we have the luxury of using these patterns for their sheer beauty. In my mind there is nothing more exciting than designing your own Aran piece, whether it be a full sweater, an afghan, or a pair of mittens. After swatching all the cables that you like, line them up next to each other and see what suits your fancy. Then find a shape and slot them in, using a basic stitch such as knit, purl, or a rib to separate the different patterns. Or you can use just one cable and center it down the front of a basic body or sleeve.

Our goal with this series of books is to challenge and inspire all those who knit or are just learning, and to entice those who have not yet tried this ever-rewarding skill. Let the fun begin!

Carla Scott

offset cables p. 91

how to use this book

The *Vogue Knitting Stitchionary, Volume 2: Cables* is divided into five chapters: Easy, Diamonds & Pretzels, Braids, Allover and Combinations. As in the first edition, we arranged the stitches in each chapter in order of difficulty, from the easiest to the hardest. In naming the stitches, for some swatches we used the most commonly recognized or descriptive names, while for others we just had fun in determining a title.

In order to accommodate your knitting preferences, we have used written instructions as well as charts to explain each stitch. All of the instructions use the *Vogue Knitting* style, with standard knitting abbreviations, easy-to-understand terminology and the internationally-recognized stitch symbols for the charts.

References to the specific cables used in the stitch are spelled out at the beginning of each instruction, so you do not have to flip back to a glossary to find the meaning of the cable.

We knitted the swatches using Aurora 8 from Karabella Yarns—a soft worsted weight 100% wool. This yarn is ideal for showing off the detailed twisting and turning of the cables. Most of the time, we used a background of purl stitches, which are not included in the instructions. We used sizes 7–8 (4.5–5mm) needles to knit the swatches. Note that if you use a different weight or textured yarn, the resulting look of the stitch may be different than what we show.

Always remember to make a gauge swatch with the yarn you are using for the project. This will make you familiar with the pattern stitch and you will know if that particular stitch worked well with the desired yarn. Because cables are so textured, it is best to use a more basic yarn to illuminate the pattern. Using a highly textured or very dark colored yarn may hide the inherent features of the cabling. And please note that some stitches are continuous, with pattern repeats, and some are panels that can be inserted into a design or combined with other stitches.

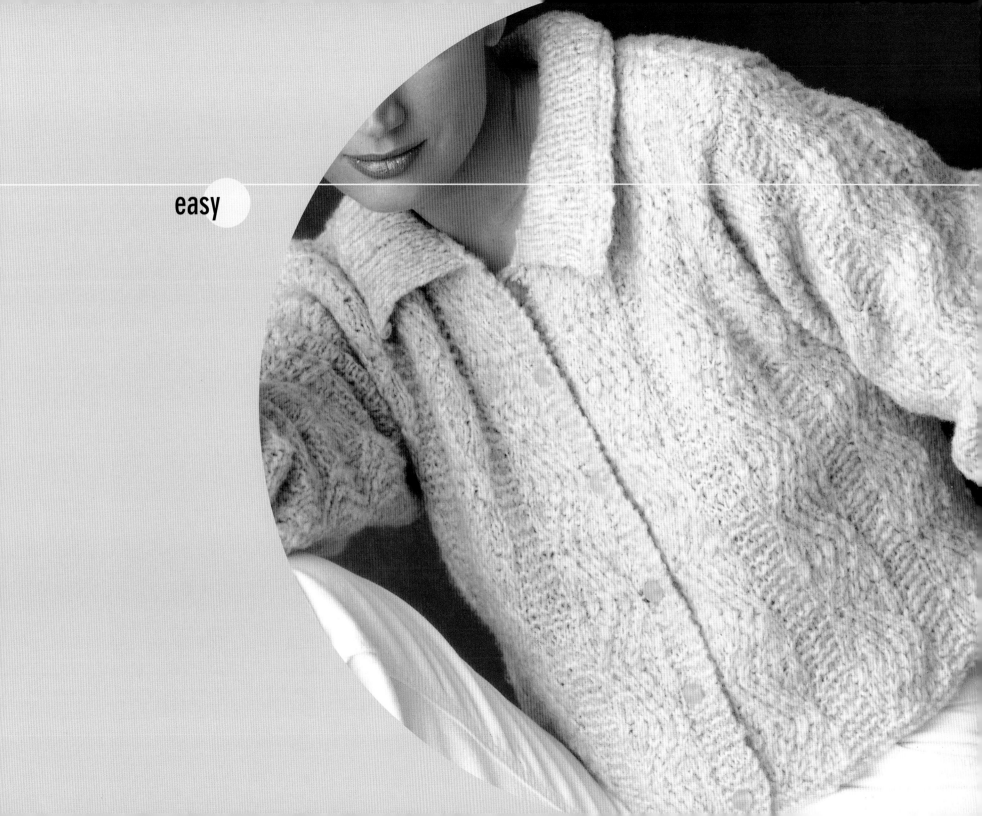

easy

1 right twist mock cable

RT K2tog leaving sts on needle, k first st, sl both sts from needle.

(multiple of 12 sts)

Row 1 (RS) *P1, RT, p1, k8; rep from * to end.

Row 2 *P8, k1, p2, k1; rep from * to end.

Rep rows 1 and 2.

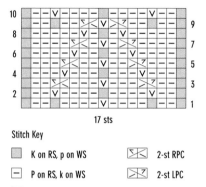

Stitch Key

▢ K on RS, p on WS

⊟ P on RS, k on WS

⧖ RT

2 tree of life cable

2-st RPC Sl 1 st to cn and hold to back, k1, p1 from cn.

2-st LPC Sl 1 st to cn and hold to front, p1, k1 from cn.

(worked over 17 sts)

Row 1 (RS) K1, p2, k1, p4, sl 1, p4, k1, p2, k1.

Row 2 P1, k2, sl 1, k4, p1, k4, sl 1, k2, p1.

Row 3 K1, p2, 2-st LPC, p3, sl 1, p3, 2-st RPC, p2, k1.

Row 4 P1, k3, sl 1, k3, p1, k3, sl 1, k3, p1.

Row 5 K1, p3, 2-st LPC, p2, sl 1, p2, 2-st RPC, p3, k1.

Row 6 P1, k4, sl 1, k2, p1, k2, sl 1, k4, p1.

Row 7 K1, p4, 2-st LPC, p1, sl 1, p1, 2-st RPC, p4, k1.

Row 8 P1, k5, sl 1, k1, p1, k1, sl 1, k5, p1.

Row 9 K1, p2, k1, p2, 2-st LPC, sl 1, 2-st RPC, p2, k1, p2, k1.

Row 10 P1, k2, sl 1, k4, p1, k4, sl 1, k2, p1.

Rep rows 1–10.

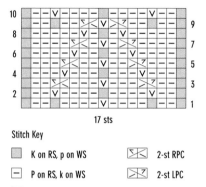

Stitch Key

▢ K on RS, p on WS

⊟ P on RS, k on WS

▽ Slip 1

⧖ 2-st RPC

⧗ 2-st LPC

3 woven twist

RT K2tog, do not sl off needle, k first st, sl both sts off needle.

LT K 2nd st tbl, do not sl off needle, k first st, sl both sts off needle.

2-st RPC Sl 1 st to cn and hold to back, k1, p1 from cn.

2-st LPC Sl 1 st to cn and hold to front, p1, k1 from cn.

(multiple of 4 sts plus 2)

Preparation row (WS) K2, *P2, k2; rep from * to end.

Row 1 P2, *LT, p2; rep from * to end.

Row 2 K2, *p2, k2; rep from * to end.

Row 3 P1, *2-st RPC, 2-st LPC; rep from *, end p1.

Row 4 K1, p1, k2*, p2, k2 rep from *, end p1, k1.

Row 5 P1, k1,*p2, RT; rep from *, end p2, k1, p1.

Row 6 K1, p1,*k2, p2; rep from * , end k2, p1, k1.

Row 7 P1, *2-st LPC, 2-st RPC; rep from *, end p1.

Row 8 *K2, p2; rep from *, end k2.

Rep rows 1–8.

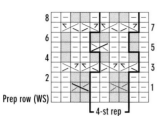

Prep row (WS)

4-st rep

Stitch Key

☐ K on RS, p on WS

☐ P on RS, k on WS

RT

LT

2-st RPC

2-st LPC

4 woven slip stitch

3-st RSC (right slipped cable) Sl 2 sts to cn and hold to back, k1, [k1, sl 1] from cn.

3-st LSC (left slipped cable) Sl 1 st to cn and hold to front, sl 1, k1, k1 from cn.

(multiple of 3 sts plus 5)

Note Sl all sts purlwise with yarn in back on RS rows and with yarn in front on WS rows.

Rows 1 and 3 (RS) K1, *k2, sl 1; rep from *, end k1.

Rows 2 and 4 K1,*sl 1, p2; rep from *, end k1.

Row 5 K1, *3-st RSC; rep from *, end k1.

Rows 6 and 8 K1, p3,*sl 1, p2; rep from *, end k1.

Row 7 K1,*k2, sl 1; rep from *, end k4.

Row 9 K1, k2,*3-st LSC; rep from *, end sl 1, k1.

Rep rows 2–9.

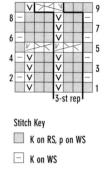

3-st rep

Stitch Key

☐ K on RS, p on WS

☐ K on WS

☑ Sl 1 purlwise wyib on RS, Sl 1 purlwise wyif on WS

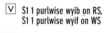

3-st RSC

3-st LSC

easy

5 brioche twist

MC K3tog loosely, but do not drop sts from LH needle, p same 3 sts tog, then k same 3 sts tog, drop sts from LH needle.

(multiple of 8 sts)

Rows 1 and 3 (RS) *P2, k3, p2, k next st into row below; rep from * to end.

Row 2 *P1, k2, p3, k2; rep from * to end.

Row 4 *P1, k2, 3-st MC, k2; rep from * to end.

Rep rows 1–4.

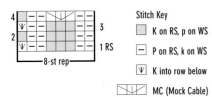

Stitch Key

- ☐ K on RS, p on WS
- ⊟ P on RS, k on WS
- ⱴ K into row below
- ⋈ MC (Mock Cable)

6 braided rib

RT P 2nd st on LH needle, leave st on needle, p first st, sl both sts from needle.

LT With RH needle behind work, k 2nd st on LH needle tbl, leave st on needle, then k first st through front loop, sl both sts from needle.

(multiple of 7 sts plus 2)

Row 1 (RS) P1, *p2, LT, k1, p2; rep from *, end p1.

Row 2 K1, *k2, RT, p1, k2; rep from *, end k1.

Rep rows 1 and 2.

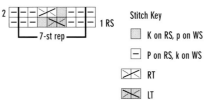

Stitch Key

- ☐ K on RS, p on WS
- ⊟ P on RS, k on WS
- ⋈ RT
- ⋈ LT

⑤ ⑥

easy

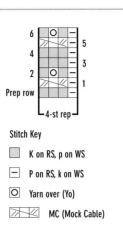

7 wrap mock cable

MC Sl 1, k2, pass sl st over k2.

(multiple of 4 sts)

Preparation row (WS) *P3, k1; rep from * to end.

Row 1 (RS) *P1, 3-st MC; rep from * to end.

Row 2 *P1, yo, p1, k1; rep from * to end.

Row 3 *P1, k3; rep from * to end.

Row 4 *P3, k1; rep from * to end.

Row 5 *P1, MC; rep from * to end.

Row 6 *P1, yo, p1, k1; rep from * to end.

Rep rows 1–6.

Stitch Key

☐ K on RS, p on WS

⊟ P on RS, k on WS

⊡ Yarn over (Yo)

⬓ MC (Mock Cable)

8 cross cable panel

2-st RC Sl 1 st to cn and hold to back, k1, k1 from cn.

2-st LC Sl 1 st to cn and hold to front, k1, k1 from cn.

2-st RPC Sl 1 st to cn and hold to back, k1, p1 from cn.

2-st LPC Sl 1 st to cn and hold to front, p1, k1 from cn.

(worked over 8 sts)

Row 1 (RS) 2-st LC, p4, 2-st RC.

Row 2 P2, k4, p2.

Row 3 K1, 2-st LPC, p2, 2-st RPC, k1.

Row 4 P1, k1, p1, k2, p1, k1, p1.

Row 5 K1, p1, 2-st LPC, 2-st RPC, p1, k1.

Row 6 P1, k2, p2, k2, p1.

Row 7 K1, p2, 2-st LC, p2, k1.

Row 8 P1, k2, p2, k2, p1.

Row 9 K1, p1, 2-st RPC, 2-st LPC, p1, k1.

Row 10 P1, k1, p1, k2, p1, k1, p1.

Row 11 K1, 2-st RPC, p2, 2-st LPC, k1.

Row 12 P2, k4, p2.

Rep rows 1–12.

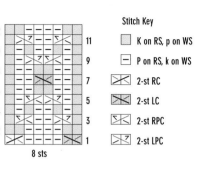

Stitch Key

☐ K on RS, p on WS

⊟ P on RS, k on WS

⧓ 2-st RC

⧓ 2-st LC

⧓ 2-st RPC

⧓ 2-st LPC

2-st RPC Sl 1 st to cn and hold to back, k1 tbl, p1 from cn.

2-st LPC Sl 1 st to cn and hold to front, p1, k1 from cn.

2-st RPC-WS Sl 1 st to cn and hold to back, p1 tbl, p1 tbl from cn.

(worked over 32 sts)

Row 1 (RS) *[2-st LPC] twice, p2, 2-st RPC, 2-st LPC, p2, [2-st RPC] twice; rep from * once more.

Row 2 [K1, p1 tbl] twice, [k2, p1 tbl] 3 times, [k1, p1 tbl, k2, p1 tbl] twice, [k2, p1 tbl] twice, k1, p1 tbl, k1.

Row 3 P1, * [2-st LPC] twice, 2-st RPC, p2, 2-st LPC, [2-st RPC] twice*, p2, rep between *'s

once more, p1.

Row 4 K2, *p1 tbl, k1, [p1 tbl] twice, k4, [p1 tbl] twice, k1, p1 tbl*, k4, rep between *'s once more, k2.

Row 5 P2, [2-st LPC] twice, p4, [2-st RPC] twice, p4, [2-st LPC] twice, p4, [2-st RPC] twice, p2.

Row 6 K3, p1 tbl, k1, p1 tbl, k4, p1 tbl, k1, [p1 tbl] twice, k4, [p1 tbl] twice, k1, p1 tbl, k4, p1 tbl, k1, p1 tbl, k3.

Row 7 P3, [2-st LPC] twice, p2, [2-st RPC] twice, 2-st LPC, p2, 2-st RPC, [2-st LPC] twice, p2, [2-st RPC] twice, p3.

Row 8 K4, [p1 tbl, k1, p1 tbl, k2] twice, p1 tbl, k2, p1 tbl, [k2, p1 tbl, k1, p1 tbl] twice, k4.

Row 9 P4, [2-st LPC] twice, [2-st RPC] twice, p2, 2-st LPC, 2-st RPC, p2, [2-st LPC] twice, [2-st RPC] twice, p4.

Row 10 K5, *p1 tbl, k1, 2-st RPC-WS, k1, p1 tbl*, k4, 2-st RPC-WS, k4, rep between *'s once more, k5.

Row 11 P4, [2-st RPC] twice, [2-st LPC] twice, p2, 2-st RPC, 2-st LPC, p2, [2-st RPC] twice, [2-st LPC] twice, p4.

Row 12 Rep row 8.

Row 13 P3, [2-st RPC] twice, p2, [2-st LPC] twice, 2-st RPC, p2, 2-st LPC, [2-st RPC] twice, p2, [2-st LPC] twice, p3.

Row 14 Rep row 6.

Row 15 P2, [2-st RPC] twice, p4, [2-st LPC]

twice, p4, [2-st RPC] twice, p4, [2-st LPC] twice, p2.

Row 16 Rep row 4.

Row 17 P1, *[2-st RPC] twice, 2-st LPC, p2, 2-st RPC, [2-st LPC] twice*, p2, rep between *'s once more, p1.

Row 18 Rep row 2.

Row 19 *[2-st RPC] twice, p2, 2-st LPC, 2-st RPC, p2, [2-st LPC] twice; rep from * once more.

Row 20 P1 tbl, k1, p1 tbl, k4, 2-st RPC-WS, k4, p1 tbl, k1, 2-st RPC-WS, k1, p1 tbl, k4, 2-st RPC-WS, k4, p1 tbl, k1, p1 tbl.

Rep rows 1–20.

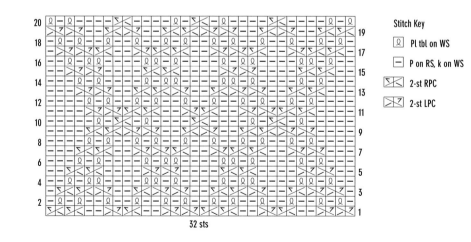

Stitch Key

- Ⴍ P1 tbl on WS
- — P on RS, k on WS
- ⊠ 2-st RPC
- ⊠ 2-st LPC

32 sts

RT K2tog leaving sts on LH needle, insert RH needle from front between 2 sts just knitted tog and k first st again, then sl both sts from needle tog.
LT With RH needle behind LH needle, skip first st and k 2nd st tbl, insert RH needle into backs of both sts and k2tog tbl.
(multiple of 14 sts)
Row 1 (RS) *[RT] 5 times, k4; rep from * to end.
Row 2 and all WS rows *K4, p10; rep from * to end.
Row 3 *K3, [RT] 3 times, k5; rep from * to end.
Row 5 *K2, [RT] 3 times, k6; rep from * to end.
Row 7 *K1, [RT] 3 times, k7; rep from * to end.
Row 9 Rep row 1.
Row 11 *[LT] 5 times, k4; rep from * to end.
Row 13 *K1, [LT] 3 times, k7; rep from * to end.
Row 15 *K2, [LT] 3 times, k6; rep from * to end.
Row 17 *K3, [LT] 3 times, k5; rep from * to end.
Row 19 *[LT] 5 times, k4; rep from * to end.
Row 20 Rep row 2.
Rep rows 1–20 .

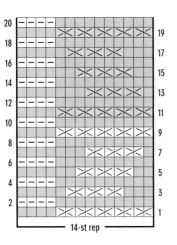

14-st rep

Stitch Key
K on RS, p on WS
— P on RS, k on WS
RT
LT

easy

RT K2tog leaving sts on LH needle, insert RH needle from front between 2 sts just knitted tog and k first st again, then sl both sts from needle tog.
(multiple of 9 sts plus 2)
Row 1 (WS) K1, *p4, k5; rep from *, end k1.
Row 2 P1, *p5, RT twice; rep from *, end p1.
Row 3 Rep row 1.
Row 4 P1, *p5, k1, RT, k1; rep from *, end p1.
Rep rows 1–4.

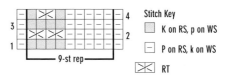

9-st rep

Stitch Key
K on RS, p on WS
— P on RS, k on WS
RT

RT K2tog leaving sts on LH needle, insert RH needle from front between 2 sts knit tog and k first st again, sl both sts from needle.

LT With RH needle behind LH needle, sk first st and k 2nd st tbl, insert RH needle into backs of both sts and k2tog tbl. (work over 78 sts)

Row 1 (RS) K1, [LT] 6 times, [RT] 7 times, p4, [RT] 7 times, LT, p4, [LT] 6 times, [RT] 7 times, k1.

Row 2 P26, k5, p16, k5, p26.

Row 3 K2, [LT] 5 times, [RT] 7 times, p4, [RT] 7 times, [LT] 2 times, p4, [LT] 5 times, [RT] 7 times, k2.

Row 4 P25, k5, p18, k5, p25.

Row 5 K3, [LT] 4 times, [RT] 7 times, p4, [RT] 7 times, [LT] 3 times, p4, [LT] 4 times, [RT] 7 times, k3.

Row 6 P24, k5, p20, k5, p24.

Row 7 K4, [LT] 3 times, [RT] 7 times, p4, [RT] 7 times, [LT] 4 times, p4, [LT] 3 times, [RT] 7 times, k4.

Row 8 P23, k5, p22, k5, p23.

Row 9 K5, [LT] 2 times, [RT] 7 times, p4, [RT] 7 times, [LT] 5 times, p4, [LT] 2 times, [RT] 7 times, k5.

Row 10 P22, k5, p24, k5, p22.

Row 11 K6, LT, [RT] 7 times, p4, [RT] 7 times, [LT] 6 times, p4, LT, [RT] 7 times, k6.

Row 12 P21, k5, p26, k5, p21.

Row 13 K7, [RT] 7 times, p4, [RT] 7 times, [LT] 7 times, p4, [RT] 7 times, k7.

Row 14 P21, k5, p26, k5, p21.

Row 15 K6, [RT] 7 times, LT, p4, [LT] 6 times, [RT] 7 times, p4, [RT] 7 times, LT, k6.

Row 16 Rep row 10.

Row 17 K5, [RT] 7 times, [LT] 2 times, p4, [LT] 5 times, [RT] 7 times, p4, [RT] 7 times, [LT] 2 times, k5.

Row 18 Rep row 8.

Row 19 K4, [RT] 7 times, [LT] 3 times, p4, [LT] 4 times, [RT] 7 times, p4, [RT] 7 times, [LT] 3 times, k4.

Row 20 Rep row 6.

Row 21 K3, [RT] 7 times, [LT] 4 times, p4, [LT] 3 times, [RT] 7 times, p4, [RT] 7 times, [LT] 4 times, k3.

Row 22 Rep row 4.

Row 23 K2, [RT] 7 times, [LT] 5 times, p4, [LT] 2 times, [RT] 7 times, p4, [RT] 7 times, [LT] 5 times, k2.

Row 24 Rep row 2.

Row 25 K1, [RT] 7 times, [LT] 6 times, p4, LT, [RT] 7 times, p4, [RT] 7 times, [LT] 6 times, k1.

Row 26 P27, k5, p14, k5, p27.

Row 27 [RT] 7 times, [LT] 7 times, p4, [RT] 7 times, p4, [RT] 7 times, [LT] 7 times.

Row 28 Rep row 26.

Rep rows 1–28.

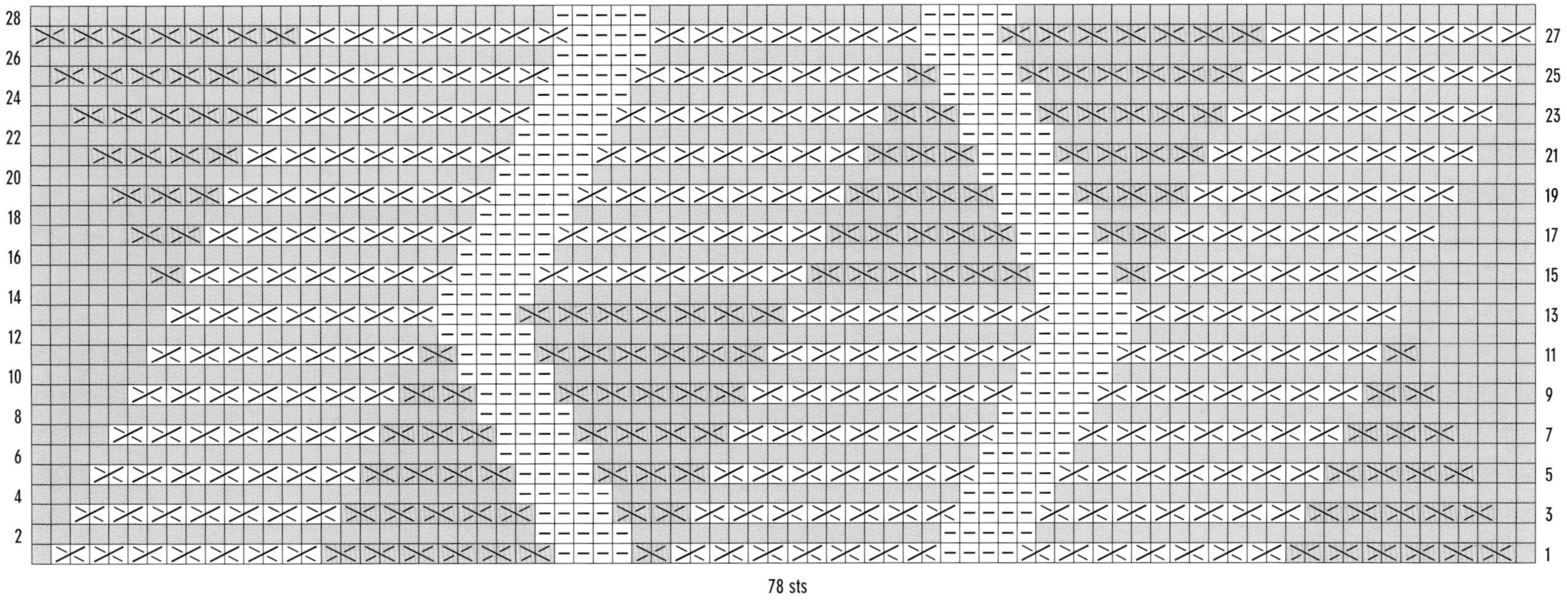

78 sts

Stitch Key

	K on RS, p on WS		RT
—	P on RS, k on WS		LT

2-st RPC (tbl) On RS: Sl 1 st to cn and hold to back, k1tbl, p1 from cn.
On WS: Sl 1 st to cn and hold to back, k1, p1 tbl from cn.

2-st LPC (tbl) On RS: Sl 1 st to cn and hold to front, p1, k1tbl from cn.
On WS: Sl 1 st to cn and hold to front, p1 tbl, k1 from cn.

2-st RC (tbl) On RS: Sl 1 st to cn and hold to back, k1tbl, k1 from cn.
On WS: Sl 1 st to cn and hold to back, p1, p1 tbl from cn.

2-st LC (tbl) On RS: Sl 1 st to cn and hold to front, k1, k1tbl from cn.
On WS: Sl 1 st to cn and hold to front, p1 tbl, p1 from cn.

3-st C (tbl) Sl 2 sts to cn and hold to front, k1tbl, with LH needle in back of cn, sl first st on cn to LH needle, k rem st on cn, k st on LH needle tbl. (worked over 15 sts)

Rows 1, 3, 11 and 13 (RS) K7, wyib sl 1, k7.

Rows 2, 4, 10, 12, and 14 Purl.

Row 5 K5, 2-st RC, wyib sl 1, 2-st LC, k5.

Row 6 P4, 2-st LC, p3, 2-st RC, p4.

Row 7 K3, 2-st RC, k2, wyib sl 1, k2, 2-st LC, k3.

Row 8 P2, 2-st LC, p7, 2-st RC, p2.

Row 9 K1, 2-st RC, k4, wyib sl 1, k4, 2-st LC, k1.

Rows 15–19 Rep rows 5–9.

Row 20 P5, 2-st LPC, p1, 2-st RPC, p5.

Row 21 K4, 2-st RPC, k1, p1, k1, 2-st LPC, k4.

Row 22 P3, 2-st LPC, [p1, k1] twice, p1, 2-st RPC, p3.

Row 23 K5, [p1, k1] 3 times, k4.

Row 24 P3, wyib sl 1, [k1, p1] 3 times, k1, wyib sl 1, p3.

Row 25 K3, 2-st LC, [p1, k1] twice, p1, 2-st RC, k3.

Row 26 P2, 2-st LPC, 2-st RC, k1, p1, k1, 2-st LC, 2-st RPC, p2.

Row 27 K5, 2-st LC, p1, 2-st RC, K5.

Row 28 P2, 2-st RC, k1, 2-st LPC, p1, 2-st RPC, k1, 2-st LC, p2.

Row 29 K3, 2-st LC, k2, p1, k2, 2-st RC, k3.

Row 30 P4, 2-st RC, k1, p1, k1, 2-st LC, p4.

Row 31 K5, 2-st LC, p1, 2-st RC, k5.

Row 32 P6, 3-st C, p6.

Row 33 K15.

Row 34 P15.

Rep rows 1–34.

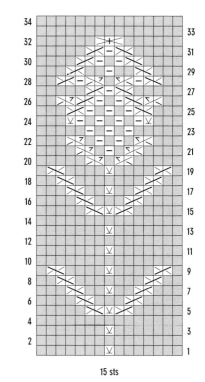

15 sts

Stitch Key

K on RS, p on WS

— P on RS, k on WS

∨ Sl 1 purlwise wyib

2-st RPC (tbl)

2-st LPC (tbl)

2-st RC (tbl)

2-st LC (tbl)

3-st C (tbl)

RT On RS rows: Skip next st on LH needle and k the 2nd st, then k the skipped st and sl both sts from LH needle.

On WS rows: Skip next st on LH needle and p the 2nd st, then p the skipped st and sl both sts from LH needle.

LT On RS rows: With RH needle behind LH needle skip next st on LH needle and k the 2nd st in back lp, then k the skipped st in front lp and sl both sts from LH needle.

On WS rows: With RH needle behind LH needle, skip next st on LH needle and p the 2nd st in back lp, then p the skipped st in front lp and sl both sts from LH needle.

(worked over 22 sts)

Row 1 (RS) [P2, k1] 3 times, p4, [k1, p2] 3 times.

Row 2 K2, [RT, k1] twice, RT, k2, [LT, k1] twice, LT, k2.

Row 3 P3, [k1, p2] twice, LT, RT, [p2, k1] twice, p3.

Row 4 K3, RT, k1, RT, [k2, LT] twice, k1, LT, k3.

Row 5 P4, k1, p2, k1, p1, RT, LT, p1, k1, p2, k1, p4.

Row 6 K4, p1, k2, p1, k1, p1, k2, p1, k1, p1, k2, p1, k4.

Row 7 P4, k1, p2, k1, p1, LT, RT, p1, k1, p2, k1, p4.

Row 8 K3, LT, k1, [LT, k2] twice, RT, k1, RT, k3.

Row 9 P3, [k1, p2] twice, RT, LT, [p2, k1] twice, p3.

Row 10 K2, [LT, k1] twice, LT, k2, [RT, k1] twice, RT, k2.

Rep rows 1–10.

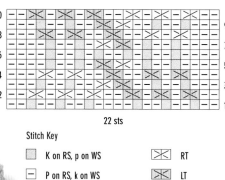

22 sts

Stitch Key

☐ K on RS, p on WS	✕ RT
— P on RS, k on WS	✕ LT

easy

4-st RC Sl 2 sts to cn and hold to back, k2, k2 from cn. (worked over 4 sts)

Row 1 (RS) 4-st RC.

Row 2 Purl.

Rep rows 1–2.

Stitch Key

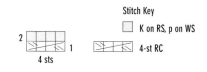

☐ K on RS, p on WS	
4 sts	✕ 4-st RC

14

15

6-st LC Sl next 3 sts to cn and hold to front, k3, k3 from cn.

(multiple of 7 sts)

Row 1 (RS) *K6, p1; rep from * to end.

Row 2 and all WS rows *K1, p6; rep from * to end.

Row 3 *6-st LC, p1; rep from * to end.

Rows 5 and 7 *K6, p1; rep from * to end.

Row 8 *K1, p6; rep from * to end.

Rep rows 1–8.

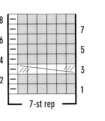

7-st rep

Stitch Key

☐ K on RS, p on WS

⊟ P on RS, k on WS

▱ 6-st LC

4-st RC Sl 2 sts to cn and hold to back, k2, k2 from cn.

4-st LC Sl 2 sts to cn and hold to front, k2, k2 from cn.

(worked over 9 sts)

Row 1 (RS) K4, p1, k4.

Row 2 P4, k1, p4.

Row 3 4-st RC, p1, 4-st LC.

Row 4 Rep row 2.

Rep rows 1–4.

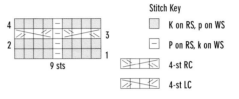

9 sts

Stitch Key

☐ K on RS, p on WS

⊟ P on RS, k on WS

▱ 4-st RC

▱ 4-st LC

18 twisted taffy

8-st RC Sl 4 sts to cn and hold to back, k4, k4 from cn.
(worked over 8 sts)
Rows 1, 3 and 5 Knit.
Row 2 and all WS rows Purl.
Row 7 8-st RC.
Row 8 Rep row 2.
Rep rows 1–8.

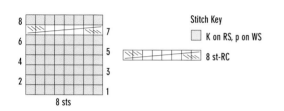

Stitch Key

☐ K on RS, p on WS

8 st-RC

19 retwisted taffy

8-st LC Sl 4 sts to cn and hold to front, k4, k4 from cn.
(worked over 8 sts)
Rows 1, 3 and 5 Knit.
Row 2 and all WS rows Purl.
Row 7 8-st LC.
Row 8 Rep row 2.
Rep rows 1–8.

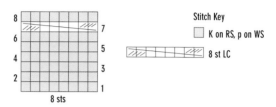

Stitch Key

☐ K on RS, p on WS

8 st LC

easy

20 relaxed cable

8-st LC Sl 4 sts to cn and hold to front, k4, k4 from cn.
(worked over 8 sts)
Rows 1, 3, 5, 7, 11, 13 and 15 (RS) Knit.
Row 2 and all WS rows Purl.
Row 9 8-st LC.
Row 16 Rep row 2.
Rep rows 1–16.

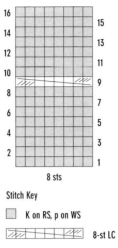

8 sts

Stitch Key

K on RS, p on WS

8-st LC

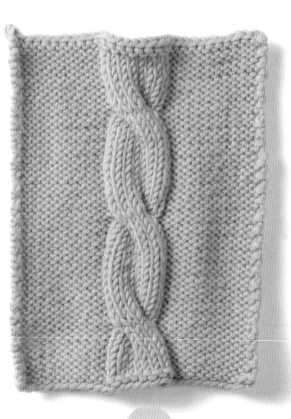

21 simple snake

6-st RPC Sl 3 sts to cn and hold to back, k3, p3 from cn.
6-st LPC Sl 3 sts to cn and hold to front, p3, k3 from cn.
(worked over 9 sts)
Row 1 (RS) 6-st LPC, p3.
Row 2 K3, p3, k3.
Row 3 P3, 6-st LPC.
Rows 4, 6 and 8 P3, k6.
Rows 5 and 7 P6, k3.
Row 9 P3, 6-st RPC.
Row 10 K3, p3, k3.
Row 11 6-st RPC, p3.
Rows 12 and 14 K6, p3.
Rows 13 and 15 K3, p6.
Row 16 Rep row 12.
Rep rows 1–16.

9 sts

Stitch Key

K on RS, p on WS

P on RS, k on WS

6-st RPC

6-st LPC

easy

16-st LC Sl 8 sts to cn and hold to front, k8, k8 from cn.
(worked over 16 sts)

Row 1 (RS) Knit.

Row 2 and all WS rows Purl.

Row 3 16-st LC.

Rows 5, 7, 9, 11, 13 and 15 Knit.

Row 16 Rep row 2.

Rep rows 1–16.

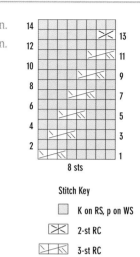

16 sts

Stitch Key

☐ K on RS, p on WS

16-st LC

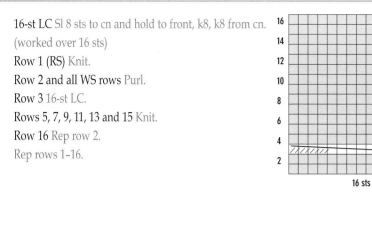

3-st RC Sl 1 st to cn and hold to back, k2, k1 from cn.

2-st RC Sl 1 st to cn and hold to back, k1, k1 from cn.
(worked over 8 sts)

Row 1 (RS) K5, 3-st RC.

Row 2 and all WS rows Purl.

Row 3 K4, 3-st RC, k1.

Row 5 K3, 3-st RC, k2.

Row 7 K2, 3-st RC, k3.

Row 9 K1, 3-st RC, k4.

Row 11 3-st RC, k5.

Row 13 2-st RC, k6.

Row 14 Purl.

Rep rows 1–14.

8 sts

Stitch Key

☐ K on RS, p on WS

⧖ 2-st RC

⧖ 3-st RC

24 scalloped cable

12-st LPC Sl 6 st to cn and hold to front, p6, k6 from cn.

(worked over 12 sts)

Row 1 (RS) P6, k6.

Row 2 P6, k6.

Row 3 12-st LPC.

Row 4 Rep row 2.

Rows 5-14 Rep rows 1 and 2 five times.

Rep rows 3–14.

Stitch Key

□ K on RS, p on WS

⊟ P on RS, k on WS

12-st LPC

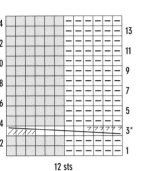

25 gathered cable

12-st TC (twist cable) Sl all 12 sts to dpn. Turn dpn one half turn clockwise. Working loosely, k sts from dpn.

(worked over 12 sts)

Row 1 (RS) Knit.

Row 2 and all WS rows Purl.

Row 3 12-st TC.

Rows 5, 7, 9, 11 and 13 Knit.

Row 14 Purl.

Rep rows 1–14.

Stitch Key

□ K on RS, p on WS

12-st TC

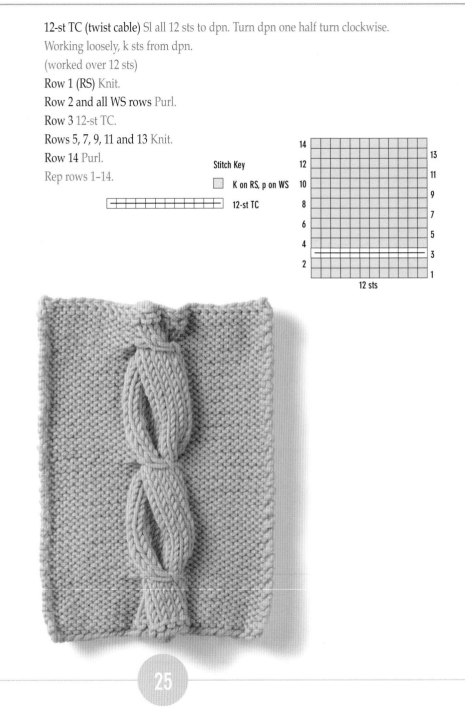

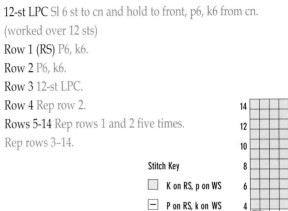

(worked over 15 sts)

Row 1 (RS) K5, p5, k5.

Rows 2-10 K the knit and p the purl sts.

Row 11 With an extra needle, work the first 5 sts in St st for 6 rows. Place sts on a safety pin for the RH strip. Cut yarn. Sl next 5 sts to holder and hold to back. Attach yarn and work the last 5 sts in st st for 6 rows. Place sts on a safety pin for the LH strip. Cut yarn. Wrap the RH strip in front of and around the LH strip to form a knot, let the RH (new LH) strip fall to the front of the work; sl sts from the safety pin of the LH (new RH) strip back to the LH needle and k5, p the sts from the holder, then sl sts from safety pin of the last strip back to LH needle and knit them.

Row 12 Rep row 2.

Rep rows 1–12.

Stitch Key

☐ K on RS, p on WS

⊟ P on RS, k on WS

▦ Tied Cable

15 sts

easy

13-st Rib RC Sl 6 sts to cn and hold to back, [k1 tbl, p1] 3 times, k1 tbl; taking care not to twist sts, cont in rib from cn as foll: [p1, k1 tbl] 3 times.

(worked over 13 sts)

Rows 1, 3, 5, 7 and 11 (RS) [K1 tbl, p1] 6 times, k1 tbl.

Row 2 and all WS rows [P1 tbl, k1] 6 times, p1 tbl.

Row 9 13-st RC.

Row 12 Rep row 2.

Rep rows 1–12.

Stitch Key

Ⴍ K tbl on RS rows, p tbl on WS rows

⊟ P on RS, k on WS

13-st rib RC

13 sts

6-st RC Sl 3 sts to cn and hold to back, k3, k3 from cn.

6-st LC Sl 3 sts to cn and hold to front, k3, k3 from cn.

(worked over 13 sts)

Rows 1 and 5 (RS) K6, p1, k6.

Row 2 and all WS rows P6, k1, p6.

Row 3 6-st RC, p1, 6-st LC.

Row 6 Rep row 2.

Rep rows 1–6.

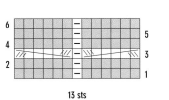

13 sts

Stitch Key

▢ K on RS, p on WS

━ P on RS, k on WS

⬚ 6-st RC

⬚ 6-st LC

3-st RC Sl 2 sts to cn and hold to back, k1, k2 from cn.

3-st LC Sl 1 st to cn and hold to front, k2, k1 from cn.

(worked over 6 sts)

Row 1 (RS) Knit.

Rows 2 and 4 Purl.

Row 3 3-st RC, 3-st LC.

Row 5 Knit.

Row 6 Rep row 2.

Rep rows 1–6.

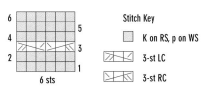

6 sts

Stitch Key

▢ K on RS, p on WS

⬚ 3-st LC

⬚ 3-st RC

28

29

30 horseshoe I

6-st RC Sl 3 sts to cn and hold to back, k3, k3 from cn.
6-st LC Sl 3 sts to cn and hold to front, k3, k3 from cn.
(worked over 12 sts)
Rows 1, 5 and 7 (RS) Knit.
Row 2 and all WS rows Purl.
Row 3 6-st RC, 6-st LC.
Row 8 Rep row 2.
Rep rows 1–8.

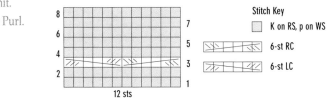

Stitch Key

☐ K on RS, p on WS

6-st RC

6-st LC

12 sts

31 horseshoe II

6-st RC Sl 3 sts to cn and
hold to back, k3, k3 from cn.
6-st LC Sl 3 sts to cn
and hold to front, k3, k3 from cn.
(worked over 12 sts)
Rows 1, 3, 7 and 9 Knit.
Row 2 and all WS rows Purl.
Row 5 6-st RC, 6-st LC.
Row 10 Rep row 2.
Rep rows 1–10.

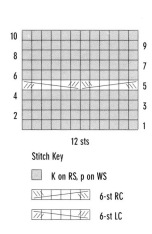

12 sts

Stitch Key

☐ K on RS, p on WS

6-st RC

6-st LC

easy

30

31

32 nested cable

10-st RC Sl 5 sts to cn and hold to back, k5, k5 from cn.

10-st LC Sl 5 sts to cn and hold to front, k5, k5 from cn.

(worked over 20 sts)

Rows 1, 3 and 5 (RS) Knit.

Rows 2, 4 and 6 Purl.

Row 7 10-st RC, 10-st LC.

Row 8 Rep row 2.

Rep rows 1–8.

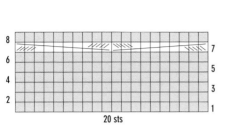

Stitch Key

K on RS, p on WS

10-st RC

10-st LC

33 drunken cable

10-st LC Sl 5 sts to cn and hold to front, k5, k5 from cn.

10-st RC Sl 5 sts to cn and hold to back, k5, k5 from cn.

(worked over 20 sts)

Rows 1, 7 and 9 (RS) Knit.

Row 2 and all WS rows Purl.

Row 3 K10, 10-st LC.

Row 5 10-st RC, k10.

Row 10 Rep row 2.

Rep rows 1–10.

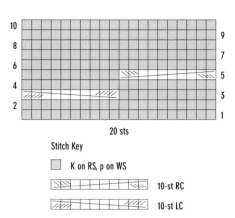

Stitch Key

K on RS, p on WS

10-st RC

10-st LC

34 ribbed horseshoe

8-st Rib RC Sl 4 sts to cn and hold to back, k1, p2, k1; then k1, p2, k1 from cn.

8-st Rib LC Sl 4 sts to cn and hold to front, k1, p2, k1; then k1, p2, k1 from cn.

(worked over 16 sts)

Rows 1, 5, 7 and 9 (RS) K1, [p2, k2] 3 times, p2, k1.

Row 2 and all WS rows P1, [k2, p2] 3 times, k2, p1.

Row 3 8-st RC, 8-st LC.

Row 10 Rep row 2.

Rep rows 1–10.

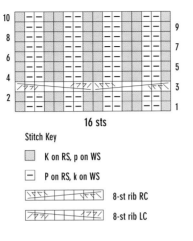

16 sts

Stitch Key

☐ K on RS, p on WS

– P on RS, k on WS

8-st rib RC

8-st rib LC

35 snow angels

6-st RC Sl 3 sts to cn and hold to back, k3, k3 from cn.

6-st LC Sl 3 sts to cn and hold to front, k3, k3 from cn.

(worked over 22 sts)

Row 1 (RS) P5, k6, p1, k6, p4.

Rows 2 and 4 K4, p6, k1, p6, k5.

Row 3 P5, 6-st RC, p1, 6-st LC, p4.

Row 5 P4, k2tog, k5, yo, p1, yo, k5, SKP, p3.

Row 6 K3, p7, k1, p7, k4.

Row 7 P3, k2tog, k6, yo, p1, yo, k6, SKP, p2.

Row 8 K2, p8, k1, p8, k3.

Row 9 P2, k2tog, k7, yo, p1, yo, k7, SKP, p1.

Row 10 K1, p9, k1, p9, k2.

Row 11 P1, k2tog, k8, yo, p1, yo, k8, SKP.

Row 12 Purl.

Rep rows 3–12.

easy

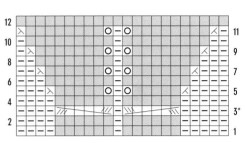

22 sts

Stitch Key

☐ K on RS, p on WS

– P on RS, k on WS

◹ K2tog

◺ SKP

○ Yo

6-st RC

6-st LC

34

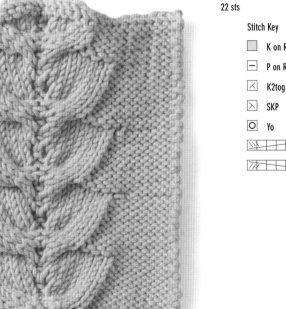

35

36 column twist

8-st RC Sl 4 sts to cn and hold to back, k4, k4 from cn.

(worked over 11 sts)

Rows 1, 5, 9, 27 and 29 (RS) P2, k7, p2.

Rows 2 and 4 K2, [p1, k1] 3 times, p1, k2.

Row 3 P2, [k1, p1] 3 times, k1, p2.

Rows 6 and 8 K2, p7, k2.

Rows 7 and 25 Purl.

Row 10 Knit.

Row 11 P2, k3, M1, k4, p2.

Rows 12, 14, 16, 18, 20 and 22 K2, p8, k2.

Rows 13, 15, 19, 21 and 23 P2, k8, p2.

Row 17 P2, 8-st RC, p2.

Row 24 K2, p3, p2tog, p3, k2.

Row 26 K2, p7, k2.

Row 28 Knit.

Row 30 Rep row 26.

Rep rows 1–30.

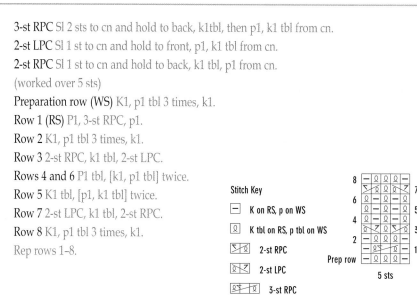

11 sts

Stitch Key

☐ K on RS, p on WS

— P on RS, k on WS

M M1 st

⬚ P2 tog on WS

⬚ 8-st RC

37 string of pearls

3-st RPC Sl 2 sts to cn and hold to back, k1tbl, then p1, k1 tbl from cn.

2-st LPC Sl 1 st to cn and hold to front, p1, k1 tbl from cn.

2-st RPC Sl 1 st to cn and hold to back, k1 tbl, p1 from cn.

(worked over 5 sts)

Preparation row (WS) K1, p1 tbl 3 times, k1.

Row 1 (RS) P1, 3-st RPC, p1.

Row 2 K1, p1 tbl 3 times, k1.

Row 3 2-st RPC, k1 tbl, 2-st LPC.

Rows 4 and 6 P1 tbl, [k1, p1 tbl] twice.

Row 5 K1 tbl, [p1, k1 tbl] twice.

Row 7 2-st LPC, k1 tbl, 2-st RPC.

Row 8 K1, p1 tbl 3 times, k1.

Rep rows 1–8.

Stitch Key

— K on RS, p on WS

Ω K tbl on RS, p tbl on WS

⬚ 2-st RPC

⬚ 2-st LPC

⬚ 3-st RPC

Prep row

5 sts

8-st RC Sl 4 sts to cn and hold to back, k4, k4 from cn.

(worked over 8 sts)

Rows 1, 3, 5, 7, 9, 11, 13, 15, 17, 19, 21 and 23 (WS) Knit.

Rows 2, 4, 6, 8 and 10 P4, k4.

Rows 12 and 24 8-st RC.

Rows 14, 16, 18, 20 and 22 K4, p4.

Rep rows 1–24.

8 sts

Stitch Key

☐ K on RS, p on WS

— P on RS, k on WS

▨ 8-st RC

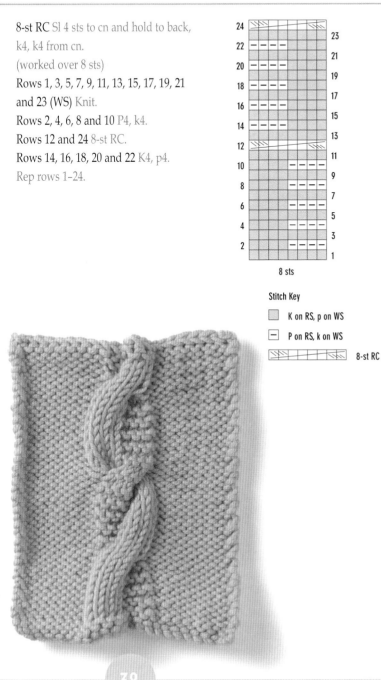

easy

6-st RCP Sl 3 sts to cn and hold to back, p1, k1, p1; k3 from cn.

6-st LCP Sl 3 sts to cn and hold to front, k3, p1, k1, p1 from cn.

6-st RCK Sl 3 sts to cn and hold to back, k1, p1, k1; k3 from cn.

6-st LCK Sl 3 sts to cn and hold to front, k3; k1, p1, k1 from cn.

(worked over 12 sts)

Rows 1, 3, 17, 19, 21 and 23 (RS) K3, [p1, k1] twice, p1, k4.

Rows 2, 4, 16, 18, 20 and 22 P3, [k1, p1] 2 times, k1, p4.

Row 5 6-st RCP, 6-st LCK.

Rows 6, 8, 10, 12 and 14 K1, p1, k1, p7, k1, p1.

Rows 7, 9, 11 and 13 P1, k1, p1, k7, p1, k1.

Row 15 6-st LCP, 6-st RCK

Row 24 Rep row 2.

Rep rows 1–24.

12 sts

Stitch Key

☐ K on RS, p on WS

— P on RS, k on WS

▨ 6-st RCP

▨ 6-st LCP

▨ 6-st RCK

▨ 6-st LCK

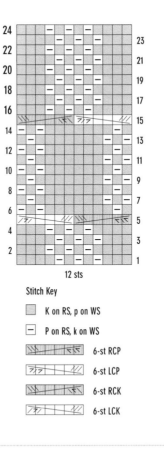

40 cruller

6-st RC Sl 3 sts to cn and hold to back, k3, k3 from cn.
(worked over 6 sts)

Rows 1, 3 and 11 (RS) K2, p2, k2.

Rows 2 and 4 P2, k2, p2.

Rows 5 and 9 6-st RC.

Rows 6, 8 and 10 Purl.

Row 7 Knit.

Row 12 Rep row 2.

Rep rows 1–12.

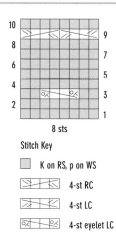

6 sts

Stitch Key

☐ K on RS, p on WS

⊟ P on RS, k on WS

▨▨▨ 6-st RC

41 wisteria

4-st eyelet LC Sl 2 sts to cn and hold to front, yo, k2tog; k2tog, yo from cn.

4-st RC Sl 2 sts to cn and hold to back, k2, k2 from cn.

4-st LC Sl 2 sts to cn and hold to front, k2, k2 from cn.

(worked over 8 sts)

Rows 1, 5 and 7 (RS) Knit.

Row 2 and all WS rows Purl.

Row 3 K2, 4-st eyelet LC, K2.

Row 9 4-st LC, 4-st RC.

Row 10 Rep row 2.

Rep rows 1–10.

8 sts

Stitch Key

☐ K on RS, p on WS

▨ 4-st RC

▨ 4-st LC

▨ 4-st eyelet LC

40

41

diamonds & pretzels

3-st RPC Sl 1 st to cn and hold to back, k2, p1 from cn.

3-st LPC Sl 2 sts to cn and hold to front, p1, k2 from cn.

5-st RPC Sl 3 sts to cn and hold to back, k2, p1, k2 from cn.

MB [(P1, yo) twice, p1] in next st, turn, k5, turn, p5, turn, ssk, k1, k2 tog, turn, p3tog. (worked over 19 sts)

Row 1 (RS) P3, 3-st LPC, [p1, k1] 3 times, p1, 3-st RC, p3.

Row 2 K4, p2, [k1, p1] 4 times, p1, k4.

Row 3 P4, 3-st LPC, [p1, k1] 2 times, p1, 3-st RPC, p4.

Row 4 K5, p2, [k1, p1] 3 times, p1, k5.

Row 5 P5, 3-st LPC, p1, k1, p1, 3-st RPC, p5.

Row 6 K6, p2, k1, p1, k1, p2, k6.

Row 7 P6, 3-st LPC, p1, 3-st RPC, p6.

Row 8 K7, p2, k1, p2, k7.

Row 9 P7, 5-st RPC, p7.

Row 10 K7, p2, k1, p2, k7.

Row 11 P6, 3-st RPC, p1, 3-st LPC, p6.

Row 12 K6, p2, k3, p2, k6.

Row 13 P5, 3-st RPC, p3, 3-st LPC, p5.

Row 14 K5, p2, k5, p2, k5.

Row 15 P4, 3-st RPC, p2, MB, p2, 3-st LPC, p4.

Row 16 K4, p2, k7, p2, k4.

Row 17 P4, 3-st LPC, p5, 3-st RPC, p4.

Row 18 K5, p2, k5, p2, k5.

19 sts

Stitch Key

▨ (grey square)	K on RS, p on WS
−	P on RS, k on WS
•	MB
◿◺	3-st RPC
◹◸	3-st LPC
◿◿◺◺	5-st RPC

42

Row 19 P5, 3-st LPC, p3, 3-st RPC, p5.
Row 20 K6, p2, k3, p2, k6.
Row 21 P6, 3-st LPC, p1, 3-st RPC, p6.
Row 22 K7, p2, k1, p2, k7.
Row 23 P7, 5-st RPC, p7.
Row 24 K7, p2, k1, p2, k7.
Row 25 P6, 3-st RPC, k1, 3-st LPC, p6.
Row 26 K6, p2, k1, p1, k1, p2, k6.
Row 27 P5, 3-st RPC, k1, p1, k1, 3-st LPC, p5.
Row 28 K5, p2, [k1, p1] 3 times, p1, k5.
Row 29 P4, 3-st RPC, [k1, p1] 2 times, k1, 3-st LPC, p4.
Row 30 K4, p2, [k1, p1] 4 times, p1, k4.
Row 31 P3, 3-st RPC, [k1, p1] 3 times, k1, 3-st LPC, p3.
Row 32 K3, p2, [k1, p1] 5 times, p1, k3.
Row 33 P2, 3-st RPC, [k1, p1] 4 times, k1, 3-st LPC, p2.
Row 34 K2, p2, [k1, p1] 6 times, p1, k2.
Row 35 P1, 3-st RPC, [k1, p1] 5 times, k1, 3-st LPC, p1.
Row 36 K1, p2, [k1, p1] 7 times, p1, k1.
Row 37 3-st RPC, [k1, p1] 6 times, k1, 3-st LPC.
Row 38 P2, [k1, p1] 8 times, p1.
Row 39 3-st LPC, [p1, k1] 6 times, p1, 3-st RPC.
Row 40 K1, p2, [k1, p1] 7 times, p1, k1.
Row 41 P1, 3-st LPC, [p1, k1] 5 times, p1, 3-st RPC, p1.
Row 42 K2, p2, [k1, p1] 6 times, p1, k2.
Row 43 P2, 3-st LPC, [p1, k1] 4 times, p1, 3-st RPC, p2.
Row 44 K3, p2, [k1, p1] 5 times, p1, k3.
Rep rows 1–44.

3-st RC Sl 1 st to cn and hold to back, k2, k1 from cn.
3-st LC Sl 2 sts to cn and hold to front, k1, k2 from cn.
3-st RPC Sl 1 to cn and hold to back, k2, p1 from cn.
3-st LPC Sl 2 sts to cn and hold to front, p1, k2 from cn.
4-st LC Sl 2 sts to cn and hold to front, k2, k2 from cn.
(worked over 14 sts)
Row 1 (RS) 3-st LPC, [p1, k1 tbl] 4 times, 3-st RPC.
Row 2 K1, p3, [k1, p1] 4 times, p1, k1.
Row 3 P1, 3-st LPC, [k1 tbl, p1] 3 times, 3-st RPC, p1.
Row 4 K2, p2, [k1, p1] 3 times, p2, k2.
Row 5 P2, 3-st LPC, [p1, k1 tbl] twice, 3-st RPC, p2.
Row 6 K3, p3, k1, p1, k1, p2, k3.
Row 7 P3, 3-st LPC, k1 tbl, p1, 3-st RPC, p3.
Row 8 K4, p2, k1, p3, k4.
Row 9 P4, 3-st LPC, 3-st RPC, p4.
Row 10 K5, p4, k5.
Row 11 P5, 4-st LC, p5.

Row 12 Rep row 10.
Row 13 P4, 3-st RC, 3-st LPC, p4.
Row 14 K4, p2, k1, p3, k4.
Row 15 P3, 3-st RPC, k1 tbl, p1, 3-st LC, p3.
Row 16 K3, p3, k1, p1, k1, p2, k3.
Row 17 P2, 3-st RC, [p1, k1 tbl] twice, 3-st LPC, p2.
Row 18 K2, p2, [k1, p1] 3 times, p2, k2.
Row 19 P1, 3-st RPC, [k1 tbl, p1] 3 times, 3-st LC, p1.
Row 20 K1, p3, [k1, p1] 4 times, p1, k1.
Row 21 3-st RC, [p1, k1 tbl] 4 times, 3-st LPC.
Row 22 P2, [k1, p1] 5 times, p2.
Rep rows 1–22.

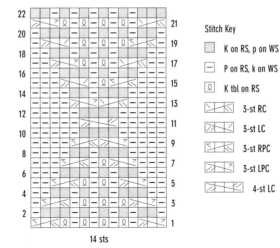

14 sts

Stitch Key

☐ K on RS, p on WS

— P on RS, k on WS

℧ K tbl on RS

⤬ 3-st RC

⤬ 3-st LC

⤬ 3-st RPC

⤬ 3-st LPC

⤬ 4-st LC

43

3-st RPC Sl 1 st to cn and hold to back, k2, p1 from cn.

3-st LPC Sl 2 sts to cn and hold to front of work, p1, k2 from cn.

5-st LPC Sl 3 sts to cn and hold to front, k2, sl the p st from cn and p it, k2 from cn. (worked over 15 sts)

Row 1 (RS) 3-st LPC, [p1, k1] 4 times, k1, 3-st RPC.

Row 2 K1, p2, [k1, p1] 5 times, p1, k1.

Row 3 P1, 3-st LPC, [p1, k1] 3 times, p1, 3-st RPC, p1.

Row 4 K2, p2, [k1, p1] 4 times, p1, k2.

Row 5 P2, 3-st LPC, [p1, k1] twice, p1, 3-st RPC, p2.

Row 6 K3, p2, [k1, p1] 3 times, p1, k3.

Row 7 P3, 3-st LPC, p1, k1, p1, 3-st RPC, P3.

Row 8 K4, p2, k1, p1, k1, p2, k4.

Row 9 P4, 3-st LPC, p1, 3-st RPC, p4.

Row 10 K5, p2, k1, p2, k5.

Row 11 P5, 5-st LPC, p5.

Row 12 K5, p2, k1, p2, k5.

Row 13 P4, 3-st RPC, k1, 3-st LPC, p4.

Row 14 K4, p2, k1, p1, k1, p2, k4.

Row 15 P3, 3-st RPC, k1, p1, k1, 3-st LPC, p3.

Row 16 K3, p2, [k1, p1] 3 times, p1, k3.

Row 17 P2, 3-st RPC, [k1, p1] twice, k1, 3-st LPC, p2.

Row 18 K2, p2, [k1, p1] 4 times, p1, k2.

Row 19 P1, 3-st RPC, [k1, p1] 3 times, k1, 3-st LPC, p1.

Row 20 K1, p2, [k1, p1] 5 times, p1, k1.

Row 21 3-st RPC, [k1, p1] 4 times, k1, 3-st LPC.

Row 22 P2, [k1, p1] 6 times, p1.

Rep rows 1–22.

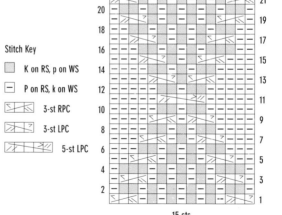

Stitch Key

☐ K on RS, p on WS

— P on RS, k on WS

▱ 3-st RPC

▱ 3-st LPC

▱ 5-st LPC

15 sts

4-st RPC Sl 1 st to cn and hold to back, k3, p1 from cn.

4-st LPC Sl 3 sts to cn and hold to front, p1, k3 from cn.

6-st RC Sl 3 sts to cn and hold to back, k3, k3 from cn.

(worked over 16 sts)

Row 1 (RS) P5, k6, p5.

Rows 2, 4, 6, 8, 10 and 12 K5, p6, k5.

Rows 3 and 11 P5, 6-st RC, p5.

Rows 5, 7 and 9 P5, k6, p5.

Row 13 P4, 4-st RPC, 4-st LPC, p4.

Row 14 K4, p3, k2, p3, k4.

Row 15 P3, 4-st RPC, p2, 4-st LPC, p3.

Rows 16 and 30 K3, p3, k4, p3, k3.

Row 17 P2, 4-st RPC, p4, 4-st LPC, p2.

Rows 18 and 28 K2, p3, k6, p3, k2.

Row 19 P1, 4-st RPC, p6, 4-st LPC, p1.

Rows 20 and 26 K1, p3, k8, p3, k1.

Row 21 4-st RPC, p8, 4-st LPC.

Rows 22 and 24 P3, k10, p3.

Row 23 K3, p10, k3.

Row 25 4-st LPC, p8, 4-st RPC.

Row 27 P1, 4-st LPC, p6, 4-st RPC, p1.

Row 29 P2, 4-st LPC, p4, 4-st RPC, p2.

Row 31 P3, 4-st LPC, p2, 4-st RPC, p3.

Row 32 K4, p3, k2, p3, k4.

Row 33 P4, 4-st LPC, 4-st RPC, p4.

Row 34 K5, p6, k5.

Rep rows 3–34.

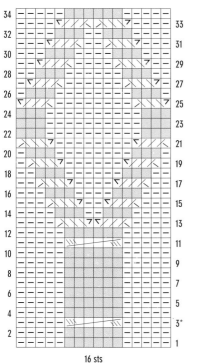

16 sts

Stitch Key

	K on RS, p on WS
−	P on RS, k on WS
	4-st RPC
	4-st LPC
	6-st RC

45

46 cat's cradle

4-st RC Sl 1 st to cn and hold to back, k3, k1 from cn.

4-st LC Sl 3 sts to cn and hold to front, k1, k3 from cn.

6-st RC Sl 3 sts to cn and hold to back, k3, k3 from cn.

6-st LC Sl 3 sts to cn and hold to front, k3, k3 from cn.

(worked over 26 sts)

Rows 1, 5 and 37 (RS) Knit.

Rows 2, 4, 6, 36 and 38 P6, k14, p6.

Rows 3 and 39 6-st RC, k14, 6-st LC.

Row 7 K3, 4-st LC, k12, 4-st RC, k3.

Rows 8 and 34 P3, k1, p3, k12, p3, k1, p3.

Row 9 K4, 4-st LC, k10, 4-st RC, k4.

Rows 10 and 32 P3, k2, p3, k10, p3, k2, p3.

Row 11 K5, 4-st LC, k8, 4-st RC, k5.

Rows 12 and 30 P3, k3, p3, k8, p3, k3, p3.

Row 13 K6, 4-st LC, k6, 4-st RC, k6.

Rows 14 and 28 P3, k4, p3, k6, p3, k4, p3.

Row 15 K7, 4-st LC, k4, 4-st RC, k7.

Rows 16 and 26 P3, k5, p3, k4, p3, k5, p3.

Row 17 K8, 4-st LC, k2, 4-st RC, k8.

Rows 18 and 24 P3, k6, p3, k2, p3, k6, p3.

Row 19 K9, 4-st LC, 4-st RC, k9.

Rows 20 and 22 P3, k7, p6, k7, p3.

Row 21 K10, 6-st LC, k10.

Row 23 K9, 4-st RC, 4-st LC, k9.

Row 25 K8, 4-st RC, k2, 4-st LC, k8.

Row 27 K7, 4-st RC, k4, 4-st LC, k7.

Row 29 K6, 4-st RC, k6, 4-st LC, k6.

Row 31 K5, 4-st RC, k8, 4-st LC, k5.

Row 33 K4, 4-st RC, k10, 4-st LC, k4.

Row 35 K3, 4-st RC, k12, 4-st LC, k3.

Row 40 Rep row 2.

Rep rows 1–40.

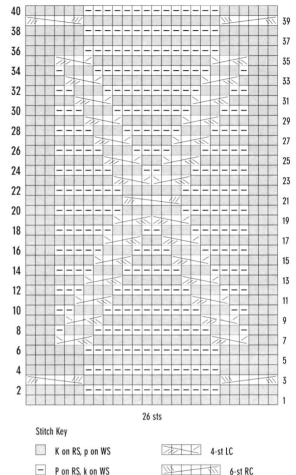

26 sts

Stitch Key

☐ K on RS, p on WS

— P on RS, k on WS

4-st RC

4-st LC

6-st RC

6-st LC

diamonds

LT With RH needle behind LH needle, sk next st on LH needle and k the 2nd st tbl, then k the skipped st and sl both sts from LH needle.

RPT With RH needle in front of LH needle, sk next st on LH needle and k the 2nd st, then p the skipped st and sl both sts from LH needle.

LPT With RH needle behind LH needle, sk next st on LH needle and p the 2nd st tbl, then k the skipped st in front lp and sl both sts from LH needle.

(worked over 14 sts)

Row 1 (RS) P6, LT, p6.

Row 2 and all WS rows K the knit and p the purl sts.

Row 3 P5, RPT, LPT, p5.

Row 5 P4, RPT, p2, LPT, p4.

Row 7 P3, RPT, p4, LPT, p3.

Row 9 P2, RPT, p6, LPT, p2.

Row 11 P1, RPT, p8, LPT, p1.

Row 13 RPT, p10, LPT.

Row 15 LPT, p10, RPT.

Row 17 P1, LPT, p8, RPT, p1.

Row 19 P2, LPT, p6, RPT, p2.

Row 21 P3, LPT, p4, RPT, p3.

Row 23 P4, LPT, p2, RPT, p4.

Row 25 P5, LPT, RPT, p5.

Row 26 Rep row 2.

Rep rows 1–26.

Stitch Key

☐ K on RS, p on WS

─ P on RS, k on WS

LT

RPT

LPT

2-st RC Sl 1 st to cn and hold to back, k1 tbl, k1 tbl from cn.

2-st LC Sl 1 st to cn and hold to front, k1 tbl, k1 tbl from cn.

2-st RPC Sl 1 st to cn and hold to back, k1 tbl, p1 from cn.

2-st LPC Sl 1 st to cn and hold to front, p1, k1 tbl from cn.

(worked over 14 sts)

Preparation row (WS) [P1 tbl twice, k4] twice, p1 tbl twice.

Row 1 2-st LC, p4, k1 tbl twice, p4, 2-st RC.

Row 2 [P1 tbl twice, k4] twice, p1 tbl twice.

Row 3 K1 tbl, 2-st LPC, p3, k1 tbl twice, p3, 2-st RPC, k1 tbl.

Row 4 P1 tbl, k1, p1 tbl, k3, p1 tbl twice, k3, p1 tbl, k1, p1 tbl.

Row 5 2-st LPC twice, p2, k1 tbl twice, p2, 2-st RPC twice.

Row 6 [K1, p1 tbl] twice, k2, p1 tbl twice, k2, [p1 tbl, k1] twice.

Row 7 P1, 2-st LPC twice, p1, k1 tbl twice, p1, 2-st RPC twice, p1.

Row 8 K2, [p1 tbl, k1] twice, p1 tbl twice, [k1, p1 tbl] twice, k2.

Row 9 P2, 2-st LPC twice, 2-st LC, 2-st RPC twice, p2.

Row 10 K3, p1 tbl, k1, p1 tbl 4 times, k1, p1 tbl, k3.

Row 11 P3, 2-st LPC, 2-st RC twice, 2-st RPC, p3.

Rows 12 and 14 K4, p1 tbl 6 times, k4.

Row 13 P4, 2-st LC 3 times, p4.

Row 15 P3, 2-st RPC, 2-st RC twice, 2-st LPC, p3.

Row 16 K3, p1 tbl, k1, p1 tbl 4 times, k1, p1 tbl, k3.

Row 17 P2, 2-st RPC twice, 2-st LC, 2-st LPC twice, p2.

Row 18 K2, [p1 tbl, k1] twice, p1 tbl twice, [p1, k1 tbl] twice, k2.

Row 19 P1, 2-st RPC twice, p1, k1 tbl twice, p1, 2-st LPC twice, p1.

Row 20 [K1, p1 tbl] twice, k2, p1 tbl twice, k2, [p1 tbl, k1] twice.

Row 21 2-st RPC twice, p2, k1 tbl twice, p2, 2-st LPC twice.

Row 22 P1 tbl, k1, p1 tbl, k3, p1 tbl twice, k3, p1 tbl, k1, p1 tbl.

Row 23 K1 tbl, 2-st RPC, p3, k1 tbl twice, p3, 2-st LPC, k1 tbl.

Row 24 [P1 tbl twice, k4] twice, p1 ibl twice.

Rep rows 1–24.

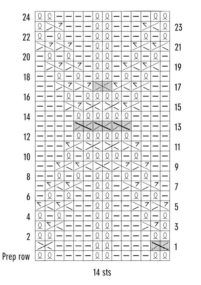

14 sts

Stitch Key

—	P on RS, k on WS
Ω	K1 tbl on RS, p1 tbl on WS
⋈	2-st RC
⋈	2-st LC
⋈	2-st RPC
⋈	2-st LPC

diamonds

2-st RC Sl 1 st to cn and hold to back, k1 tbl, k1 tbl from cn.

2-st LC Sl 1 st to cn and hold to front, k1 tbl, k1 tbl from cn.

2-st RPC Sl 1 st to cn and hold to back, k1 tbl, p1 from cn.

2-st LPC Sl 1 st to cn and hold to front, p1, k1 tbl from cn.

(worked over 11 sts)

Preparation row (WS) K1, p1 tbl twice, [k1, p1 tbl] 4 times.

Row 1 [K1 tbl, p1] 4 times, 2-st LC, p1.

Row 2 K1, p1 tbl twice, [k1, p1 tbl] 4 times.

Row 3 K1 tbl, [p1, k1 tbl] 3 times, 2-st RPC, 2-st LPC.

Rows 4 and 6 P1 tbl, k2, p1 tbl twice, [k1, p1 tbl] 3 times.

Row 5 [K1 tbl, p1] 3 times, 2-st RC, p2, k1 tbl.

Row 7 K1 tbl, [p1, k1 tbl] twice, 2-st RPC, 2-st LPC, 2-st RPC.

Rows 8 and 10 K1, p1 tbl twice, k2, p1 tbl twice, [k1, p1 tbl] twice.

Row 9 [K1 tbl, p1] twice, 2-st LC, p2, 2-st LC, p1.

Row 11 K1 tbl, p1, k1 tbl, [2-st RPC, 2-st LPC] twice.

Rows 12 and 14 P1 tbl, [k2, p1 tbl twice] twice, k1, p1 tbl.

Row 13 K1 tbl, p1, [2-st RC, p2] twice, k1 tbl.

Row 15 K1 tbl, [2-st RPC, 2-st LPC] twice, 2-st RPC.

Rows 16 and 18 K1, [p1 tbl twice, k2] twice, p1 tbl twice.

Row 17 [2-st LC, p2] twice, 2-st LC, p1.

Row 19 K1 tbl, [2-st LPC, 2-st RPC] twice, 2-st LPC.

Rows 20 and 22 P1 tbl, [k2, p1 tbl twice] twice, k1, p1 tbl.

Row 21 K1 tbl, p1, [2-st RC, p2] twice, k1 tbl.

Row 23 K1 tbl, p1, k1 tbl, [2-st LPC, 2-st RPC] twice.

Rows 24 and 26 K1, p1 tbl twice, k2, p1 tbl twice, [k1, p1 tbl] twice.

Row 25 [K1 tbl, p1] twice, 2-st LC, p2, 2-st LC, p1.

Row 27 K1 tbl, [p1, k1 tbl] twice, 2-st LPC, 2-st RPC, 2-st LPC.

Rows 28 and 30 P1 tbl, k2, p1 tbl twice, [k1, p1 tbl] 3 times.

Row 29 [K1 tbl, p1] 3 times, 2-st RC, p2, k1 tbl.

Row 31 K1 tbl, [p1, k1 tbl] 3 times, 2-st LPC, 2-st RPC.

Row 32 K1, p1 tbl twice, [k1, p1 tbl] 4 times.

Rep rows 1–32.

Stitch Key

−	P on RS, k on WS
Q	K1 tbl on RS, p1 tbl on WS
⤫	2-st RC
⤫	2-st LC
⤫	2-st RPC
⤫	2-st LPC

2-st RC Sl 1 st to cn and hold to back, k1 tbl, k1 tbl from cn.

2-st LC Sl 1 st to cn and hold to front, k1 tbl, k1 tbl from cn.

2-st RPC Sl 1 st to cn and hold to back, k1 tbl, p1 from cn.

2-st LPC Sl 1 st to cn and hold to front, p1, k1 tbl from cn.

(worked over 11 sts)

Preparation row (WS) [P1 tbl, k1] 4 times, p1 tbl twice, k1.

Row 1 P1, 2-st RC, [p1, k1 tbl] 4 times.

Row 2 [P1 tbl, k1] 4 times, p1 tbl twice, k1.

Row 3 2-st RPC, 2-st LPC, k1 tbl, [p1, k1 tbl] 3 times.

Rows 4 and 6 [P1 tbl, k1] 3 times, p1 tbl twice, k2, p1 tbl.

Row 5 K1 tbl, p2, 2-st LC, [p1, k1 tbl} 3 times.

Row 7 2-st LPC, 2-st RPC, 2-st LPC, k1 tbl, [p1, k1 tbl] twice.

Rows 8 and 10 [P1 tbl, k1] twice, p1 tbl twice, k2, p1 tbl twice, k1.

Row 9 P1, 2-st RC, p2, 2-st RC, [p1, k1 tbl] twice.

Row 11 [2-st RPC, 2-st LPC] twice, k1 tbl, p1, k1 tbl.

Rows 12 and 14 P1 tbl, k1, [p1 tbl twice, k2] twice. p1 tbl.

Row 13 K1 tbl, [p2, 2-st LC] twice, p1, k1 tbl.

Row 15 [2-st LPC, 2-st RPC] twice, 2-st LPC, k1 tbl.

Rows 16 and 18 [P1 tbl twice, k2] twice, p1 tbl twice, k1.

Row 17 P1, [2-st RC, p2] twice, 2-st RC.

Row 19 [2-st RPC, 2-st LPC] twice, 2-st RPC, k1 tbl.

Rows 20 and 22 P1 tbl, k1, [p1 tbl twice, k2] twice, p1 tbl.

Row 21 K1 tbl, [p2, 2-st LC] twice, p1, k1 tbl.

Row 23 [2-st LPC, 2-st RPC] twice, k1 tbl, p1, k1 tbl.

Rows 24 and 26 [P1 tbl, k1] twice, p1 tbl twice, k2, p1 tbl twice, k1.

Row 25 P1, 2-st RC, p2, 2-st RC, [p1, k1 tbl] twice.

Row 27 2-st RPC, 2-st LPC, 2-st RPC, k1 tbl, [p1, k1 tbl] twice.

Rows 28 and 30 [P1 tbl, k1] 3 times, p1 tbl twice, k2, p1 tbl.

Row 29 K1 tbl, p2, 2-st LC, [p1, k1 tbl] 3 times.

Row 31 2-st LPC, 2-st RPC, [k1 tbl, p1] 3 times, k1 tbl.

Row 32 [P1 tbl, k1] 4 times, p1 tbl twice, k1.

Rep rows 1–32.

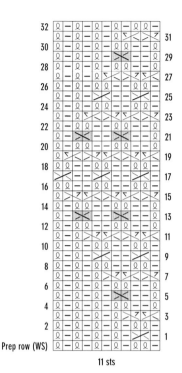

11 sts

Stitch Key

⊡ P on RS, k on WS

Ⓠ K1 tbl on RS, p1 tbl on WS

⤬ 2-st RC

⤫ 2-st LC

⤬ 2-st RPC

⤬ 2-st LPC

diamonds

4-st RPC Sl 2 sts to cn and hold to back, k2, p2 from cn.

4-st LPC Sl 2 sts to cn and hold to front, p2, k2 from cn.

4-st RC Sl 2 sts to cn and hold to back, k2, k2 from cn.

4-st LC Sl 2 sts to cn and hold to front, k2, k2 from cn.

5-st LPC Sl 3 sts to cn and hold to front, k2, sl p st back to LH needle and p it, k2 from cn.

(worked over 21 sts inc to 25)

Row 1 (RS) P10, M1, inc 2, M1, p10.

Row 2 K10, p2, k1, p2, k10.

Row 3 P8, 4-st RPC, p1, 4-st LPC, p8.

Rows 4 and 22 K8, k2, p5, k2, k8.

Row 5 P6, 4-st RC, p5, 4-st LC, p6.

Rows 6 and 20 K6, p4, k5, p4, k6.

Row 7 P4, 4-st RPC, 4-st LPC, p1, 4-st RPC, 4-st LPC, p4.

Rows 8 and 18 K4, p2, k4, p2, k1, p2, k4, p2, k4.

Row 9 P2, 4-st RC, p4, 5-st LPC, p4, 4-st LC, p2.

Rows 10 and 16 K2, p4, k4, p2, k1, p2, k4, p4, k2.

Row 11 4-st RPC, 4-st LPC, 4-st RPC, p1, 4-st LPC, 4-st RPC, 4-st LPC.

Rows 12 and 14 P2, k4, p4, k5, p4, k4, p2.

Row 13 K2, p4, 4-st RC, p5, 4-st RC, p4, k2.

Row 15 4-st LPC, 4-st RPC, 4-st LPC, p1, 4-st RPC, 4-st LPC, 4-st RPC.

Row 17 P2, 4-st LC, p4, 5-st LPC, p4, 4-st RC, p2.

Row 19 P4, 4-st LPC, 4-st RPC, p1, 4-st LPC, 4-st RPC, p4.

Row 21 P6, 4-st LC, p5, 4-st RC, p6.

Row 23 P8, 4-st LPC, p1, 4-st RPC, p8.

Row 24 K10, p5tog, k10.

Rep rows 1–24.

21 sts inc'd to 25 sts

Stitch Key

▢ K on RS, p on WS	4-st LPC
− P on RS, k on WS	4-st RC
Inc 2	4-st LC
M1	5-st LPC
4-st RPC	P5tog

MB K into front, back and front of next st, turn, k3, turn, p3, turn, k3, turn, SK2P.

2-st RC Sl 1 st to cn and hold to back, k1, k1 from cn.

2-st LC Sl 1 st to cn and hold to front, k1, k1 from cn.

2-st RPC Sl 1 st to cn and hold to back, k1, p1 from cn.

2-st LPC Sl 1 st to cn and hold to front, p1, k1 from cn.

3-st RC Sl next 2 sts to cn and hold to back, k1, k2 from cn.

(worked over 11 sts)

Row 1 (RS) P4, 3-st RC, p4.

Row 2 K4, p3, k4.

Row 3 P3, 2-st RC, k1, 2-st LC, p3.

Rows 4 and 18 K3, p5, k3.

Row 5 P2, 2-st RC, k1, MB, k1, 2-st LC, p2.

Rows 6 and 16 K2, p7, k2.

Row 7 P1, 2-st RC, k5, 2-st LC, p1.

Rows 8 and 14 K1, p9, k1.

Row 9 2-st RC, k7, 2-st LC.

Rows 10 and 12 P11.

Row 11 K3, MB, k3, MB, k3.

Row 13 2-st LPC, k7, 2-st RPC.

Row 14 K1, p9, k1.

Row 15 P1, 2-st LPC, k5, 2-st RPC, p1.

Row 17 P2, 2-st LPC, k1, MB, k1, 2-st RPC, p2.

Row 19 P3, 2-st LPC, k1, 2-st RPC, p3.

Row 20 Rep row 2.

Rep rows 1–20.

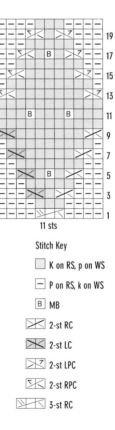

11 sts

Stitch Key

☐ K on RS, p on WS

− P on RS, k on WS

B MB

⧅ 2-st RC

⧅ 2-st LC

⧅ 2-st LPC

⧅ 2-st RPC

⧅ 3-st RC

diamonds

3-st RPC Sl 1 st to cn and hold to back, k2, p1 from cn.

3-st LPC Sl 2 sts to cn and hold to front, p1, k2 from cn.

4-st RC Sl 2 sts to cn and hold to back, k2, k2 from cn.

4-st LC Sl 2 sts to cn and hold to front, k2, k2 from cn.

(worked over 20 sts, inc to 24, dec to 20)

Preparation row (WS) K3, p4, k6, p4, k3.

Row 1 (RS) P3, 4-st LC, p3, yo twice, p3, 4-st LC, p3.

Row 2 K3, p4, k1, k2tog, k4 (dropping extra yo), p4, k3.

Row 3 P2, 3-st RPC, 3-st LPC, yo twice, p4,

yo twice, 3-st RPC, 3-st LPC, p2.

Row 4 K2, p2, k2, p2, k1 (dropping extra yo), k2tog, ssk, k1 (dropping extra yo), p2, k2, p2, k2.

Row 5 P1, 3-st RPC, p2, 3-st LPC, p2, 3-st RPC, p2, 3-st LPC, p1.

Row 6 K1, p2, k4, p2, k2, p2, k4, p2, k1.

Row 7 3-st RPC, yo twice, p4, yo twice, 3-st LPC, 3-st RPC, yo twice, p4, yo twice, 3-st LPC.

Row 8 P2, k2 (dropping extra yo), k2tog, ssk, k2 (dropping extra yo), p4, k2 (dropping extra yo), k2tog, ssk, k2 (dropping extra yo), p2.

Row 9 K2, p3, yo twice, p3, 4-st RC, p3, yo twice, p3, k2.

Row 10 P2, k1, ssk, k4 (dropping extra yo), p4,

k4 (dropping extra yo), ssk, k1, p2.

Row 11 3-st LPC, yo twice, p4, yo twice, 3-st RPC, 3-st LPC, yo twice, p4, yo twice, 3-st RPC.

Row 12 K1, p2, k1, (dropping extra yo), ssk, k2tog, k1 (dropping extra yo), p2, k2, p2, k1 (dropping extra yo), ssk, k2tog, k1 (dropping extra yo), p2, k1.

Row 13 P1, 3-st LPC, p2, 3-st RPC, p2, 3-st LPC, p2, 3-st RPC, p1.

Row 14 K2, p2, k2, p2, k4, p2, k2, p2, k2.

Row 15 P2, 3-st LPC, 3-st RPC, yo twice, p4, yo twice, 3-st LPC, 3-st RPC, p2.

Row 16 K3, p4, k2 (dropping extra yo), k2tog, ssk, k2 (dropping extra yo), p4, k3.

Rep rows 1–16.

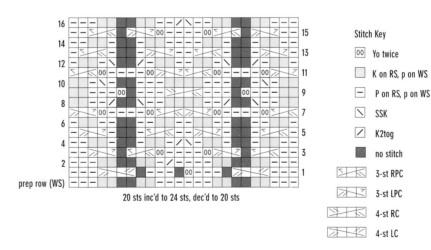

prep row (WS)

20 sts inc'd to 24 sts, dec'd to 20 sts

Stitch Key

00	Yo twice
☐	K on RS, p on WS
—	P on RS, p on WS
╲	SSK
╱	K2tog
■	no stitch
⧅	3-st RPC
⧄	3-st LPC
⧅	4-st RC
⧄	4-st LC

2-st RC Sl 1 st to cn and hold in back, k1, k1 from cn.

2-st LC Sl 1 st to cn and hold in front, k1, k1 from cn.

2-st RPC Sl 1 st to cn and hold in back, k1, p1 from cn.

2-st LPC Sl 1 st to cn and hold in front, p1, k1 from cn.

6-st RC Sl 2 sts to cn and hold in back, k4, k2 from cn.

6-st LC Sl 4 sts to cn and hold in front, k2, k4 from cn.

6-st RPC Sl 2 sts to cn and hold in back, k4, p2 from cn.

6-st LPC Sl 4 sts to cn and hold in front, p2, k4 from cn.

9-st RC Sl 4 st to cn and hold in back, k5, k4 from cn.

9-st LPC Sl 5 sts to cn and hold in front, k4, sl p st from cn and p it, k4 from cn.

(worked over 59 sts)

Row 1 (WS) P14, k1, p29, k1, p14.

Row 2 2-st LC, k8, 9-st LPC, k9, 2-st RC, 2-st LC, k8, 9-st LPC, k10.

Row 3 P14, k1, p29, k1, p14.

Row 4 K1, 2-st LC, k5, 6-st RPC, p1, 6-st LPC, k6, 2-st RC, k2, 2-st LC, k5, 6-st RPC, p1, 6-st LPC, k6, 2-st RC.

Row 5 P12, k5, p25, k5, p12.

Row 6 K2, 2-st LC, k2, 6-st RPC, p5, 6-st LPC, k3, 2-st RC, k4, 2-st LC, k2, 6-st RPC, p5, 6-st LPC, k3, 2-st RC, k1.

Row 7 P10, k9, p21, k9, p10.

Row 8 K3, 2-st LC, k5, p9, 6-st LPC, 2-st RC, k6, 2-st LC, k5, p9, 6-st LPC, 2-st RC, k2.

Row 9 P8, k11, p19, k11, p10.

Row 10 K4, 2-st LC, k4, 2-st LPC, p7, 2-st RPC, k13, 2-st LC, k4, 2-st LPC, p7, 2-st RPC, k8.

Row 11 P8, k1, p1, k7, p1, k1, p19, k1, p1, k7, p1, k1, p10.

Row 12 K4, 6-st RPC, p1, 2-st LPC, p5, 2-st RPC, p1, k13, 6-st RPC, p1, 2-st LPC, p5, 2-st RPC, p1, k8.

Row 13 P8, k2, p1, k5, p1, k4, p17, k2, p1, k5, p1, k4, p8.

Row 14 K2, 6-st RPC, p4, 2-st LPC, p3, 2-st RPC, p2, 6-st LPC, k5, 6-st RPC, p4, 2-st LPC, p3, 2-st RPC, p2, 6-st LPC, k2.

Row 15 P6, k5, p1, k3, p1, k7, p13, k5, p1, k3, p1, k7, p6.

Row 16 6-st RPC, p7, 2-st LC, p1, 2-st RPC, p5, 6-st LPC, k1, 6-st RPC, p7, 2-st LC, p1, 2-st RPC, p5, 6-st LPC.

Row 17 P4, k8, p1, k1, p2, k9, p9, k8, p1, k1, p2, k9, p4.

Row 18 K4, p8, 2-st RPC, 2-st LPC, p9, 9-st RC, p8, 2-st RPC, 2-st LPC, p9, k4.

Row 19 P4, k9, p1, k2, p1, k8, p9, k9, p1, k2, p1, k8, p4.

Row 20 6-st LC, p5, 2-st RPC, p2, 2-st LPC, p6, 6-st RC, k1, 6-st LC, p5, 2-st RPC, p2, 2-st

LPC, p6, 6-st RC.

Row 21 P6, k6, p1, k4, p1, k5, p13, k6, p1, k4, p1, k5, p6.

Row 22 K2, 6-st LC, p2, 2-st RPC, p4, 2-st LPC, p3, 6-st RC, k5, 6-st LC, p2, 2-st RPC, p4, 2-st LPC, p3, 6-st RC, k2.

Row 23 P8, k3, p1, k6, p1, k2, p17, k3, p1, k6, p1, k2, p8.

Row 24 K8, p1, 2-st RPC, p6, 2-st LPC, 6-st RC, k13, p1, 2-st RPC, p6, 2-st LPC, 6-st RC, k4.

Row 25 P11, k8, p1, k1, p20, k8, p1, k1, p8.

Row 26 K2, 2-st RC, k4, 2-st RPC, p9, k4, 2-st LC, k7, 2-st RC, k4, 2-st RPC, p9, k4, 2-st LC, k4.

Row 27 P10, k10, p20, k10, p9.

Row 28 K1, 2-st RC, k1, 6-st LC, p9, k5, 2-st LC, k5, 2-st RC, k1, 6-st LC, p9, k5, 2-st LC, k3.

Row 29 P10, k9, p21, k9, p10.

Row 30 2-st RC, k4, 6-st LC, p5, 6-st RC, k2, 2-st LC, k3, 2-st RC, k4, 6-st LC, p5, 6-st RC, k2, 2-st LC, k2.

Row 31 P12, k5, p25, k5, p12.

Row 32 K8, 6-st LC, p1, 6-st RC, k5, 2-st LC, k1, 2-st RC, k7, 6-st LC, p1, 6-st RC, k5, 2-st LC, k1.

Rep rows 1–32.

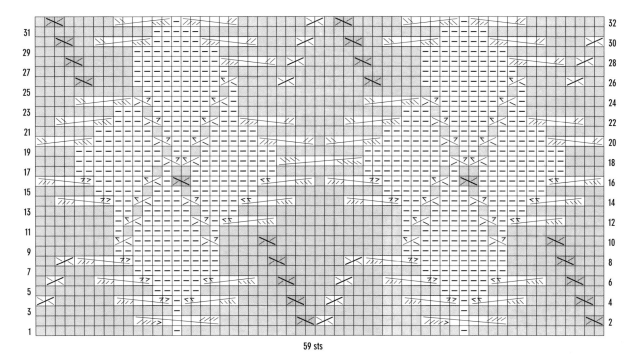

59 sts

Stitch Key

Symbol	Meaning	Symbol	Meaning
	K on RS, p on WS		6-st RC
–	P on RS, k on WS		6-st LC
	2-st RC		6-st RPC
	2-st LC		6-st LPC
	2-st RPC		9-st RC
	2-st LPC		9-st LPC

2-st RC (WS) Sl 1 st to cn and hold to RS of work, k1, k1 from cn.

2-st LC (WS) Sl 1 st to cn and hold to WS of work, k1, k1 from cn.

2-st RPC Sl 1 st to cn and hold to back, k1, p1 from cn.

2-st LPC Sl 1 st to cn and hold to front, p1, k1 from cn.

3 RC Sl 1 st to cn and hold to back, k2, k1 from cn.

3-st LC Sl 2 sts to cn and hold to front, k1, k2 from cn.

3-st RPC Sl 1 st to cn and hold to back, k2, p1 from cn.

3-st LPC Sl 2 sts to cn and hold to front, p1, k2 from cn.

4-st LC Sl 2 sts to cn and hold to front, k2, k2 from cn.

(Worked over 14 sts)

Preparation row (WS) K5, p4, k5.

Row 1 (RS) P5, 4-st LC, p5.

Row 2 K5, p4, k5.

Row 3 P4, 3-st RC, 3-st LC, p4.

Row 4 K4, p6, k4.

Row 5 P3, 3-st RPC, k2, 3-st LPC, p3.

Row 6 K3, p2, k1, p2, k1, p2, k3.

Row 7 P2, 3-st RPC, k4, 3-st LPC, p2.

Row 8 K2, p2, k1, p4, k1, p2, k2.

Row 9 P1, 3-st RPC (twice), 3-st LPC (twice), p1.

Row 10 K1, p2, k1, p2, k2, p2, k1, p2, k1.

Row 11 3-st RPC (twice), p2, 3-st LPC (twice).

Row 12 P2, k1, p2, k4, p2, k1, p2.

Row 13 K1, 2-st LPC, 3-st LPC, p2, 3-st RPC, 2-st RPC, k1.

Row 14 P1, k1, p1, k1, p2, k2, p2, k1, p1, k1, p1.

Row 15 K1, p1, 2-st LPC, 3-st LPC, 3-st RPC, 2-st RPC, p1, k1.

Row 16 P1, k2, p1, k1, p4, k1, p1, k2, p1.

Row 17 2-st LPC, 2-st RPC, p1, 4-st LC, p1, 2-st LPC, 2-st RPC.

Row 18 K1, 2-st RC, k2, p4, k2, 2-st LC, k1.

Rep rows 1–18.

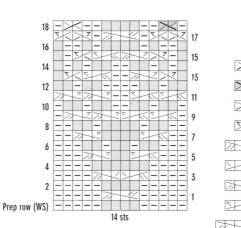

Stitch Key

☐	K on RS, p on WS
−	P on RS, k on WS
⧅	2-st RC
⧄	2-st LC
⧄	2-st LPC
⧅	2-st RPC
⧄	3-st LC
⧅	3-st RC
⧄	3-st LPC
⧅	3-st RPC
⧄	4-st LC

18 16 14 12 10 8 6 4 2

17 15 13 11 9 7 5 3 1

Prep row (WS)

14 sts

pretzels

Double-increase K1, p1 and k1 into st.

Dec 4 sts On WS, make 1 st from 5 as follows: drop yarn, s1 3 sts purlwise to RH needle, *pass 2nd st on RH needle over the first (center) st, sl center st back to LH needle and pass 2nd st on LH needle over it *, sl center st back to RH needle and rep between *'s once. Then, with dropped yarn, k1 into this st.

3-st RPC Sl 1 st to cn and hold in back, k2, p1 from cn.

3-st LPC Sl 2 sts to cn and hold in front, p1, k2 from cn.

4-st RC Sl 2 sts to cn and hold in back, k2, k2 from cn.

4-st LC Sl 2 sts to cn and hold in front, k2, k2 from cn.

4-st RPC Sl 2 sts to cn and hold in back, k2, p2 from cn.

4-st LPC Sl 2 sts to cn and hold in front, p2, k2 from cn.

(worked over 22 sts, inc'd to 26 sts)
Preparation row (WS) K7, p4, k5, p4, k2.
Row 1 P2, 4-st RC, p5, 4-st RC, p7.
Row 2 K7, p4, k5, p4, k2.
Row 3 P1, [3-st RPC, 3-st LPC, p3] twice, M1, double inc, M1, p2 — 32sts.
Row 4 K2, p2, k1, p2, [k3, p2, k2, p2] twice, k1.
Row 5 3-st RPC, p2, 4-st LPC, 3-st RPC, p2, 3-st LPC, 4-st RPC, p1, 4-st LPC.
Rows 6 and 8 P2, k5, p4, k4, p4, k5, p2.

Row 7 K2, p5, 4-st LC, p4, 4-st LC, p5, k2.
Row 9 4-st LPC, p1, 4-st RPC, 3-st LPC, p2, 3-st RPC, 4-st LPC, p2, 3-st RPC.
Row 10 K1, [p2, k2, p2, k3] twice, dec 4, k2 — 28 sts.
Row 11 P6, 3-st LPC, 3-st RPC, p3, 3-st LPC, 3-st RPC, p1.
Rows 12 and 14 K2, p4, k5, p4, k7.
Row 13 P7, 4-st RC, p5, 4-st RC, p2.
Row 15 P2, M1, double inc, M1, p3, 3-st RPC, 3-st LPC, p3, 3-st RPC, 3-st LPC, p1 — 32 sts.
Row 16 K1, [p2, k2, p2, k3] twice, p2, k1, p2, k2.

Row 17 4-st RPC, p1, 4-st LPC, 3-st RPC, p2, 3-st LPC, 4-st RPC, p2, 3-st LPC.
Rows 18 and 20 P2, k5, p4, k4, p4, k5, p2.
Row 19 K2, p5, 4-st LC, p4, 4-st LC, p5, k2.
Row 21 3-st LPC, p2, 4-st RPC, 3-st LPC, p2, 3-st RPC, 4-st LPC, p1, 4-st RPC.
Row 22 K2, dec 4, [k3, p2, k2, p2] twice, k1 — 28 sts.
Row 23 P1, 3-st LPC, 3-st RPC, p3, 3-st LPC, 3-st RPC, p6.
Row 24 K7, p4, k5, p4, k2.
Rep rows 1–24.

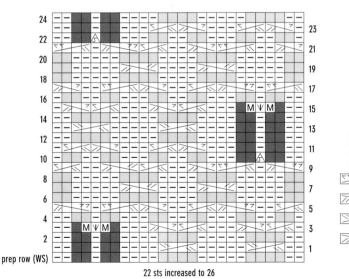

22 sts increased to 26

Stitch Key

- No stitch
- K on RS, p on WS
- P on RS, k on WS
- M M1
- V Double inc
- A Dec 4 sts
- 3-st RPC
- 3-st LPC
- 4-st RPC
- 4-st LPC
- 4-st RC
- 4-st LC

56

6-st RPC Sl 3 sts to cn and hold to back, k3, p3 from cn.

6-st LPC Sl 3 sts to cn and hold to front, p3, k3 from cn.

6-st RC Sl 3 sts to cn and hold to back, k3, k3 from cn.

6-st LC Sl 3 sts to cn and hold to front, k3, k3 from cn.

(worked over 30 sts)

Row 1 (RS) K3, p9, k6, p9, k3.

Row 2 P3, k9, p6, k9, p3.

Row 3 6-st LPC, p6, 6-st LC, p6, 6-st RPC.

Row 4 K3, p3, k6, p6, k6, p3, k3.

Row 5 P3, 6-st LPC, 6-st RC, 6-st LC, 6-st RPC, p3.

Row 6 K6, p18, k6.

Row 7 P6, 6-st RPC, 6-st LC, 6-st LPC, p6.

Row 8 K6, p3, k3, p6, k3, p3, k6.

Row 9 P3, 6-st RPC, p3, k6, p3, 6-st LPC, p3.

Row 10 K2, p4, k6, p6, k6, p4, k2.

Row 11 6-st RPC, p6, k6, p6, 6-st LPC.

Rep rows 2-11.

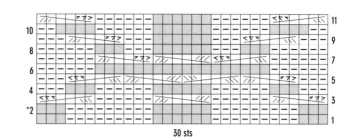

30 sts

Stitch Key

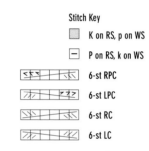

☐ K on RS, p on WS

— P on RS, k on WS

6-st RPC

6-st LPC

6-st RC

6-st LC

58 river run

3-st RPC Sl 1 st to cn and hold to back, k2, p1 from cn.

3-st LPC Sl 2 sts to cn and hold to front, p1, k2 from cn.

4-st RC Sl 2 sts to cn and hold to back, k2, k2 from cn.

4-st LC Sl 2 sts to cn and hold to front, k2, k2 from cn.

(worked over 24 sts)

Row 1 (RS) P1, [4-st RC, p2] 3 times, 4-st RC, p1.

Row 2 K1, [p4, k2] 3 times, p4, k1.

Row 3 [3-st RPC, 3-st LPC] 4 times.

Rows 4 and 6 P2, [k2, p4] 3 times, k2, p2.

Row 5 K2, [p2, 4-st LC] 3 times, p2, k2.

Row 7 [3-st LPC, 3-st RPC] 4 times.

Row 8 Rep row 2.

Rep rows 1–8.

Stitch Key

- K on RS, p on WS
- P on RS, k on WS
- 3-st RPC
- 3-st LPC
- 4-st RC
- 4-st LC

24 sts

59 candelabra

2-st RC (tbl) Sl 1 st to cn and hold to back, k1tbl, k1tbl from cn.

2-st LC (tbl) Sl 1 st to cn and hold to front, k1tbl, k1tbl from cn.

2-st RPC (tbl) Sl 1 st to cn and hold to back, k1tbl, p1from cn.

2-st LPC (tbl) Sl 1 st to cn and hold to front, p1, k1tbl from cn.

(worked over 10 sts)

Preparation row (WS) K4, p1 tbl twice, k4.

Row 1 (RS) P4, 2-st LC, k4.

Row 2 K4, p1 tbl twice, k4.

Row 3 P3, 2-st RC, 2-st LC, p3.

Row 4 K3, p1 tbl 4 times, k3.

Row 5 P2, 2-st RPC, 2-st LC, 2-st LPC, p2.

Row 6 K2, p1 tbl, k1, p1 tbl twice, k1, p1 tbl, k2.

Row 7 P1, 2-st RPC twice, 2-st LPC twice, p1.

Row 8 [K1, p1 tbl] twice, k2, [p1 tbl, k1] twice.

Row 9 2-st RPC, p6, 2-st LPC.

Row 10 P1 tbl, [k2, p1 tbl] 3 times.

Row 11 K1 tbl, p2, 2-st LPC, 2-st RPC, p2, k1 tbl.

Row 12 P1 tbl, k3, p1 tbl twice, k3, p1 tbl.

Rep rows 1–12.

Prep row (WS)

10 sts

Stitch Key

- P on RS, k on WS
- K tbl on RS, p tbl on WS
- 2-st RC
- 2-st LC
- 2-st RPC
- 2-st LPC

pretzels

58

59

51

6-st RC Sl 3 sts to cn and hold in back, k3, k3 from cn.

6-st LC Sl 3 sts to cn and hold in front, k3, k3 from cn.

6-st RPC Sl 3 sts to cn and hold in back, k3, p3 from cn.

6-st LPC Sl 3 sts to cn and hold in front, p3, k3 from cn.

(worked over 21 sts)

Preparation row (WS) P9, k9, p3.

Row 1 6-st LC, p6, 6-st LPC, k3.

Row 2 P6, k9, p6.

Row 3 K3, 6-st LC, p6, 6-st LPC.

Row 4 P3, k9, p9.

Row 5 K6, 6-st LC, p6, k3.

Row 6 P3, k6, p12.

Row 7 K9, 6-st LPC, p3, k3.

Row 8 [P3, k3] twice, p9.

Row 9 K3, 6-st RC, p3, k3, 6-st RC.

Row 10 P9, k3, p9.

Row 11 6-st RPC, k3, p3, 6-st RC, k3.

Row 12 P9, [k3, p3] twice.

Row 13 K3, p3, 6-st LPC, k9.

Row 14 P12, k6, p3.

Row 15 K3, p6, 6-st LPC, k6.

Row 16 P9, k9, p3.

Rep rows 1–16.

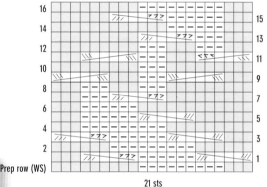

Prep row (WS)

21 sts

Stitch Key

☐ K on RS, p on WS

⊟ P on RS, k on WS

▨ 6-st RC

▨ 6-st LC

▨ 6-st RPC

▨ 6-st LPC

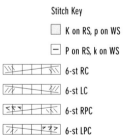

4-st RC Sl 2 sts to cn and hold to back, k2, k2 from cn.

10-st RC Sl 5 sts to cn and hold to back, k5, k5 from cn.

(worked over 10 sts)

Rows 1 and 3 (RS) K2, p1, k4, p1, k2.

Rows 2 and 4 P2, k1, p4, k1, p2.

Row 5 10-st RC.

Rows 6 and 8 Purl.

Row 7 Knit.

Row 9 K2, p1, 4-st RC, p1, k2.

Rows 10 and 12 Rep row 2.

Row 11 Rep row 1.

Rows 13-20 Rep rows 9-12 twice.

Rep rows 5–20.

10 sts

Stitch Key

☐ K on RS, p on WS

⊟ P on RS, k on WS

▨ 4-st RC

▨ 10-st RC

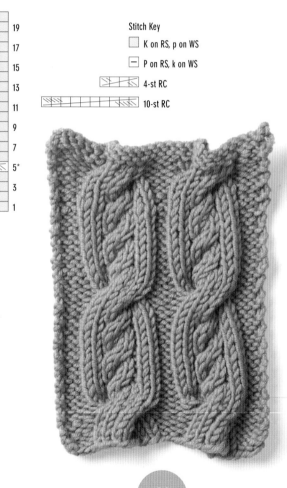

pretzels

3-st RPC Sl 1 st to cn and hold to back, k2, p1 from cn.

3-st LPC Sl 2 sts to cn and hold to front, p1, k2 from cn.

4-st RC Sl 2 sts to cn and hold to back, k2, k2 from cn.

4-st LC Sl 2 sts to cn and hold to front, k2, k2 from cn.

(panel of 28 sts)

Preparation row (WS) K2, p2, [k4, p4] twice, k4, p2, k2.

Row 1 (RS) P2, 3-st LPC, [p2, 3-st RPC, 3-st LPC] twice, p2, 3-st RPC, p2.

Row 2 K3, [p2, k2] 5 times, p2, k3.

Row 3 P3, 3-st LPC, 3-st RPC, p2, k6, p2, 3-st LPC, 3-st RPC, p3.

Rows 4 and 6 K4, [p4, k4] 3 times.

Row 5 P4, [4-st RC, k4] 3 times.

Row 7 P3, [3-st RPC, 3-st LPC, k2] 3 times, p1.

Rows 8 and 10 K3, [p2, k2] 5 times, p2, k3.

Row 9 P3, [k2, p2] 6 times, p1.

Row 11 P3, [3-st LPC, 3-st RPC, p2] 3 times, p1.

Rows 12 and 14 K4, [p4, k4] 3 times.

Row 13 P4, [4-st RC, p4] 3 times.

Row 15 P3, [3-st RPC, 3-st LPC, p2] 3 times, p1.

Row 16 K3, p6, [k2, p2] twice, k2, p6, k3.

Row 17 P2, [3-st RPC, p2, 3-st LPC] 3 times, p2.

Row 18 K2, p2, [k4, p4] twice, k4, p2, k2.

Row 19 P1, 3-st RPC, [p4, 4-st LC] twice, p4, 3-st LPC, p1.

Row 20 K1, p2, k5, p4, k4, p4, k5, p2, k1.

Row 21 3-st RPC, p4, [3-st RPC, 3-st LPC, p2] twice, p2, 3-st LPC.

Rows 22 and 24 P2, k5, [p2, k2] 3 times, p2, k5, p2.

Row 23 K2, p5, [k2, p2] 3 times, k2, p5, k2.

Row 25 3-st LPC, p4, [3-st LPC, 3-st RPC, p2] twice, p2, 3-st RPC.

Row 26 K1, p2, k5, p4, k4, p4, k5, p2, k1.

Row 27 P1, 3-st LPC, p4, [4-LC, p4] twice, 3-st RPC, p1.

Row 28 K2, p2, [k4, p4] twice, k4, p2, k2.

Rep rows 1–28.

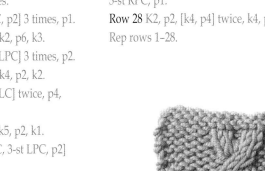

Stitch Key

☐	K on RS, p on WS
⊟	P on RS, k on WS
◹◺	3-st RPC
◺◹	3-st LPC
◹◺	4-st RC
◺◹	4-st LC

28 sts

Bind 2 Yo, p2, pass yo over p2.

Dec 4 (decrease 4) Wyif sl 3, drop yarn to front, *pass 2nd st on RH needle over first (center st), sl center st back to LH needle and pass 2nd st on LH needle over center st*, sl center st back to RH needle and rep between *'s once more, pick up yarn and k center stitch.

3-st RPC Sl 1 st to cn and hold in back, k2, p1 from cn.

3-st LPC Sl 2 sts to cn and hold in front, p1, k2 from cn.

4-st RC Sl 2 sts to cn and hold in back, k2, k2 from cn.

4-st LC Sl 2 sts to cn and hold in front, k2, k2 from cn.

4-st RPC Sl 2 sts to cn and hold in back, k2, p2 from cn.

4-st LPC Sl 2 sts to cn and hold in front, p2, k2 from cn.

5-st LPC Sl 3 sts to cn and hold in front, k2, sl last st from cn to LH needle and p it, k2 from cn.

(worked over 25 sts)

Preparation row (WS) P2, k4, p4, k5, p4, k4, p2.

Row 1 (RS) K2, p4, 4-st RC, p5, 4-st RC, p4, k2.

Row 2 P2, k4, p4, k5, p4, k4, p2.

Row 3 4-st LPC, 4-st RPC, 4-st LPC, p1, 4-st RPC, 4-st LPC, 4-st RPC.

Rows 4 and 6 K2, p4, k4, p2, k1, p2, k4, p4, k2.

Row 5 P2, 4-st LC, p4, 5-st LPC, p4, 4-st LC, p2.

Row 7 P1, 3-st RPC, 4-st LPC, 4-st RPC, p1, 4-st LPC, 4-st RPC, 3-st LPC, p1.

Rows 8 and 10 K1, bind 2, k3, p4, k5, p4, k3, bind 2, k1.

Row 9 P1, k2, p3, 4-st RC, p5, 4-st RC, p3, k2, p1.

Row 11 P1, k2, p2, 3-st RPC, 4-st LPC, p1, 4-st RPC, 3-st LPC, p2, k2, p1.

Row 12 K1, bind 2, k2, bind 2, k3, dec 4 , k3, bind 2, k2, bind 2, k1- 21 sts.

Rows 13, 15, 17, 19, 21 and 23 P1, k2, p2, k2, p7, k2, p2, k2, p1.

Rows 14, 16, 18, 20, 22 and 24 K1, bind 2, k2, bind 2, k7, bind 2, k2, bind 2, k1.

Row 25 P1, k2, p2, k2, p3, M1, inc 2, M1, p3, k2, p2, k2, p1 – 25 sts.

Row 26 K1, bind 2, k2, bind 2, k3, p2, k1, p2, k3, bind 2, k2, bind 2, k1.

Row 27 P1, k2, p2, 3-st LPC, 4-st RPC, p1, 4-st LPC, 3-st RPC, p2, k2, p1.

Rows 28 and 30 K1, bind 2, k3, p4, k5, p4, k3, bind 2, k1.

Row 29 P1, k2, p3, 4-st RC, p5, 4-st RC, p3, k2, p1.

Row 31 P1, 3-st LPC, 4-st RPC, 4-st LPC, p1, 4-st RPC, 4-st LPC, 3-st RPC, p1.

Rows 32 and 34 K2, p4, k4, p2, k1, p2, k4, p4, k2.

Row 33 P2, 4-st LC, p4, 5-st LPC, p4, 4-st LC, p2.

Row 35 4-st RPC, 4-st LPC , 4-st RPC, p1, 4-st LPC , 4-st RPC, 4-st LPC.

Row 36 P2, k4, p4, k5, p4, k4, p2.

Rep rows 1–36.

pretzels

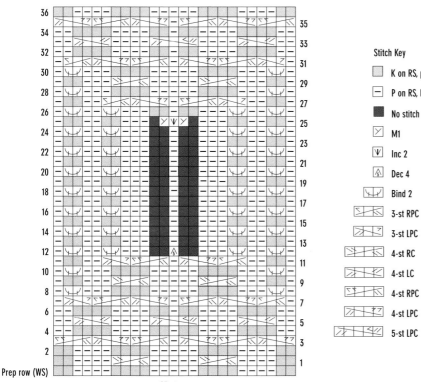

Prep row (WS)

25 sts

Stitch Key

- ☐ K on RS, p on WS
- − P on RS, k on WS
- ■ No stitch
- ☒ M1
- Ⅴ Inc 2
- ⋀ Dec 4
- ⊔ Bind 2
- 3-st RPC
- 3-st LPC
- 4-st RC
- 4-st LC
- 4-st RPC
- 4-st LPC
- 5-st LPC

5-st RPC Sl 2 sts to cn and hold to back, k3, p2 from cn.

5-st LPC Sl 3 sts to cn and hold to front, p2, k3 from cn.

6-st RC Sl 3 sts to cn and hold to back, k3, k3 from cn.

6-st LC Sl 3 sts to cn and hold to front, k3, k3 from cn.

(worked over 15 sts)

Row 1 (RS) K3, p4, 6-st RC, p2.

Row 2 K2, p6, k4, p3.

Row 3 5-st LPC, 5-st RPC, 5-st LPC.

Rows 4 and 6 P3, k4, p6, k2.

Row 5 P2, 6-st LC, p4, k3.

Row 7 5-st RPC, 5-st LPC, 5-st RPC.

Row 8 K2, p6, k4, p3.

Rep rows 1–8.

15 sts

Stitch Key

- ☐ K on RS, p on WS
- − P on RS, k on WS
- 5-st RPC
- 5-st LPC
- 6-st RC
- 6-st LC

5-st RPC Sl 1 st to cn and hold to back, k4, p1 from cn.

5-st LPC Sl 4 sts to cn and hold to front, p1, k4 from cn.

6-st RPC Sl 2 sts to cn and hold to back, k4, p2 from cn.

6-st LPC Sl 4 sts to cn and hold to front, p2, k4 from cn.

8-st RC Sl 4 sts to cn and hold to back, k4, k4 from cn.

8-st LC Sl 4 sts to cn and hold to front, k4, k4 from cn.

(worked over 40 sts)

Preparation row (WS) P4, k6, p8, k4, p8, k6, p4.

Row 1 K4, p6, 8-st RC, p4, 8-st RC, p6, k4.

Row 2 P4, k6, p8, k4, p8, k6, p4.

Row 3 K4, p4, 6-st RPC, 5-st LPC, p2, 5-st RPC, 6-st LPC, p4, k4.

Row 4 P4, k4, p4, k1, p1, k1, p4, k2, p4, k1, p1, k1, p4, k4, p4.

Row 5 K4, p2, 6-st RPC, k1, p1, k1, 5-st LPC, 5-st RPC, k1, p1, k1,

6-st LPC, p2, k4.

Row 6 P4, k2, p4, [k1, p1] twice, k1, p10, [k1, p1] twice, k1, p4, k2, p4.

Row 7 K4, 6-st RPC, [k1, p1] 3 times, 8-st LC, [k1, p1] 3 times, 6-st LPC, k4.

Row 8 P8, [k1, p1] 3 times, k1, p10, [k1, p1] 3 times, k1, p8.

Row 9 8-st LC, [k1, p1] 3 times, 6-st RPC, 6-st LPC, [p1, k1] 3 times, 8-st RC.

Row 10 P8, [k1, p1] twice, k1, p5, k4, p5, [k1, p1] twice, k1, p8.

Row 11 K4, 5-st LPC, p1, k1, p1, 6-st RPC, p4, 6-st LPC, p1, k1, p1, 5-st RPC, k4.

Row 12 P4, [k1, p5] twice, k8, [p5, k1] twice, p4.

Row 13 K4, p1, 5-st LPC, 6-st RPC, p8, 6-st LPC, 5-st RPC, p1, k4.

Rows 14 and 16 P4, k2, p8, k12, p8, k2, p4.

Row 15 K4, p2, 8-st RC, p12, 8-st RC, p2, k4.

Row 17 K4, p1, 5-st RPC, 6-st LPC, p8, 6-st RPC, 5-st LPC, p1, k4.

Row 18 [P4, k1] twice, p1, k1, p4, k8, p4, k1, p1, [k1, p4] twice.

Row 19 K4, 5-st RPC, k1, p1, k1, 6-st LPC, p4, 6-st RPC, k1, p1, k1, 5-st LPC, k4.

Row 20 P9, k1, [p1, k1] twice, p4, k4, p4, k1, [p1, k1] twice, p9.

Row 21 8-st LC, [p1, k1] 3 times, 6-st LPC, 6-st RPC, [k1, p1] 3 times, 8-st RC.

Row 22 P9, k1, [p1, k1] 3 times, p8, [k1, p1] 3 times, k1, p9.

Row 23 K4, 6-st LPC, [p1, k1] 3 times, 8-st LC, [p1, k1] 3 times, 6-st RPC, k4.

Row 24 P4, k2, p5, k1, [p1, k1] twice, p8, [k1, p1] twice, k1, p5, k2, p4.

Row 25 K4, p2, 6-st LPC, p1, k1, p1, 5-st RPC, 5-st LPC, p1, k1, p1, 6-st RPC, k2, p4.

Row 26 P4, k4, p5, k1, p5, k2, p5, k1, p5, k4, p4.

Row 27 K4, p4, 6-st LPC, 5-st RPC, p2, 5-st LPC, 6-st RPC, p4, k4.

Row 28 P4, k6, p8, k4, p8, k6, p4.

Rep rows 1–28.

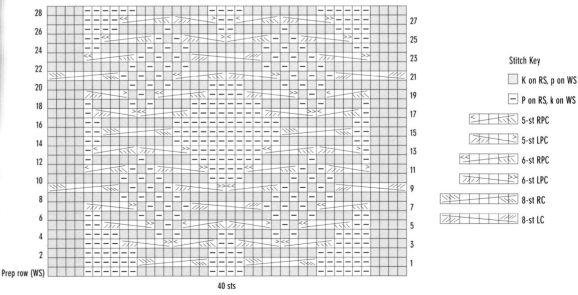

Prep row (WS)

40 sts

Stitch Key

☐ K on RS, p on WS

− P on RS, k on WS

5-st RPC

5-st LPC

6-st RPC

6-st LPC

8-st RC

8-st LC

pretzels

3-st RPC Sl 1 st to cn and hold to back, k2, p1 from cn.

3-st LPC Sl 2 sts to cn and hold to front, p1, k2 from cn.

4-st RC Sl 2 sts to cn and hold to back, k2, k2 from cn.

4-st LC Sl 2 sts to cn and hold to front, k2, k2 from cn.

6-st CL Sl 6 sts to cn, wrap yarn 3 times around these sts under cn in a counter-clockwise direction (looking down from top), sl 6 sts back to LH needle, k2, p2, k2.

(worked over 16 sts)

Preparation row (WS) K2, p4, k4, p4, k2.

Rows 1 and 9 (RS) P2, 4-st RC, p4, 4-st LC, p2.

Rows 2, 8 and 10 K2, p4, k4, p4, k2.

Rows 3 and 11 P1, 3-st RPC, 3-st LPC, p2, 3-st RPC, 3-st LPC, p1.

Rows 4, 6, 12 and 26 K1, [p2, k2] 3 times, p2, k1.

Row 5 P1, k2, p2, 6-st CL, p2, k2, p1.

Rows 7 and 27 P1, 3-st LPC, 3-st RPC, p2, 3-st LPC, 3-st RPC, p1.

Row 13 3-st RPC, p2, 3-st LPC, 3-st RPC, p2, 3-st LPC.

Rows 14, 16, 18, 20, 22 and 24 K2, p4, k4, p4, k2.

Rows 15, 19 and 23 K2, p4, 4-st RC, p4, k2.

Rows 17 and 21 K2, p4, k4, p4, k2.

Row 25 3-st LPC, p2, 3-st RPC, 3-st LPC, p2, 3-st RPC.

Row 28 Rep row 2.

Rep rows 1–28.

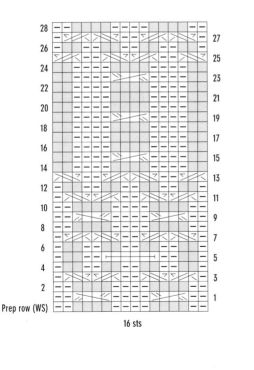

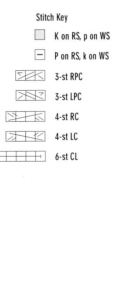

Stitch Key

2-st RPC Sl 1 st to cn and hold to back, k1, p1 from cn.

2-st LPC Sl 1 st to cn and hold to front, p1, k1 from cn.

3-st RC Sl 1 st to cn and hold to back, k2, k1 from cn.

3-st LC Sl 2 sts to cn and hold to front, k1, k2 from cn.

3-st RPC Sl 1 st to cn and hold to back, k2, p1 from cn.

3-st LPC Sl 2 sts to cn and hold to front, p1, k2 from cn.

3-st C Sl 2 sts to cn and hold to back, k1, place p st from cn to LH needle a p it, k1 from cn.

4-st RC Sl 1 st to cn and hold to back, k3, k1 from cn.

4-st LC Sl 3 sts to cn and hold to front, k1, k3 from cn.

4-st RPC Sl 1 st to cn and hold to back, k3, p1 from cn.

4-st LPC Sl 3 sts to cn and hold to front, p1, k3 from cn.

5-st RC Sl 2 sts to cn and hold to back, k3, k2 from cn.

5-st LC Sl 3 sts to cn and hold to front, k2, k3 from cn.

5-st RPC Sl 2 sts to cn and hold to back, k3, p2 from cn.

5-st LPC Sl 3 sts to cn and hold to front, p2, k3 from cn.

5-st C Sl 3 sts to cn and hold to back, k2, place p st from cn to LH needle and p it, k2 from cn. (worked over 23 sts)

Preparation row (WS) P3, k4, p2, k5, p2, k4, p3.

Row 1 (RS) 4-st LPC, p2, 3-st RC, p5, 3-st LC, p2, 4-st RPC.

Row 2 K1, p3, k2, p3, k5, p3, k2, p3, k1.

Row 3 P1, 4-st LPC, 3-st RPC, 2-st LPC, p3, 2-st RPC, 3-st LPC, 4-st RPC, p1.

Row 4 K2, p5, k2, p1, k3, p1, k2, p5, k2.

Row 5 P2, 5-st LC, p2, 2-st LPC, p1, 2-st RPC, p2, 5-st RC, p2.

Row 6 K2, p5, k3, p1, k1, p1, k3, p5, k2.

Row 7 P1, 3-st RPC, 4-st LPC, p2, 3-st C, p2, 4-st RPC, 3-st LPC, p1.

Row 8 K1, p2, k2, p3, k2, p1, k1, p1, k2, p3, k2, p2, k1.

Row 9 3-st RPC, p2, 4-st LPC, 2-st RPC, p1, 2-st LPC, 4-st RPC, p2, 3-st LPC.

Rows 10 and 12 P2, k4, p4, k3, p4, k4, p2.

Row 11 K2, p4, 4-st LC, p3, 4-st RC, p4, k2.

Row 13 3-st LPC, p2, 2-st RPC, 4-st LPC, p1, 4-st RPC, 2-st LPC, p2, 3-st RPC.

Row 14 K1, p2, k2, p1, k2, p3, k1, p3, k2, p1, k2, p2, k1.

Row 15 P1, 3-st LPC, 2-st RPC, p2, k3, p1, k3, p2, 2-st LPC, 3-st RPC, p1.

Row 16 K2, p3, k3, p3, k1, p3, k3, p3, k2.

Row 17 P2, 3-st LPC, p3, k3, p1, k3, p3, 3-st RPC, p2.

Row 18 K3, p2, k3, p3, k1, p3, k3, p2, k3.

Row 19 P3, 3-st LPC, p2, k3, p1, k3, p2, 3-st RPC, p3.

Row 20 K4, p2, k2, p3, k1, p3, k2, p2, k4.

Row 21 P4, 3-st LPC, 4-st RPC, p1, 4-st LPC, 3-st RPC, p4.

Rows 22 and 24 K5, p5, k3, p5, k5.

Row 23 P5, 5-st RC, p3, 5-st LC, p5.

Row 25 P3, 5-st RPC, 3-st LPC, p1, 3-st RPC, 5-st LPC, p3.

Row 26 K3, p3, k3, p2, k1, p2, k3, p3, k3.

Row 27 P1, 5-st RPC, p3, 5-st C, p3, 5-st LPC, p1.

Row 28 K1, p3, k5, p2, k1, p2, k5, p3, k1.

pretzels

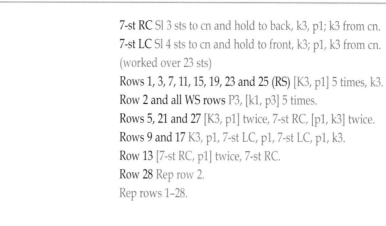

7-st RC Sl 3 sts to cn and hold to back, k3, p1; k3 from cn.

7-st LC Sl 4 sts to cn and hold to front, k3; p1, k3 from cn.

(worked over 23 sts)

Rows 1, 3, 7, 11, 15, 19, 23 and 25 (RS) [K3, p1] 5 times, k3.

Row 2 and all WS rows P3, [k1, p3] 5 times.

Rows 5, 21 and 27 [K3, p1] twice, 7-st RC, [p1, k3] twice.

Rows 9 and 17 K3, p1, 7-st LC, p1, 7-st LC, p1, k3.

Row 13 [7-st RC, p1] twice, 7-st RC.

Row 28 Rep row 2.

Rep rows 1–28.

Stitch Key

▨ K on RS, p on WS	4-st RC
▭ P on RS, k on WS	4-st LC
2-st RPC	4-st RPC
2-st LPC	4-st LPC
3-st RC	5-st RC
3-st LC	5-st LC
3-st RPC	5-st RPC
3-st LPC	5-st LPC
3-st C	5-st C

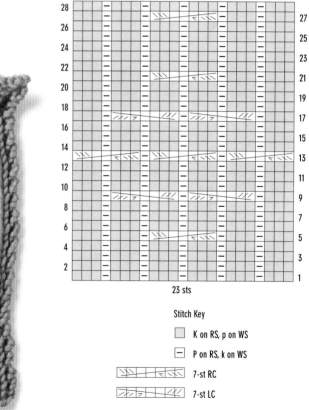

23 sts

Stitch Key

▭ K on RS, p on WS	
▭ P on RS, k on WS	
7-st RC	
7-st LC	

3-st RPC Sl 1 st to cn and hold to back, k2, p1 from cn.

3-st LPC Sl 2 sts to cn and hold to front, p1, k2 from cn.

4-st RC Sl 2 sts to cn and hold to back, k2, k2 from cn.

4-st LC Sl 2 sts to cn and hold to front, k2, k2 from cn.

Wrapped Sts K2, p2, k2, sl these 6 sts from RH needle to cn and wrap yarn 6 times counter-clockwise around the sts, sl back to RH needle.

(worked over 16 sts)

Rows 1 and 17 (RS) P2, 4-st RC, p4, 4-st LC, p2.

Rows 2, 16, and 18 K2, p4, k4, p4, k2.

Rows 3 and 19 P1, 3-st RPC, 3-st LPC, p2, 3-st RPC, 3-st LPC, p1.

Rows 4, 14, 20 and 22 K1, [p2, k2] 3 times, p2, k1.

Row 5 3-st RPC, p2, 3-st LPC, 3-st RPC, p2, 3-st LPC.

Rows 6, 8, 10 and 12 P2, k4, p4, k4, p2.

Rows 7 and 11 K2, p4, 4-st RC, p4, k2.

Row 9 K2, p4, k4, p4, k2.

Row 13 3-st LPC, p2, 3-st RPC, 3-st LPC, p2, 3-st RPC.

Rows 15 and 23 P1, 3-st LPC, 3-st RPC, p2, 3-st LPC, 3-st RPC, p1.

Row 21 P1, k2, p2, Wrapped Sts, p2, k2, p1.

Row 24 Rep row 2.

Rep rows 1–24.

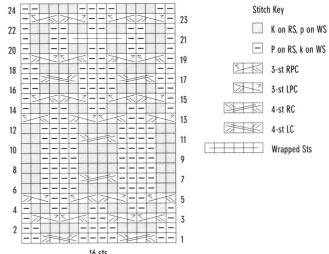

Stitch Key

☐ K on RS, p on WS

— P on RS, k on WS

3-st RPC

3-st LPC

4-st RC

4-st LC

Wrapped Sts

16 sts

pretzels

3-st RPC Sl 1 st to cn and hold to back, k2, p1 from cn.

3-st LPC Sl 2 sts to cn and hold to front, p1, k2 from cn.

4-st RC Sl 2 sts to cn and hold to back, k2, k2 from cn.

4-st LC Sl 2 sts to cn and hold to front, k2, k2 from cn.

(worked over 18 sts)

Rows 1, 3, 23 and 25 (RS) K2, p3, k2, p4, k2, p3, k2.

Rows 2, 4, 22 and 24 P2, k3, p2, k4, p2, k3, p2.

Row 5 [3-st LPC, p2] twice, 3-st RPC, p2, 3-st RPC.

Rows 6 and 20 K1, p2, k3, p2, k2, p2, k3, p2, k1.

Row 7 P1, 3-st LPC, P2, 3-st LPC, 3-st RPC, p2, 3-st RPC, p1.

Rows 8 and 18 K2, p2, k3, p4, k3, p2, k2.

Row 9 P2, 3-st LPC, p2, 4-st RC, p2, 3-st RPC, p2.

Rows 10 and 16 K3, p2, k2, p4, k2, p2, k3.

Row 11 P3, [3-st LPC, 3-st RPC] twice, p3.

Rows 12 and 14 K4, p4, k2, p4, k4.

Row 13 P4, 4-st LC, p2, 4-st LC, p4.

Row 15 P3, [3-st RPC, 3-st LPC] twice, p3.

Row 17 P2, 3-st RPC, p2, 4-st RC, p2, 3-st LPC, p2.

Row 19 P1, 3-st RPC, p2, 3-st RPC, 3-st LPC, p2, 3-st LPC, p1.

Row 21 [3-st RPC, p2] twice, 3-st LPC, p2, 3-st LPC.

Row 26 Rep row 2.

Rep rows 1–26.

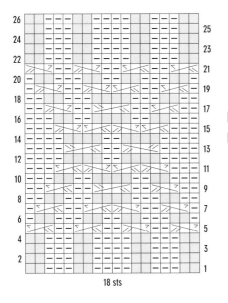

18 sts

Stitch Key

☐ K on RS, p on WS

⊟ P on RS, k on WS

▱ 3-st RPC

▱ 3-st LPC

▱ 4-st RC

▱ 4-st LC

3-st C Wyib sl 1, k2, psso k2 sts.

7-st LC Sl next 4 sts onto cn and hold to front, k3, sl p st from cn to LH needle and p it, k3 from cn.

9-st RC Sl 6 sts from cn and hold to back, k3, sl the 2nd set of 3 sts from cn to LH needle and k them, k3 from cn.

(worked over 37 sts)

Row 1 (RS) *3-st C, p2, k3, p2, 3-st C*, p2, k3, p1, k3, p2; rep between *'s once.

Row 2 *P1, yo, p1, k2, p3, k2, p1, yo, p1*, k2, p3, k1, p3, k2; rep between *'s once.

Row 3 [K3, p2] 3 times, k3, p1, [k3, p2] 3 times, k3.

Row 4 [P3, k2] 3 times, p3, k1, [p3, k2] 3 times, p3.

Row 5 Rep row 1.

Row 6 Rep row 2.

Row 7 [K3, p2] 3 times, 7-st LC, [p2, k3] 3 times.

Row 8 Rep row 4.

Row 9 3-st C, p2, *M1, k3, p2, 3-st C, p2, k3,

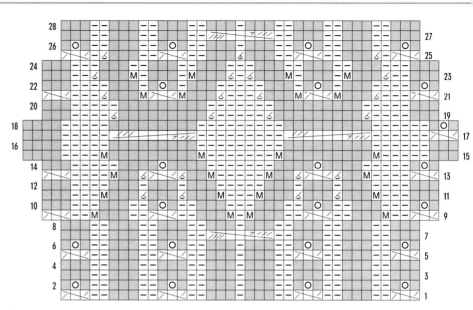

37 sts

Stitch Key

▢	K on RS, p on WS
−	P on RS, k on WS
O	Yarn over
M	M1
◿	P2tog
◿	P3tog
▱	3-st C
▱	7-st LC
▱	9-st RC

M1*, p1; rep between *'s once, p2, 3-st C.

Row 10 P1, yo, p1, *k3, p3, k2, p1, yo, p1, k2, p3; rep from * once, k3, p1, yo, p1 — 41 sts.

Row 11 K3, p3, *M1, k3, p2tog, k3, p2tog, k3, M1, p3; rep from * once, k3.

Row 12 P3, k4, [p3, k1] twice, p3, k5, [p3, k1] twice, p3, k4, p3.

Row 13 3-st C, p4, *M1, k2, p2tog, 3-st C, p2tog, k2, M1*, p5; rep between *'s once, p4, 3-st C.

Row 14 P1, yo, p1, k5, *p4, yo, p4*, k7; rep between *'s once, k5, p1, yo, p1.

Row 15 K3, p5, M1, k9, M1, p7, M1, k9, M1, p5, k3 — 45 sts.

Row 16 P3, k6, p9, k9, p9, k6, p3.

Row 17 3-st C, p6, 9-st RC, p9, 9-st RC, p6, 3-st C.

Row 18 P1, yo, p1, k6, p9, k9, p9, k6, p1, yo, p1.

Row 19 K3, p4, p2tog, k9, p2tog, p5, p2tog, k9, p2tog, p4, k3 — 41 sts.

Row 20 P3, k5, p9, k7, p9, k5, p3.

Row 21 3-st C, p3, *p2tog, k3, M1, 3-st C, M1, k3, p2tog, p3; rep from * once, 3-st C.

Row 22 P1, yo, p1, k4, p3, k1, p1, yo, p1, k1, p3, k5, p3, k1, p1, yo, p1, k1, p3, k4, p1, yo, p1.

Row 23 K3, p2, *p2tog, k3, M1, p1, k3, p1, M1, k3, p2tog*, p1; rep between *'s once, p2, k3.

Row 24 P3, *k3, p3, [k2, p3] twice; rep from * once, k3, p3.

Row 25 3-st C, p1, p2tog, *k3, p2, 3-st C, p2, k3*, p3tog; rep between *'s once, p2tog, p1, 3-st C.

Row 26 Rep row 2 — 37 sts.

Row 27 Rep row 7.

Row 28 Rep row 4.

Rep rows 1–28.

5-st RPC Sl 2 sts to cn and hold to back, k3, p2 from cn.

5-st LPC Sl 3 sts to cn and hold to front, p2, k3 from cn.

6-st RC Sl 3 sts to cn and hold to back, k3, k3 from cn.

6-st LC Sl 3 sts to cn and hold to front, k3, k3 from cn.

(worked over 20 sts)

Rows 1 and 5 (RS) K3, p4, k6, p4, k3.

Rows 2, 4 and 6 P3, k4, p6, k4, p3.

Row 3 K3, p4, 6-st LC, p4, k3.

Row 7 5-st LPC, p2, k6, p2, 5-st RPC.

Rows 8 and 14 K2, p3, k2, p6, k2, p3, k2.

Row 9 P2, 5-st LPC, 6-st LC, 5-st RPC, p2.

Rows 10 and 12 K4, p12, k4.

Row 11 P4, 6-st RC twice, p4.

Row 13 P2, 5-st RPC, 6-st LC, 5-st LPC, p2.

Row 15 5-st RPC, p2, k6, p2, 5-st LPC.

Row 16 Rep row 2.

Rep rows 1–16.

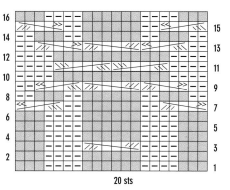

20 sts

Stitch Key

☐ K on RS, p on WS

– P on RS, k on WS

5-st RPC

5-st LPC

6-st RC

6-st LC

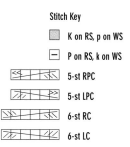

73 puckered cable

4-st RC Sl 1 st to cn and hold to back, k3, k1 from cn.

4-st LC Sl 3 sts to cn and hold to front, k1, k3 from cn.

6-st RC Sl 3 sts to cn and hold to back, k3, k3 from cn.

(worked over 20 sts)

Preparation row (WS) Purl.

Row 1 (RS) K3, 4-st LC, k6, 4-st RC, k3.

Row 2 and all WS rows Purl.

Row 3 K4, 4-st LC, k4, 4-st RC, k4.

Row 5 K5, 4-st LC, k2, 4-st RC, k5.

Row 7 K6, 4-st LC, 4-st RC, k6.

Rows 9 and 21 K7, 6-st RC, k7.

Row 11 and 23 K6, 4-st RC, 4-st LC, k6.

Row 13 4-st LC, k1, 4-st RC, k2, 4-st LC, k1, 4-st RC.

Row 15 Knit.

Row 17 4-st RC, k1, 4-st LC, k2, 4-st RC, k1, 4-st LC.

Row 19 K6, 4-st LC, 4-st RC, k6.

Row 25 K5, 4-st RC, k2, 4-st LC, k5.

Row 27 K4, 4-st RC, k4, 4-st LC, k4.

Row 29 K3, 4-st RC, k6, 4-st LC, k3.

Row 30 Purl.

Rep rows 1–30.

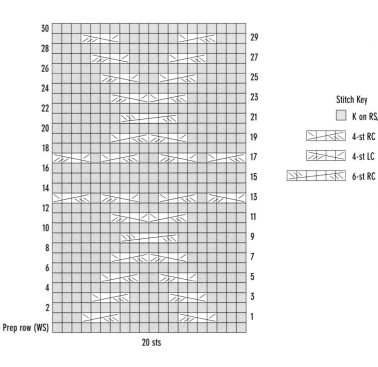

Stitch Key

- ☐ K on RS, p on WS
- 4-st RC
- 4-st LC
- 6-st RC

Prep row (WS)

20 sts

73

74 broken horseshoe

6-st RPC Sl 4 sts to cn and hold to back, k2; p2, k2 from cn.

6-st LPC Sl 2 sts to cn and hold to front, k2, p2; k2 from cn.

(worked over 16 sts)

Rows 1, 3, 5, 9 and 11 (RS) P2, k2, p2, k4, p2, k2, p2.

Rows 2, 4, 6, 8 and 10 K2, p2, k2, p4, k2, p2, k2.

Row 7 P2, 6-st RPC, 6-st LPC, p2.

Rows 12-16 Knit.

Rep rows 1–16.

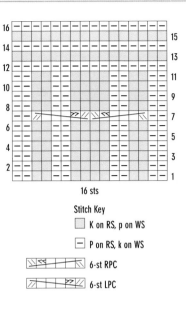

16 sts

Stitch Key

☐ K on RS, p on WS

⊟ P on RS, k on WS

6-st RPC

6-st LPC

75 dew drop

8-st RC Sl 4 sts to cn and hold to back, k4, k4 from cn.

8-st LC Sl 4 sts to cn and hold to front, k4, k4 from cn.

(woked over 16 sts)

Rows 1, 3, 5, 7 and 9 (RS) K4, p3, k2, p3, k4.

Rows 2, 4, 6, 8, 10 P4, k3, p2, k3, p4.

Row 11 8-st LC, 8-st RC.

Row 12 Purl.

Rep rows 1–12.

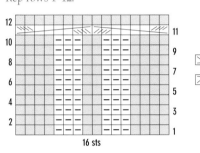

16 sts

Stitch Key

☐ K on RS, p on WS

⊟ P on RS, k on WS

8-st RC

8-st LC

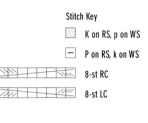

pretzels

4-st RPC Sl 2 sts to cn and hold to back, k2, p2 from cn

4-st LPC Sl 2 sts to cn and hold to front, p2, k2 from cn.

(worked over 8 sts)

Rows 1 and 3 (RS) P2, k4, p2.

Rows 2 and 4 K2, p4, k2.

Row 5 4-st RPC, 4-st LPC.

Rows 6, 8 and 10 P2, k4, p2.

Rows 7 and 9 K2, p4, k2.

Row 11 4-st LPC, 4-st RPC.

Row 12 K2, p4, k2.

Rep rows 1–12.

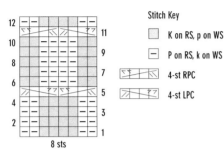

Stitch Key

⬜ K on RS, p on WS

— P on RS, k on WS

4-st RPC

4-st LPC

3-st RPC Sl 1 st to cn and hold to back, k2, p1 from cn.

3-st LPC Sl 2 sts to cn and hold to front, p1, k2 from cn.

4-st RPC Sl 2 sts to cn and hold to back, k2, p2 from cn.

4-st LPC Sl 2 sts to cn and hold to front, p2, k2 from cn.

4-st RC Sl 2 sts to cn and hold to back, k2, k2 from cn.

4-st LC Sl 2 sts to cn and hold to front, k2, k2 from cn.

(worked over 20 sts)

Row 1 (RS) K2, p6, k4, p6, k2.

Row 2 and all WS rows K the knit sts and p the purl sts.

Row 3 3-st LPC, p4, 3-st RPC, 3-st LPC, p4, 3-st RPC.

Row 5 P1, 4-st LPC, 4-st RPC, p2, 4-st LPC, 4-st RPC, p1.

Row 7 P3, 4-st RC, p6, 4-st LC, p3.

Row 9 P1, 4-st RPC, 4-st LPC, p2, 4-st RPC, 4-st LPC, p1.

Row 11 3-st RPC, p4, 3-st LPC, 3-st RPC, p4, 3-st LPC.

Row 12 P2, k6, p4, k6, p2.

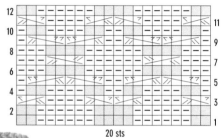

20 sts

Stitch Key

⬜ K on RS, p on WS

— P on RS, k on WS

3-st RPC

3-st LPC

4 st RPC

4-st LPC

4-st RC

4-st LC

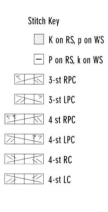

pretzels

3-st LPC Sl 2 sts to cn and hold to front, p1, k2 from cn.

3-st RPC Sl 1 st to cn and hold to back, k2, p1 from cn.

12-st RC Sl 6 sts to cn and hold to back, k2, p2, k2, then k2, p2, k2 from cn.

(worked over 16 sts)

Rows 1, 3, 5 and 7 (RS) K2, p2, k2, p4, k2, p2, k2.

Rows 2, 4, 6 and 8 P2, k2, p2, k4, p2, k2, p2.

Row 9 3-st LPC, p1, 3-st LPC, p2, 3-st RPC, p1, 3-st RPC.

Row 10 K1, [p2, k2] 3 times, p2, k1.

Row 11 P1, 3-st LPC, p1, 3-st LPC, 3-st RPC, p1, 3-st RPC, p1.

Rows 12 and 14 K2, p2, k2, p4, k2, p2, k2.

Row 13 P2, 12-st RC, p2.

Row 15 [P1, 3-st RPC] twice, [3-st LPC, p1] twice.

Row 16 P3, [k2, p2] twice, k2, p3.

Row 17 [3-st RPC, p1] twice, [p1, 3-st LPC] twice.

Rows 18, 20, 22, 24 and 26 P2, k2, p2, k4, p2, k2, p2.

Rows 19, 21, 23, 25, and 27 K2, p2, k2, p4, k2, p2, k2.

Row 28 P2, k2, p2, k4, p2, k2, p2.

Rep rows 9–28.

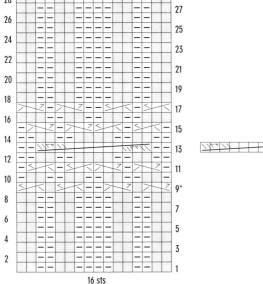

16 sts

Stitch Key

☐ K on RS, p on WS

⊟ P on RS, k on WS

▷◁ 3-st LPC

◁▷ 3-st RPC

▷◁▷◁ 12-st RC

Bind 3 Sl 1 st wyib, k1, yo, k1, psso the k1, yo, k1.

5-st LPC Sl 3 sts to cn and hold to front, p2, k3 from cn.

5-st RPC Sl 2 sts to cn and hold to back, k3, p2 from cn.

6-st LC Sl 3 sts to cn and hold to front, k3, k3 from cn.

6-st RC Sl 3 sts to cn and hold to back, k3, k3 from cn.

(worked over 30 sts)

Rows 1, 3, 5, 7 and 9 (WS) P3, [k2, p3] twice, k4, [p3, k2] twice, p3.

Rows 2, 4, 6 and 8 Bind 3, [p2, bind 3] twice, p4, [bind 3, p2] twice, bind 3.

Row 10 5-st LPC 3 times, 5-st RPC 3 times.

Row 11 K2, [p3, k2] twice, p6, [k2, p3] twice, k2.

Row 12 P2, 5-st LPC twice, 6-st RC, 5-st RPC twice, p2.

Row 13 K4, p3, k2, p12, k2, p3, k4.

Row 14 P4, 5-st LPC, 6-st LC twice, 5-st RPC, p4.

Rows 15 and 17 K6, p18, k6.

Row 16 P6, 6-st RC 3 times, p6.

Row 18 P4, 5-st RPC, 6-st LC twice, 5-st LPC, p4.

Row 19 K4, p3, k2, p12, k2, p3, k4.

Row 20 P2, 5-st RPC twice, 6-st RC, 5-st LPC twice, p2.

Row 21 K2, [p3, k2] twice, p6, [k2, p3] twice, k2.

Row 22 5-st RPC 3 times, 5-st LPC 3 times.

Rows 23, 25, 27 and 29 P3, [k2, p3] twice, k4, [p3, k2] twice, p3.

Rows 24, 26, 28 and 30 Bind 3, [p2, bind 3] twice, p4, [bind 3, p2] twice, bind 3.

Rep rows 1–30.

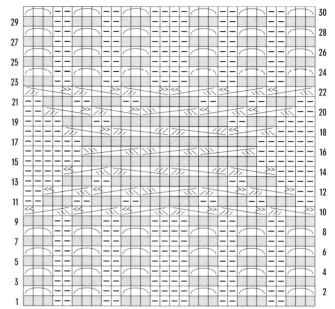

30 sts

Stitch Key

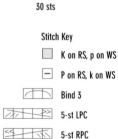

K on RS, p on WS

P on RS, k on WS

Bind 3

5-st LPC

5-st RPC

6-st LC

6-st RC

2-st RC Sl 1 st to cn and hold to back, k1, k1 from cn.

2-st LC Sl 1 st to cn and hold to front, k1, k1 from cn.

2-st RPC Sl 1 st to cn and hold to back, k1, p1 from cn.

2-st LPC Sl 1 st to cn and hold to front, p1, k1 from cn.

(worked over 20 sts)

Row 1 (WS) K4, p2, k2, p4, k2, p2, k4.

Row 2 P4, 2-st LC, p2, 2-st LPC, 2-st RPC, p2, 2-st LC, p4.

Rows 3 and 5 K4, p2, k3, p2, k3, p2, k4.

Row 4 P4, k2, p3, 2-st LC, p3, k2, p4.

Row 6 P4, 2-st LC, p2, 2-st RC, 2-st LC, p2, 2-st LC, p4.

Row 7 K4, p2, k2, p4, k2, p2, k4.

Row 8 P3, 2-st RC, 2-st LC, 2-st RC, p2, 2-st LC, 2-st RC, 2-st LC, p3.

Row 9 K3, p14, k3.

Row 10 [P2, 2-st RC] twice, p4, 2-st RC, p2, 2-st LC, p2.

Row 11 K2, p16, k2.

Row 12 P1, 2-st RC, p2, 2-st RC, 2-st LC, p2, 2-st RC, 2-st LC, p2, 2-st LC, p1.

Row 13 K1, p18, k1.

Row 14 [2-st RC, p2] twice, 2-st LC, 2-st RC, [p2, 2-st LC] twice.

Rows 15 and 17 Purl.

Row 16 P9, 2-st LC, p9.

Row 18 2-st LPC, p2, 2-st LC, p2, 2-st RC, 2-st LC, p2, 2-st RC, p2, 2-st RPC.

Row 19 K1, p18, k1.

Row 20 P1, 2-st LPC, p2, [2-st LC, 2-st RC, p2] twice, 2-st RPC, p1.

Row 21 K2, p16, k2.

Row 22 P2, 2-st LPC, p2, 2-st RC, p4, 2-st LC, p2, 2-st RPC, p2.

Row 23 K3, p14, k3.

Row 24 P3, 2-st LPC, 2-st RPC, 2-st LPC, p2, 2-st RPC, 2-st LPC, 2-st RPC, p3.

Rep rows 1–24.

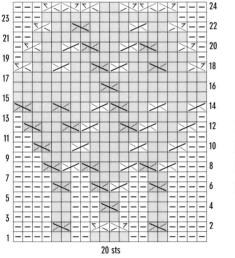

20 sts

Stitch Key

- ⬜ K on RS, p on WS
- ⊟ P on RS, k on WS
- ⤬ 2-st RC
- ⤬ 2-st LC
- ⤬ 2-st RPC
- ⤬ 2-st LPC

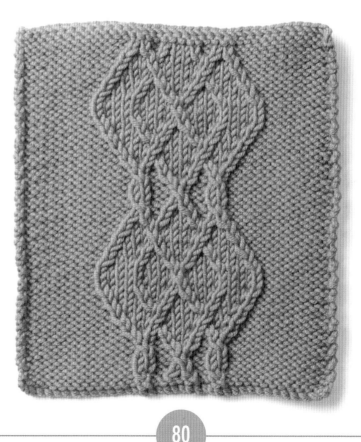

5-st RPC Sl 1 st to cn and hold to back, k4, p1 from cn.

5-st LPC Sl 4 sts to cn and hold to front, p1, k4 from cn.

6-st RPC Sl 2 sts to cn and hold to back, k4, p2 from cn.

6-st LPC Sl 4 sts to cn and hold to front, p2, k4 from cn.

7-st RPC Sl 3 sts to cn and hold to back, k4, p3 from cn.

7-st LPC Sl 4 sts to cn and hold to front, p3, k4 from cn.

8-st RC Sl 4 sts to cn and hold to back, k4, k4 from cn.

8-st LC Sl 4 sts to cn and hold to front, k4, k4 from cn.

8-st RPC Sl 4 sts to cn and hold to back, k4, p4 from cn.

8-st LPC Sl 4 sts to cn and hold to front, p4, k4 from cn.

(panel of 54 sts, inc'd to 58 sts, dec'd to 54 sts)

Rows 1 and 3 (WS) K9, p8, k6, p8, k6, p8, k9.

Row 2 P9, 8-st RC, [p6, 8-st RC] twice, p9.

Row 4 P6, [7-st RPC, 7-st LPC] 3 times, p6.

Row 5 K4, [M1, k1] twice, p4, [k6, p8] twice, k6, p4, [k1, M1] twice, k4.

Row 6 P4, 8-st RC, [p6, 8-st LC] 3 times, p4.

Row 7 K4, [p8, k6] 3 times, p8, k4.

Row 8 P2, 6-st RPC, [7-st LPC, 7-st RPC] 3 times, 6-st LPC, p2.

Row 9 K2, p4, k5, [p8, k6] twice, p8, k5, p4, k2.

Row 10 P1, 5-st RPC, p5, [8-st RC, p6] twice, 8-st RC, k5, 5-st LPC, p1.

Row 11 K1, p4, [k6, p8] 3 times, k6, p4, k1.

Row 12 5-st RPC, p3, 7-st RPC, 7-st LPC, p3, k8, p3, 7-st RPC, 7-st LPC, p3, 5-st LPC.

Rows 13 and 15 P4, k4, p4, k6, p4, k3, p8, k3, p4, k6, p4, k4, p4.

Row 14 K4, p4, k4, p6, k4, p3, 8-st RC, p3, k4, p6, k4, p4, k4.

Row 16 5-st LPC, p3, 7-st LPC, 7-st RPC, p3, k8, p3, 7-st LPC, 7-st RPC, p3, 5-st RPC.

Row 17 K1, p4, [k6, p8] 3 times, k6, p4, k1.

Row 18 P1, 5-st LPC, p5, [8-st RC, p6] twice, 8-st RC, p5, 5-st RPC, p1.

Row 19 K2, p4, k5, [p8, k6] twice, p8, k5, p4, k2.

Row 20 P2, 6-st LPC, 7-st RPC, [7-st LPC, 7-st RPC] twice, 7-st LPC, 6-st RPC, p2.

Row 21 K4, [p8, k6] 3 times, p8, k4.

Row 22 P4, 8-st LPC, p6 [8-st LC, p6] twice, 8-st RPC, p4.

Row 23 K4, p2tog twice, p4, [k6, p8] twice, k6, p4, p2tog tbl twice, k4.

Row 24 P6, [7-st LPC, 7-st RPC] 3 times, p6.

Rows 25, 27, 29 and 31 K9, [p8, k6] twice, p8, k9.

Rows 26 and 30 P9, [8-st RC, k6] twice, 8-st RC, p9.

Row 28 P9, [k8, p6] twice, k8, p9.

Row 32 P9, [k8, p6] twice, k8, p9.

Rep rows 1–32.

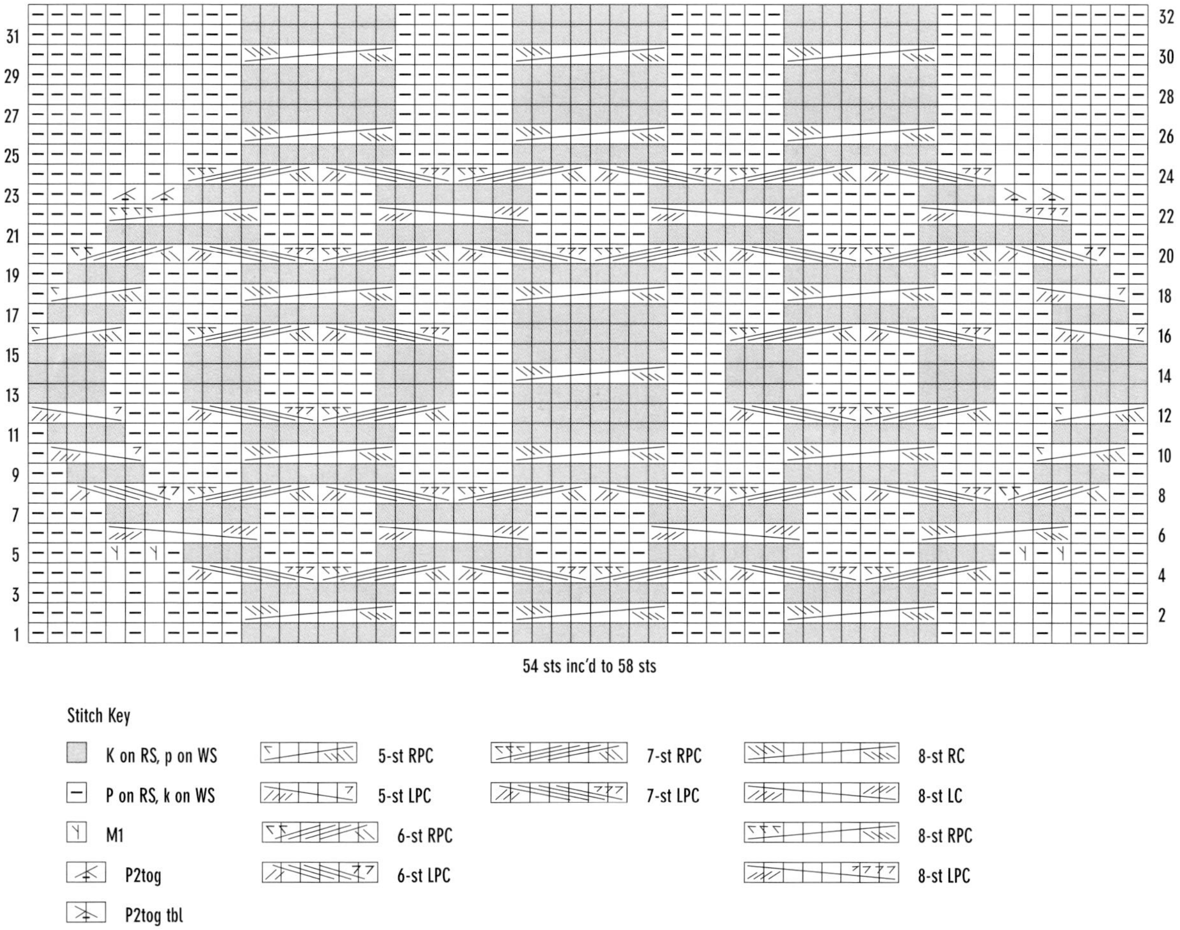

The chart rows are numbered 1–32. Left-side labels (odd rows): 31, 29, 27, 25, 23, 21, 19, 17, 15, 13, 11, 9, 7, 5, 3, 1. Right-side labels (even rows): 32, 30, 28, 26, 24, 22, 20, 18, 16, 14, 12, 10, 8, 6, 4, 2.

54 sts inc'd to 58 sts

Stitch Key

▨	K on RS, p on WS		5-st RPC		7-st RPC		8-st RC
—	P on RS, k on WS		5-st LPC		7-st LPC		8-st LC
Υ	M1		6-st RPC				8-st RPC
⤡	P2tog		6-st LPC				8-st LPC
⤢	P2tog tbl						

4-st RPC Sl 1 st to cn and hold to back, k3, p1 from cn.

4-st LPC Sl 3 sts to cn and hold to front, p1, k3 from cn.

6-st RC Sl 3 sts to cn and hold to back, k3, k3 from cn.

6-st LC Sl 3 sts to cn and hold to front, k3, k3 from cn.

(worked over 18 sts)

Preparation row (WS) P3, k6, p6, k3.
Row 1 (RS) P3, 6-st LC, p6, k3.
Row 2 P3, k6, p6, k3.
Row 3 P2, 4-st RPC, 4-st LPC, p4, 4-st RPC.
Row 4 K1, p3, k4, p3, k2, p3, k2.
Row 5 P1, 4-st RPC, p2, 4-st LPC, p2, 4-st RPC, p1.
Row 6 K2, p3, k2, p3, k4, p3, k1.

Row 7 4-st RPC, p4, 4-st LPC, 4-st RPC, p2.
Rows 8 and 10 K3, p6, k6, p3.
Row 9 K3, p6, 6-st LC, p3.
Row 11 4-st LPC, k4, 4-st RPC, 4-st LPC, p2.
Row 12 [P2, k3] twice, k4, p3, k1.
Row 13 P1, 4-st LPC, p2, 4-st RPC, p2, 4-st LPC, p1.
Row 14 K1, p3, k4, [p3, k2] twice.

Row 15 P2, 4-st LPC, 4-st RPC, p4, 4-st LPC.
Rows 16, 18, 20 and 22 P3, k6, p6, k3.
Rows 17 and 21 P3, 6-st LC, p6, k3.
Row 19 P3, k6, p6, k3.
Row 23 P2, 4-st RPC, 4-st LPC, p4, 4-st RPC.
Row 24 K1, p3, k4, [p3, k2] twice.
Row 25 P1, 4-st RPC, p2, 4-st LPC, p2, 4-st RPC, p1.
Row 26 [K2, p3] twice, k4, p3, k1.
Row 27 4-st RPC, p4, 4-st LPC, 4-st RPC, p2.
Rows 28, 30, 32 and 34 K3, p6, k6, p3.
Rows 29 and 33 K3, p6, 6-st RC, p3.
Row 31 K3, p6, k6, p3.
Row 35 4-st LPC, p4, 4-st RPC, 4-st LPC, p2.
Row 36 [K2, p3] twice, k4, p3, k1.
Row 37 P1, 4-st LPC, p2, 4-st RPC, p2, 4-st LPC, p1.
Row 38 K1, p3, k4, [p3, k2] twice.
Row 39 P2, 4-st LPC, 4-st RPC, p4, 4-st LPC.
Rows 40 and 42 P3, k6, p6, k3.
Row 41 P3, 6-st LC, p6, k3.
Row 43 P3, k6, p6, k3.
Row 44 P3, k6, p6, k3.
Rep rows 1–44.

Stitch Key

▢	K on RS, p on WS
—	P on RS, k on WS
	4-st RPC
	4-st LPC
	6-st RC
	6-st LC

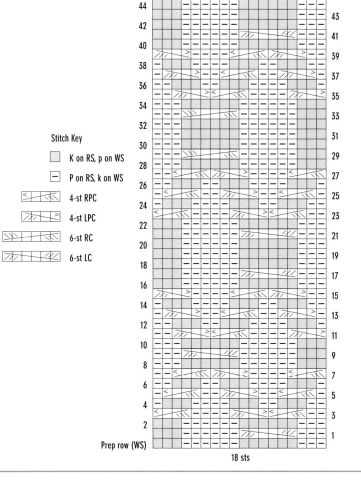

Prep row (WS)

18 sts

pretzels

2-st RPC Sl 1 st to cn and hold to back, k1, p1 from cn.

2-st LPC Sl 1 st to cn and hold to front, p1, k1 from cn.

3-st RPC Sl 2 sts to cn and hold to back, k1, place p st from cn to LH needle and p it, k1 from cn.

4-st RPC Sl 1 st to cn and hold to back, k3, p1 from cn.

4-st LPC Sl 3 sts to cn and hold to front, p1, k3 from cn.

5-st RPT Sl 2 sts to cn and hold to back, k3; p1, k1 from cn.

5-st LPT Sl 3 sts to cn and hold to front, k1, p1; k3 from cn.

5-st RPC Sl 2 sts to cn and hold to back, k3, p2 from cn.

5-st LPC Sl 3 sts to cn and hold to front, p2, k3 from cn.

6-st RPC Sl 3 sts to cn and hold to back, k3, p3 from cn.

6-st LPC Sl 3 sts to cn and hold to front, p3, k3 from cn.

(worked over 21 sts)

Row 1 (RS) P6, k3, p3, k3, p6.

Row 2 K6, p3, k3, p3, k6.

Row 3 P4, 5-st RPT, p3, 5-st LPT, p4.

Row 4 K4, p3, k1, p1, k3, p1, k1, p3, k4.

Row 5 P2, 5-st RPC, p1, 2-st LPC, p1, 2-st RPC, p1, 5-st LPC, p2.

Row 6 K2, p3, k4, p1, k1, p1, k4, p3, k2.

Row 7 5-st RPC, p4, 3-st RPC, p4, 5-st LPC.

Row 8 P3, k6, p1, k1, p1, k6, p3.

Row 9 K3, p5, 2-st RPC, p1, 2-st LPC, p5, k3.

Row 10 P3, k5, p1, k3, p1, k5, p3.

Row 11 5-st LPC, p2, 2-st RPC, p3, 2-st LPC, p2, 5-st RPC.

Row 12 K2, p3, k2, p1, k5, p1, k2, p3, k2.

Row 13 P2, 6-st LPC, p5, 6-st RPC, p2.

Row 14 K5, p3, k5, p3, k5.

Row 15 P5, 4-st LPC, p3, 4-st RPC, p5.

Row 16 K6, p3, k3, p3, k6.

Rep rows 1–16.

21 sts

Stitch Key

☐ K on RS, p on WS

— P on RS, k on WS

2-st RPC

2-st LPC

3-st RPC

4-st RPC

4-st LPC

5-st RPT

5-st LPT

5-st RPC

5-st LPC

6-st RPC

6-st LPC

4-st RC Sl 2 sts to cn and hold to back, k2, k2 from cn.

4-st LC Sl 2 sts to cn and hold to front, k2, k2 from cn.

4-st RPC Sl 2 sts to cn and hold in back, k2, p2 from cn.

4-st LPC Sl 2 sts to cn and hold in front, p2, k2 from cn.

(multiple of 32)

Preparation row (WS) K5, p4, [k2, p2] twice, [k4, p2] twice, k3.

Row 1 P3, 4-st LPC, 4-st RPC, p4, k2, p2, k2, 4-st RPC, 4-st LPC, p3.

Row 2 K3, p2, k4, p4, k2, p2, k6, p4, k5.

Row 3 P5, 4-st RC, p4, 4-st RPC, p2, 4-st RC, p4, 4-st LPC, p1.

Row 4 K1, p2, k6, p4, k4, p2, k4, p4, k5.

Row 5 P5, k2, 4-st LPC, 4-st RPC, p2, 4-st RPC, 4-st LPC, p4, k2, p1.

Row 6 K1, p2, [k4, p2] twice, k4, p4, k2, p2, k5.

Row 7 P5, 4-st LPC, 4-st LC, p2, 4-st RPC, p4, 4-st LPC, 4-st RPC, p1.

Rows 8 and 10 K3, p4, k8, p2, k2, p6, k7.

Row 9 P7, 4-st RC, k2, p2, k2, p8, 4-st LC, p3.

Row 11 P5, 4-st RPC, 4-st LC, p2, 4-st LPC, p4, 4-st RPC, 4-st LPC, p1.

Row 12 K1, [p2, k4] 3 times, p4, k2, p2, k5.

Row 13 P5, k2, 4-st RPC, 4-st LPC, p2, 4-st LPC, 4-st RPC, p4, k2, p1.

Row 14 K1, p2, k6, p4, k4, p2, k4, p4, k5.

Row 15 P5, 4-st RC, p4, 4-st LPC, p2, 4-st RC, p4, 4-st RPC, p1.

Row 16 K3, p2, k4, p4, k2, p2, k6, p4, k5.

Row 17 P3, 4-st RPC, 4-st LPC, p4, k2, p2, k2, 4-st LPC, 4-st RPC, p3.

Row 18 K5, p4, [k2, p2] twice, [k4, p2] twice, k3.

Row 19 P1, 4-st RPC, p4, 4-st LPC, 4-st RPC, p2, 4-st LPC, 4-st LC, p5.

Rows 20 and 22 K5, p6, k6, p4, k8, p2, k1.

Row 21 P1, k2, p8, 4-st LC, p6, 4-st RC, k2, p5.

Row 23 P1, 4-st LPC, p4, 4-st RPC, 4-st LPC, p2, 4-st RPC, 4-st LC, p5.

Row 24 K5, p4, [k2, p2] twice, [k4, p2] twice, k3.

Rep rows 1–24.

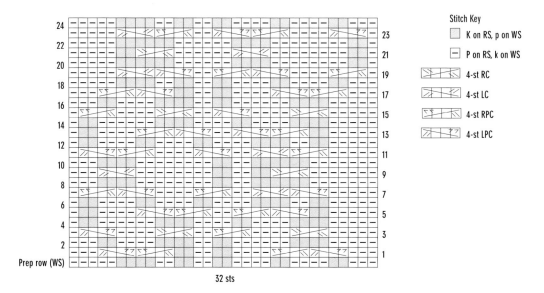

Stitch Key

K on RS, p on WS

— P on RS, k on WS

4-st RC

4-st LC

4-st RPC

4-st LPC

32 sts

4-st RC Slip 2 sts to cn and hold to back, k2, k2 from cn.

4-st LC Slip 2 sts to cn and hold to front, k2, k2 from cn.

4-st RPC Slip 2 sts to cn and hold to back, k2, p2 from cn.

4-st LPC Slip 2 sts to cn and hold to front, p2, k2 from cn.

(worked over 16 sts)

Preparation row (WS) K6, p4, k6.

Row 1 (RS) P6, 4-st RC, p6.

Row 2 K6, p4, k6.

Row 3 P4, 4-st RPC, 4-st LPC, p4.

Row 4 K4, p2, k4, p2, k4.

Row 5 P2, 4-st RC, p4, 4-st LC, p2.

Row 6 K2, p4, k4, p4, k2.

Row 7 [4-st RPC, 4-st LPC] twice.

Rows 8 and 10 P2, k4, p4, k4, p2.

Row 9 K2, p4, 4-st RC, p4, k2.

Row 11 4-st LC, 4-st RPC, 4-st LPC, 4-st RC.

Row 12 P6, k4, p6.

Row 13 K2, 4-st LPC, p4, 4-st RPC, k2.

Row 14 P2, k2, p2, k4, p2, k2, p2.

Row 15 K2, p2, 4-st LPC, 4-st RPC, p2, k2.

Row 16 and 18 P2, k4, p4, k4, p2.

Row 17 K2, p4, 4-st RC, p4, k2.

Row 19 [4-st LPC, 4-st RPC] twice.

Row 20 K2, p4, k4, p4, k2.

Row 21 P2, 4-st LPC, p4, 4-st RPC, p2.

Row 22 K4 [p2, k4] twice.

Row 23 P4, 4-st LPC, 4-st RPC, p4.

Rows 24 and 26 K6, p4, k6.

Row 25 P6, 4-st RC, p6.

Row 27 P4, 4-st RPC, 4-st LPC, p4.

Rows 28, 30, 32 and 34 K4, p2, k4, p2, k4.

Rows 29, 31 and 33 P4, k2, p4, k2, p4.

Row 35 P4, 4-st LPC, 4-st RPC, p4.

Row 36 K6, p4, k6.

Rep rows 1–36.

Stitch Key

K on RS, p on WS

P on RS, k on WS

4-st RC

4-st LC

4-st RPC

4-st LPC

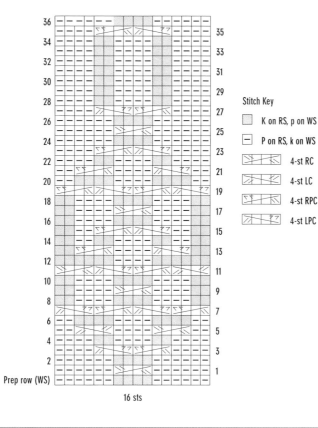

16 sts

RT K2tog, do not sl off needle, k first st, sl both sts from needle.

LT K 2nd st tbl, do not sl off needle, k first st, sl both sts from needle.

RPT Sl 1 to cn, hold to back of work, k1, p1 from cn.

LPT Sl 1 to cn, hold to front of work, p1, k1 from cn. (worked over 8 sts)

Preparation row (WS) K1, p2, k2, p2, k1.

Rows 1 and 9 [RPT, LPT] twice.

Rows 2, 4, 10 and 12 P1, k2, p2, k2, p1.

Rows 3 and 11 K1, p2, LT, p2, k1.

Rows 5 and 13 [LPT, RPT] twice.

Rows 6, 8 and 14 K1, p2, k2, p2, k1.

Rows 7 and 15 P1, RT, p2, RT, p1.

Rows 16, 18, 20, 22, 24, 26, 28 and 30 K1, p2, k2, p2, k1.

Rows 17, 19, 21, 23, 25, 27 and 29 P1, k2, p2, k2, p1.

Row 31 P1, RT, p2, RT, p1.

Row 32 K1, p2, k2, p2, k1.

Rep rows 1–32.

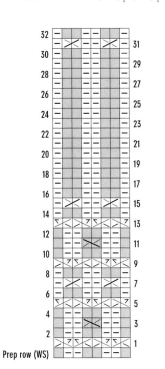

Prep row (WS)

Stitch Key

K on RS, p on WS

— P on RS, k on WS

RT

LT

RPT

LPT

braids

87 beanstalk

6-st LC Sl 3 sts to cn and hold to front, k3, k3 from cn.
6-st RC Sl 3 sts to cn and hold to back, k3, k3 from cn.
(worked over 9 sts)
Rows 1 and 3 (RS) Knit.
Row 2 and all WS rows Purl.
Row 5 6-st LC, k3.
Rows 7 and 9 Knit.
Row 11 K3, 6-st RC.
Row 12 Purl.
Rep rows 1–12.

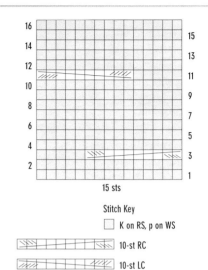

9 sts

Stitch Key

☐ K on RS, p on WS

6-st LC

6-st RC

87

88 plaited cable

10-st RC Sl 5 sts to cn and hold to back, k5,
k5 from cn.
10-st LC Sl 5 sts to cn and hold to front, k5,
k5 from cn.
(worked over 15 sts)
Row 1 (RS) Knit.
Row 2 and all WS rows Purl.
Row 3 10-st RC, k5.
Rows 5, 7 and 9 Knit.
Row 11 K5, 10-st LC.
Rows 13 and 15 Knit.
Row 16 Purl.
Rep rows 1–16.

15 sts

Stitch Key

☐ K on RS, p on WS

10-st RC

10-st LC

88

89 chicken scratch

3-st RPC Sl 2 sts to cn and hold to back, k1tbl, then p1, k1tbl from cn.

3-st LPC Sl 1 st to cn and hold to front, k1 tbl, p1, then k1 tbl from cn.

(worked over 5 sts)

Preparation row (WS) P1 tbl, [k1, p1 tbl] twice.

Row 1 (RS) K1 tbl, p1, 3-st RPC.

Row 2 P1 tbl, [k1, p1 tbl] twice.

Row 3 3-st LPC, p1, k1 tbl.

Row 4 P1 tbl, [k1, p1 tbl] twice.

Rep rows 1–4.

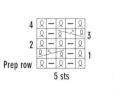

Stitch Key

Ⓠ K tbl on RS, p tbl on WS

▬ P on RS, k on WS

  3-st RPC

  3-st LPC

90 long and winding

10-st rib RC Sl 5 sts to cn and hold to back, rib next 5 sts, rib 5 from cn.

10-st rib LC Sl 5 sts to cn and hold to front, rib next 5 sts, rib 5 from cn.

(worked over 15 sts)

Rows 1 and 3 (RS) [K1, p1] 2 times, k2, p1, k1, p1, k2, [p1, k1] 2 times.

Row 2 and all WS rows K the knit sts and p the purl sts.

Row 5 10-st rib LC, [k1, p1] 2 times, k1.

Rows 7 and 9 [K1, p1] 2 times, k2, p1, k1, p1, k2, [p1, k1] 2 times.

Row 11 [K1, p1] 2 times, k1, 10-st rib RC.

Row 12 Rep row 2.

Rep rows 1–12.

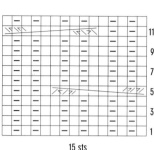

15 sts

Stitch Key

☐ K on RS, p on WS

▬ P on RS, k on WS

  10-st rib RC

  10-st rib LC

91 garlic braid

4-st RC Sl 2 sts to cn and hold to back, k2, k2 from cn.
4-st LC Sl 2 sts to cn and hold to front, k2, k2 from cn.
(worked over 8 sts)
Rows 1 and 3 (WS) Purl.
Row 2 [4-st RC] twice.
Row 4 K2, 4-st LC, k2.
Rep rows 1–4.

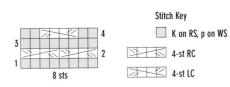

Stitch Key

⬜ K on RS, p on WS

▱ 4-st RC

▱ 4-st LC

92 pippi

12-st RC (worked over 2 rows) Row 3 K12,
[turn work, p6, turn, k6] twice, sl these 6 sts to
cn and hold to RS of work, wyib sl 6 sts from
RH needle back to LH needle and k these 6 sts.
Row 4 P6, p6 from cn.
12-st LC (worked over 2 rows) Row 7 K6, [turn
work, p6, turn, k6] twice, sl these 6 sts to cn
and hold to RS of work, wyib sl 6 sts from LH
needle to RH needle.
Row 8 P6 from cn, p6.
(worked over 18 sts)
Rows 1 and 5 (RS) Knit.
Rows 2 and 6 Purl.
Row 3 12-st RC, k6.
Row 4 P6, 12-st RC.
Row 7 K6, 12-st LC.
Row 8 12-st LC, p6.
Rep rows 1–8.

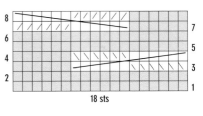

18 sts

Stitch Key

⬜ K on RS, p on WS

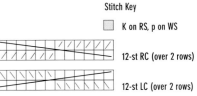

12-st RC (over 2 rows)

12-st LC (over 2 rows)

93 basic braid

6-st RC Sl 3 sts to cn and hold to back, k3, k3 from cn.

6-st LC Sl 3 sts to cn and hold to front, k3, k3 from cn.

(worked over 9 sts)

Rows 1 and 5 (RS) Knit.

Row 2 and all WS rows Purl.

Row 3 6-st RC, k3.

Row 7 K3, 6-st LC.

Row 8 Purl.

Rep rows 1–8.

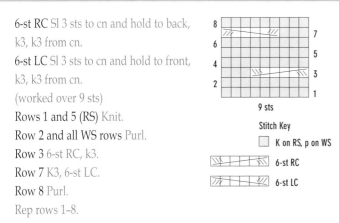

9 sts

Stitch Key

☐ K on RS, p on WS

6-st RC

6-st LC

94 double fantasy

9-st RPC Sl 5 sts to cn and hold to back, k4, then sl the p st from cn back to LH needle and p it, k4 from cn.

9-st LPC Sl 5 sts to cn and hold to front, k4, then sl the p st from cn back to LH needle and p it, k4 from cn.

(worked over 24 sts)

Rows 1, 5, 9 and 11 (RS) K4, [p1, k4] 4 times.

Row 2 and all WS rows [P4, k1] 4 times, p4.

Row 3 K4, [p1, 9-st LPC] twice.

Row 7 [9-st RPC, p1] twice, k4.

Row 12 P4, [k1, p4] 4 times.

Rep rows 1–12.

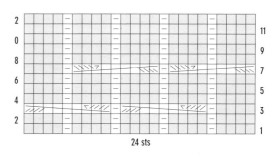

24 sts

Stitch Key

☐ K on RS, p on WS

– P on RS, k on WS

9-st RPC

9-st LPC

braids

93

94

95 crossroads

7-st RPC Sl 4 sts to cn and hold to back, k3, then p1, k3 from cn.

7-st LPC Sl 3 sts to cn and hold to front, k3, p1, then k3 from cn.

(worked over 23 sts)

Rows 1, 3, 5, 7, 9 and 11 (RS) K3, [p1, k3] 5 times.

Row 2 and all WS rows [P3, k1] 5 times, p3.

Rows 13 and 29 [K3, p1] twice, 7-st RPC, [p1, k3] twice.

Rows 15, 19, 23 and 27 K3, [p1, k3] 5 times.

Rows 17 and 25 K3, p1, [7-st LPC, p1] twice, k3.

Row 21 7-st RPC, [p1, 7-st RPC] twice.

Row 30 [P3, k1] 5 times, p3.

Rep rows 1–30.

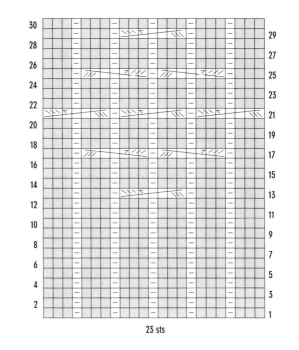

23 sts

Stitch Key

▢	K on RS, p on WS
−	P on RS, k on WS
	7-st RPC
	7-st LPC

95

96 fudge swirl

8-st LPC Sl 3 sts to cn and hold to front, k3, p2, then k3 from cn.

(worked over 18 sts)

Rows 1, 3, 19, 21, 23, 25 and 27 (RS) [K3, p2] 3 times, k3.

Row 2 and all WS rows P3, [k2, p3] 3 times.

Rows 5, 9, 13 and 17 K3, p2, 8-st LPC, p2, k3.

Rows 7, 11 and 15 8-st LPC, p2, 8-st LPC,

Row 28 P3, [k2, p3] 3 times.

Rep rows 1–28.

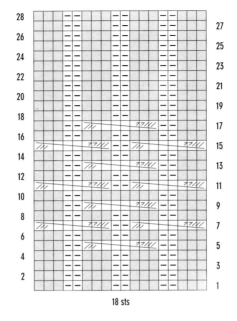

18 sts

Stitch Key

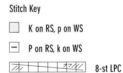

K on RS, p on WS

− P on RS, k on WS

8-st LPC

97 peek-a-boo

3-st RPC Sl 1 st to cn and hold to back, k2, p1 from cn.
3-st LPC Sl 2 sts to cn and hold to front, p1, k2 from cn.
4-st RC Sl 2 sts to cn and hold to back, k2, k2 from cn.
4-st LC Sl 2 sts to cn and hold to front, k2, k2 from cn.
5-st RPC Sl 3 sts to cn and hold to back, k2, p3 from cn.
(worked over 10 sts)
Row 1 (RS) P2, k6, p2.
Rows 2, 4, 6, 16, 18, 20, 22 and 24 K2, p6, k2.
Row 3 P2, 4-st LC, k2, p2.
Row 5 P2, k2, 4-st RC, p2.
Row 7 P1, 5-st RPC, 3-st LPC, p1.

Row 8 K1, p2, k4, p2, k1.
Row 9 3-st RPC, p4, 3-st LPC.
Row 10 P2, k6, p2.
Row 11 3-st LPC, p4, 3-st RPC.
Row 12 K1, p2, k4, p2, k1.
Row 13 P1, 3-st LPC, p2, 3-st RPC, p1.
Row 14 K2, [p2, k2] twice.
Rows 15, 19 and 23 P2, 4-st LC, k2, p2.
Rows 17, 21 and 25 P2, k2, 4-st RC, p2.
Row 26 K2, p6, k2.
Rep rows 3–26.

98 turkey scratch

2-st RC Sl 1 st to cn and hold to back, k1, k1 from cn.
2-st LC Sl 1 st to cn and hold to front, k1, k1 from cn.
(worked over 3 sts)
Row 1 (RS) 2-st RC, k1.
Row 2 Purl.
Row 3 K1, 2-st LC.
Row 4 Purl.
Rep rows 1-4.

Stitch Key
☐ K on RS, p on WS
⧄ 2-st RC
⧄ 2-st LC

10 sts

Stitch Key
☐ K on RS, p on WS
— P on RS, k on WS
⧄ 3-st RPC
⧄ 3-st LPC
⧄ 4-st RC
⧄ 4-st LC
⧄ 5-st RPC

97

98

allover

99 ice storm

4-st RC Sl 2 sts to cn and hold to back, k2, k2 from cn.

(multiple of 6 sts plus 2)

Rows 1 and 3 (RS) Knit.

Row 2 Purl.

Row 4 *K2, p4; rep from *, end k2.

Row 5 P2, *4-st RC, p2; rep from * to end.

Row 6 Purl.

Rep rows 1–6.

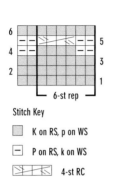

Stitch Key

☐ K on RS, p on WS

⊟ P on RS, k on WS

▨ 4-st RC

99

100 windswept

4-st LC Sl 2 sts to cn and hold to front, k2, k2 from cn.

(multiple of 5 sts plus 1)

Row 1 (RS) *P1, k4; rep from * to last st, p1.

Row 2 K1, *p4, k1; rep from * to end.

Row 3 *P1, 4-st LC; rep from * to last st, p1.

Row 4 Rep row 2.

Rep rows 1–4.

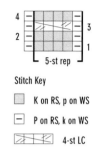

Stitch Key

☐ K on RS, p on WS

⊟ P on RS, k on WS

▨ 4-st LC

100

101 quail

3-st RC Sl 2 sts to cn and hold to back, k1, k2 from cn.

3-st LC Sl 1 st to cn and hold to front, k2, k1 from cn.

(multiple of 18 sts plus 3)

Rows 1, 3 and 5 (WS) K3, *p2, [wyif sl 1] twice, p2, k3, p6, k3; rep from * to end.

Rows 2, 4 and 6 (RS) *P3, k6, p3, 3-st RC, 3-st LC; rep from *, end p3.

Rows 7, 9 and 11 K3, *p6, k3, p2, [wyif sl 1] twice, p2, k3; rep from * to end.

Rows 8, 10 and 12 *P3, 3-st RC, 3-st LC, p3, k6; rep from *, end p3.

Rep rows 1–12.

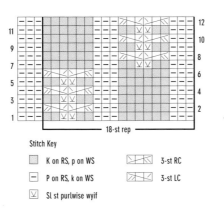

18-st rep

Stitch Key

☐ K on RS, p on WS

□ P on RS, k on WS

Ⅴ Sl st purlwise wyif

3-st RC

3-st LC

102 firefly

4-st RC Sl 2 sts to cn and hold to back, k2, k2 from cn.

(multiple of 10 sts plus 1)

Rows 1, 5, 7, 9, 13, 17, 19 and 21 (RS) *P1, k4; rep from *, end p1.

Row 2 and all WS rows K1, *p4, k1; rep from * to end.

Rows 3 and 23 *P1, 4-st RC, p1, k4; rep from *, end p1.

Rows 11 and 15 *P1, k4, p1, 4-st RC; rep from *, end p1.

Row 24 Rep row 2.

Rep rows 1–24.

10-st rep

Stitch Key

☐ K on RS, p on WS

□ P on RS, k on WS

4-st RC

103 candy stripes

4-st LC Sl 2 sts to cn and hold to front, k2, k2 from cn.
6-st LC Sl 3 sts to cn and hold to front, k3, k3 from cn.
(multiple of 14 sts plus 2)
Rows 1 and 5 (RS) *P2, 4-st LC, p2, k6; rep from *, end p2.

Rows 2 and 4 K2, *p6, k2, p4, k2; rep from * to end.
Row 3 *P2, 4-st LC, p2, 6-st LC; rep from *, end p2.
Row 6 Rep row 2.
Rep rows 1–6.

Stitch Key

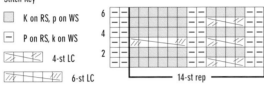

▢	K on RS, p on WS
—	P on RS, k on WS
⧄	4-st LC
⧄	6-st LC

14-st rep

103

104 lifted cables

(multiple of 24 sts plus 4 selvage sts)
Note Work 2 sts at beg and end of every row in St st selvage sts. This pattern does not have a chart.
Rows 1–6 Work in St st.
Row 7 K2 (selvage sts), *sl next 12 sts to cn and hold to front, k12; rep from * to last 2 sts, k2 (selvage sts).

Row 8 Join sep ball of yarn to each 12-st section on cn and sl these sts to extra needle. Purl all sts.
Rows 9–26 Work each 12 st section in St st.
Row 27 (joining row) K2 (selvage sts), *k12, k12 from first 12 sts section on extra needle; rep from * to last 2 sts, k2 (selvage sts).
Row 28 (WS) Purl.
Rep rows 1–28.

104

105 gingerbread

4-st LC Sl 2 sts to cn and hold to front, k2, k2 from cn.

(multiple of 10 sts plus 1)

Rows 1 and 5 (RS) *P1, k4; rep from *, end p1.

Rows 2 and 4 K1, *p1, k2, p1, k1, p4, k1; rep from * to end.

Row 3 *P1, 4-st LC, p1, k4; rep from *, end p1.

Row 6 Rep row 2.

Rep rows 1–6.

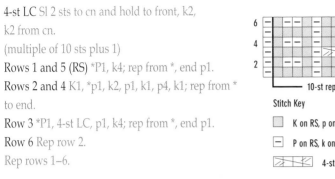

Stitch Key

- ▢ K on RS, p on WS
- — P on RS, k on WS
- ▱ 4-st LC

106 sand cables

6-st RC Sl 3 sts to cn and hold to back, k3, k3 from cn.

6-st LC (WS) Sl 3 sts to cn and hold to front, p3, p3 from cn.

(multiple of 12 sts)

Rows 1 and 3 (RS) Knit.

Rows 2 and 4 Purl.

Row 5 *6-st RC, k6; rep from * to end.

Rows 6 and 8 Purl.

Rows 7 and 9 Knit.

Row 10 (WS) *6-st LC, p6; rep from * to end.

Rep rows 1–10.

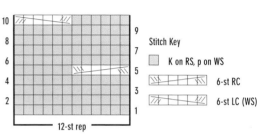

Stitch Key

- ▢ K on RS, p on WS
- ▱ 6-st RC
- ▱ 6-st LC (WS)

allover

105

106

12-st RC Sl 6 sts to cn and hold to back, k6, k6 from cn.

12-st LC Sl 6 sts to cn and hold to front, k6, k6 from cn.

(multiple of 36 sts plus 18)

Rows 1–12 Work in St st.

Row 13 (RS) *K3, 12-st LC, k21; rep from * to last 18 sts, k3, 12-st LC, k3.

Rows 14–24 Work in St st.

Row 25 *K21, 12-st RC, k3; rep from * to last 18 sts, k18.

Row 26 Purl.

Rep rows 1–26.

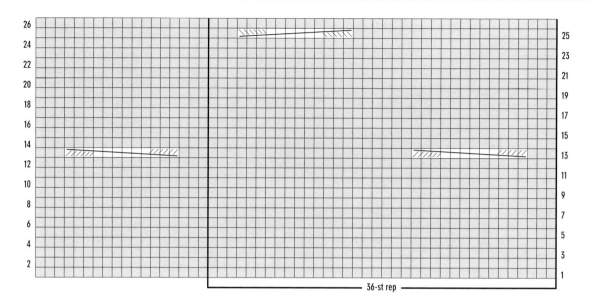

36-st rep

Stitch Key

☐ K on RS, p on WS

12-st RC

12-st LC

108 offset cables

4-st LC Sl 2 sts to cn and hold to front, k2, k2 from cn.

(multiple of 8 sts)

Rows 1 and 5 (RS) Knit.

Row 2 and all WS rows Purl.

Row 3 *4-st LC, k4; rep from * to end.

Row 7 *K4, 4-st LC; rep from * to end.

Row 8 Purl.

Rep rows 1–8.

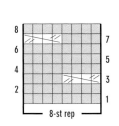

8-st rep

Stitch Key

☐ K on RS, p on WS

▱ 4-st LC

109 wavelengths

4-st LC Sl 1 st to cn and hold to front, k3, k1 from cn.

(multiple of 8 sts plus 4)

Rows 1 and 3 (RS) Knit.

Row 2 and all WS rows Purl.

Row 5 *4-st LC, k4; rep from *, end 4-st LC.

Rows 7 and 9 Knit.

Row 11 *K4, 4-st LC; rep from *, end k4.

Row 12 Purl.

Rep rows 1–12.

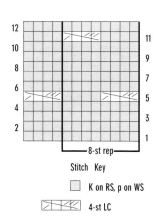

8-st rep

Stitch Key

☐ K on RS, p on WS

▱ 4-st LC

allover

108

109

110 knot cable

6-st KC (Knot Cable) Sl 4 sts to cn and hold to front, k2, sl 2 p sts back to LH needle, hold 2 sts on cn to back of work, p2 from LH needle, k2 from cn.
(multiple of 22 sts plus 1)

Rows 1, 3, and 7 (RS) *K1, [p2, k2] twice, p2, k1, [p2, k2] twice, p2; rep from *, end k1.

Row 2 and all WS rows P1, *[k2, p2] twice, k2, p1; rep from * to end.

Row 5 *K1, p2, 6-st KC, p2, k1, [p2, k2] twice, p2; rep from *, end k1.

Row 9 *K1, [p2, k2] twice, p2, k1, p2, 6-st KC, p2; rep from *, end k1.

Row 10 Rep row 2.

Rep rows 1–10.

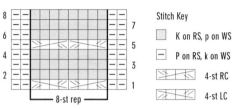

Stitch Key

▢ K on RS, p on WS

– P on RS, k on WS

6-st KC

111 honeycomb

4-st RC Sl 2 sts to cn and hold to back, k2, k2 from cn.

4-st LC Sl 2 sts to cn and hold to front, k2, k2 from cn.
(multiple of 8 sts plus 4)

Row 1 (RS) P2, *4-st RC, 4-st LC; rep from * to last 2 sts, p2.

Row 2 and all WS rows K2, p to last 2 sts, k2.

Rows 3 and 7 P2, k to last 2 sts, p2.

Row 5 P2, *4-st LC, 4-st RC; rep from * to last 2 sts, p2.

Row 8 Rep row 2.

Rep rows 1–8.

Stitch Key

▢ K on RS, p on WS

– P on RS, k on WS

4-st RC

4-st LC

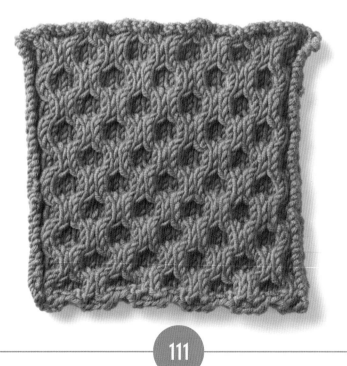

112 watson and crick

9-st LPC Sl 3 sts to cn and hold to front, sl next 3 sts to second cn and hold to back, k3, p3 from second cn, k3 from first cn.
(multiple of 24 sts plus 3)
Rows 1, 3, 7, 9, 11 and 15 (RS) P3, *k3, p3; rep from * to end.
Row 2 and all WS rows *K3, p3, rep from * , end k3.
Row 5 P3, *[k3, p3] twice, 9-st LPC, p3; rep from * to end.

Row 13 P3, *9-st LPC, [p3, k3] twice; rep from *, end p3.
Row 16 Rep row 2.
Rep rows 1–16.

24-st rep

Stitch Key

☐ K on RS, p on WS

⊟ P on RS, k on WS

9-st LPC

113 long cable

6-st LC Sl 3 sts to cn and hold to front, k3, k3 from cn.
(multiple of 14 sts plus 1)
Rows 1, 5, 7, 9, 11, 13, 15, 19, 21, 23, 25 and 27 (RS) *P1, k6; rep from * to last st, p1.
Row 2 and all WS rows *K1, p6; rep from *, end k1.
Row 3 *P1, 6-st LC, p1, k6; rep from *, end p1.
Row 17 *P1, k6, p1, 6-st LC; rep from *, end p1.
Row 28 Rep row 1.
Rep rows 1–28.

allover

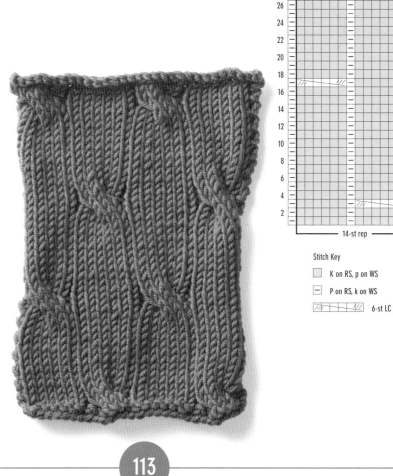

14-st rep

Stitch Key

☐ K on RS, p on WS

⊟ P on RS, k on WS

6-st LC

112

113

4-st LC Sl 2 sts to cn and hold to front, k2, k2 from cn.

(multiple of 16 sts plus 12)

Rows 1, 3, 5, 9, 13, 17, 21, 23, 25, 29, 33 and 37 (RS) *P4, k4; rep from * to last 4 sts, p4.

Row 2 and all WS rows K4, *p4, k4; rep from * to end.

Rows 7, 11, 15 and 19 *P4, 4-st LC, p4, k4; rep from * to last 12 sts, p4, 4-st LC, p4.

Rows 27, 31, 35 and 39 *P4, k4, p4, 4-st LC; rep from * to last 12 sts, p4, k4, p4.

Row 40 Rep row 2.

Rep rows 1–40.

Stitch Key

◻ K on RS, p on WS

— P on RS, k on WS

▨ 4-st LC

40
38
36
34
32
30
28
26
24
22
20
18
16
14
12
10
8
6
4
2

39
37
35
33
31
29
27
25
23
21
19
17
15
13
11
9
7
5
3
1

16 - sts rep

4-st RC Sl 2 sts to cn and hold to back, k2, k2 from cn.

4-st LC Sl 2 sts to cn and hold to front, k2, k2 from cn.

(multiple of 20 sts)

Rows 1, 5, 9 and 13 *P1, k8, p1; rep from * to end.

Row 2 and all WS rows *K1, p8, k1; rep from * to end.

Rows 3 and 7 *P1, 4-st RC, 4-st LC, p2, 4-st LC, 4-st RC, p1; rep from * to end.

Rows 11 and 15 *P1, 4-st LC, 4-st RC, p2, 4-st RC, 4-st LC, p1; rep from * to end.

Row 16 Rep row 2.

Rep rows 1–16.

116 staggered cables

4-st RC Sl 2 sts to cn and hold to back, k2, k2 from cn.

6-st LC Sl 3 sts to cn and hold to front, k3, k3 from cn.

(multiple of 12 sts plus 2)

Rows 1, 5, 9, 13, 17, 19, 23 and 25 (RS) P2, *k10, p2; rep from * to end.

Row 2 and all WS rows *K2, p10; rep from *, end k2.

Rows 3, 7 and 11 P2, *4-st RC, k6, p2; rep from * to end.

Rows 15, 21 and 27 P2, *k4, 6-st LC, p2; rep from * to end.

Row 28 Rep row 2.

Rep rows 1–28.

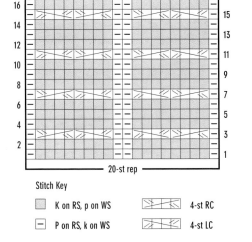

20-st rep

Stitch Key

▨ K on RS, p on WS	⬚ 4-st RC
⊟ P on RS, k on WS	⬚ 4-st LC

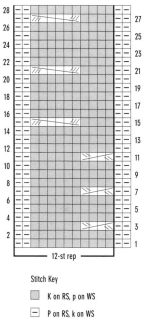

12-st rep

Stitch Key

▨ K on RS, p on WS

⊟ P on RS, k on WS

⬚ 4-st RC

⬚ 6-st LC

116

95

10-st RC Sl 5 sts to cn and hold to back, k5, k5 from cn.

10-st LC Sl 5 sts to cn and hold to front, k5, k5 from cn.

(multiple of 18 sts plus 10)

Rows 1, 3 and 5 (RS) Knit.

Row 2 and all WS rows Purl.

Rows 7, 15 and 23 K9, *10-st LC, k8; rep from * to last st, end k1.

Rows 9, 11, 13, 17, 19, 21, 25, 27, 29, and 31 Knit.

Rows 33, 41 and 49 *10-st RC, k8; rep from * to last 10 sts, end 10-st RC.

Rows 35, 37, 39, 43, 45, 47 and 51 Knit.

Row 52 Purl.

Rep rows 1–52.

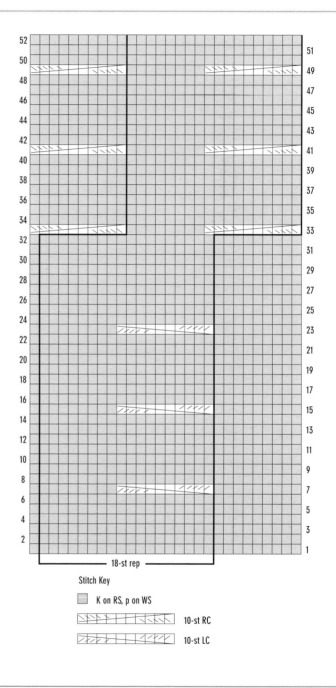

Stitch Key

☐ K on RS, p on WS

▨ 10-st RC

▨ 10-st LC

117

118 disappearing cable

6-st RC Sl 3 sts to cn and hold to back, k3, k3 from cn.
6-st LC Sl 3 sts to cn and hold to front, k3, k3 from cn.
(multiple of 24 sts plus 3)
Rows 1, 5, 7, 11, 13, 17, 19, 23, 25, 29, 31, 35, 37, 41, 43, 47 (RS) Knit.
Row 2 and all WS rows Purl.
Row 3 *6-st LC, k6; rep from *, end k3.
Row 9 *K1, 6-st LC, k6, 6-st LC, k5; rep from *, end k3.
Row 15 *K2, 6-st LC, k6, 6-st LC, k4; rep from *, end k3.
Row 21 *K3, 6-st LC, k6, 6-st LC, k3; rep from * end k3.
Row 27 K3, *k6, 6-st RC; rep from * to end.

Row 33 K3, *k5, 6-st RC, k6, 6-st RC, k1; rep from * to end.
Row 39 K3, *k4, 6-st RC, k6, 6-st RC, k2; rep from * to end.
Row 45 K3, *k3, 6-st RC, k6, 6-st RC, k3; rep from * to end.
Row 48 Purl.
Rep rows 1–48.

Stitch Key

☐ K on RS, p on WS

▨ 6-st RC

▨ 6-st LC

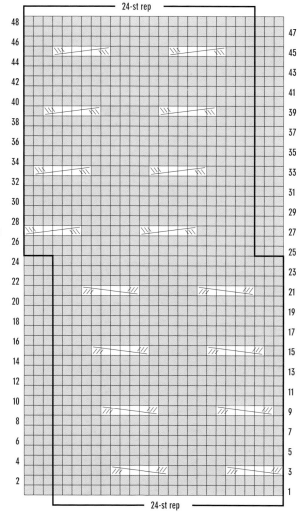

allover

118

97

119 simple staggered cables

6-st RC Sl 3 sts to cn and hold to back, k3, k3 from cn.
6-st LC Sl 3 sts to cn and hold to front, k3, k3 from cn.
(multiple of 16 sts plus 2)
Rows 1, 3, 7, 9, 13, 15, 19 and 21 (RS) *P2, k14; rep
from *, end p2.
Row 2 and WS rows K2, *p14, k2; rep from * to end.
Row 5 *P2, k8, 6-st RC; rep from *, end p2.
Rows 11 and 17 *P2, 6-st LC, k8; rep from *, end p2.
Row 23 *P2, k8, 6-st RC; rep from *, end p2.
Row 24 Rep row 2.
Rep rows 1–24.

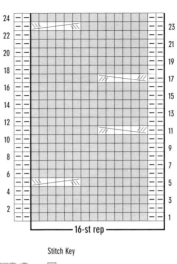

16-st rep

Stitch Key

□ K on RS, p on WS

⊟ P on RS, k on WS

6-st RC

6-st LC

119

120 braid panels

RT K2tog leaving sts on needle, insert
needle between sts and k first st, sl
both sts from needle.
LT Insert RH needle in back of 2nd st
on LH needle and k st tbl, leave sts on
needle, k2tog tbl.
(multiple of 10 sts)
Rows 1, 5, 9, 13 and 17 (RS) *K5, p1,
RT, k1, p1; rep from * to end.
Row 2 and all WS rows Purl.
Rows 3, 7, 11, 15 and 19 *K5, p1,
k1, LT, p1; rep from * to end.
Rows 21, 25, 29, 33 and 37 *P1,
RT, k1, p1, k5; rep from * to end.
Rows 23, 27, 31, 35 and 39 *P1,
k1, LT, p1, k5; rep from * to end.
Row 40 Purl.
Rep rows 1–40.

120

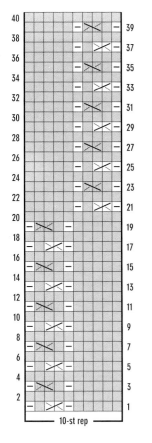

6-st RC Sl 3 sts to cn and hold to back, k3, k3 from cn.

6-st LC Sl 3 sts to cn and hold to front, k3, k3 from cn.

(cast on multiple of 20 sts plus 2)

Row 1 (RS) *P2, [k into front and back of st] twice, k4, [k into front and back of st] twice, p10; rep from *, end p2.

Rows 2, 4, 8, 10 and 14 K2, *k10, p12, k2; rep from * to end.

Rows 3, 9 and 15 *P2, k12, p10; rep from *, end p2.

Rows 5 and 11 *P2, k12, p2, k8; rep from *, end p2.

Rows 6 and 12 K2, *p8, k2, p12, k2; rep from * to end.

Rows 7 and 13 *P2, 6-st RC, 6-st LC, p10; rep from *, end p2.

Row 16 K2, *k10, p2, [k2tog] 4 times, p2, k2; rep from * to end.

Row 17 K2, *p12, [k into front and back of st] twice, k4, [k into front and back of st] twice; rep from * to end.

Rows 18, 20, 24, 26 and 30 *P12, k12; rep from *, end p2.

Rows 19, 25 and 31 K2, *p12, k12; rep from * to end.

Rows 21 and 27 K2, *p2, k8, p2, k12; rep from * to end.

Rows 22 and 28 *P12, k2, p8, k2; rep from *, end p2.

Rows 23 and 29 K2, *p12, 6-st RC, 6-st LC; rep from * to end.

Row 32 *P2, [k2tog] 4 times, p2, k12; rep from *, end p2.

Rep rows 1–32.

10-st rep

Stitch Key

- ☐ K on RS, p on WS
- ⊟ P on RS, k on WS
- ⧓ RT
- ⧓ LT

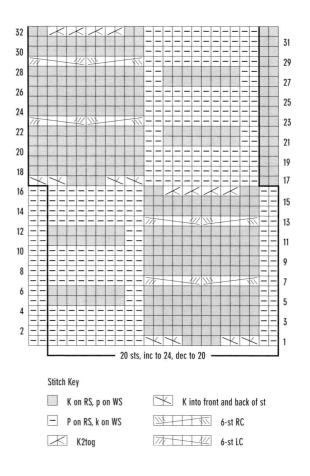

20 sts, inc to 24, dec to 20

Stitch Key

- ☐ K on RS, p on WS
- ⊟ P on RS, k on WS
- ⧓ K2tog
- ⧓ K into front and back of st
- ⧓ 6-st RC
- ⧓ 6-st LC

8-st RC Sl 4 sts to cn and hold to back, k4, k4 from cn.

8-st LC Sl 4 sts to cn and hold to front, k4, k4 from cn.

(multiple of 30 plus 14)

Rows 1, 3, 7, 9, 11, 15 and 17 P3, *k8, p3, k16, p3; rep from *, end k8, p3.

Rows 2, 4, 6, 8, 10, 12, and 14 K3, p8, *k3, p16, k3, p8; rep from *, end k3.

Row 5 P3, *8-st RC, p3, 8-st RC, 8-st LC, p3; rep from *, end 8-st LC, p3.

Row 13 P3, *8-st RC, p3, 8-st LC, 8-st RC, p3; rep from *, end 8-st LC, p3.

Row 16 Knit.

Row 18 Knit.

Rep rows 1–18.

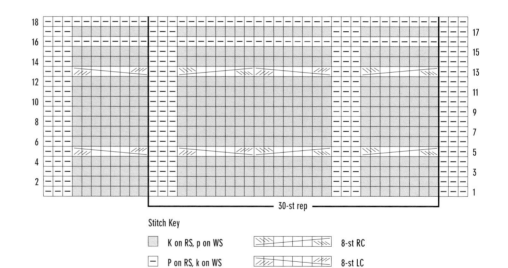

30-st rep

Stitch Key

☐ K on RS, p on WS	▨▨ 8-st RC
☐ P on RS, k on WS	▨▨ 8-st LC

123 mirror image

6-st RPC Sl 3 sts to cn and hold to back, p3, k3 from cn.

6-st LPC Sl 3 sts to cn and hold to front, k3, p3 from cn.

Note: This is a mirror-image pattern.

Mark center of row.

(multiple of 18 sts plus 18)

Rows 1, 3 and 5 (RS) *P6, k3; rep from * to center; **k3, p6; rep from ** to end.

Rows 2, 4 and 6 *K6, p3; rep from * to center; **p3, k6; rep from ** to end.

Row 7 *P3, 6-st LPC; rep from * to center; **6-st RPC, p3; rep from ** to end.

Rows 8, 10 and 12 *K3, p3, k3; rep from * to end.

Rows 9 and 11 *P3, k3, p3; rep from * to end.

Row 13 *6-st LPC, p3; rep from * to center; **p3, 6-st RPC; rep from ** to end.

Rows 14, 16 and 18 *P3, k6; rep from * to center; **k6, p3; rep from ** to end.

Rows 15 and 17 *K3, p6; rep from * to center; **p6, k3; rep from ** to end.

Row 19 P6, *6-st LPC, p3; rep from *, end k3 at center; k3, **p3, 6-st RPC; rep from **; end p6.

Row 20 *P6, k3; rep from * to center; **k3, p6; rep from ** to end.

Rep rows 3–20.

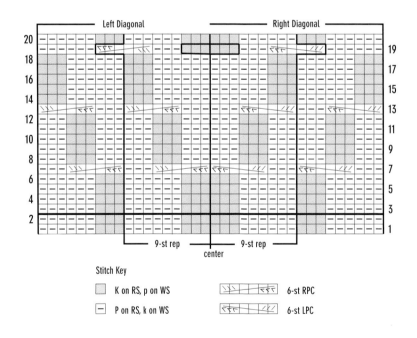

Stitch Key

☐ K on RS, p on WS

─ P on RS, k on WS

6-st RPC

6-st LPC

124 acorns

RT K2tog, leave sts on LH needle, insert RH needle from front between the 2 sts just knit tog and knit the first st again. Sl both sts to RH needle tog.

LT With RH needle behind LH needle, skip one st and k the second st tbl, then insert RH needle into the backs of both sts and k2tog tbl.

(multiple of 8 sts)

Rows 1 and 7 (WS) *P1, k2, p2, k2, p1; rep from * to end.

Row 2 *K1, p1, RT, LT, p1, k1; rep from * to end.

Row 3 *P1, k1, p1, k2, p1, k1, p1; rep from * to end.

Row 4 *K1, RT, p2, LT, k1; rep from * to end.

Row 5 *P2, k4, p2; rep from * to end.

Row 6 Knit.

Row 8 *LT, p1, k2, p1, RT; rep from * to end.

Row 9 *K1, p1, k1, p2, k1, p1, k1; rep from * to end.

Row 10 *P1, LT, k2, RT, p1; rep from * to end.

Row 11 *K2, p4, k2; rep from * to end.

Row 12 Knit.

Rep rows 1–12.

125 waves

4-st RC Sl 2 sts to cn and hold to back, k2, k2 from cn.

4-st LC Sl 2 sts to cn and hold to front, k2, k2 from cn.

(multiple of 6 sts)

Rows 1 and 5 (RS) Knit.

Row 2 and all WS rows Purl.

Row 3 *K2, 4-st RC; rep from * to end.

Row 7 *4-st LC, k2; rep from * to end.

Row 8 Purl.

Rep rows 1–8.

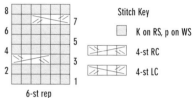

Stitch Key

☐ K on RS, p on WS

⊠ 4-st RC

⊠ 4-st LC

6-st rep

8-st rep

Stitch Key

☐ K on RS, p on WS

☐ P on RS, k on WS

⊠ 2-st RT

⊠ 2-st LT

124

125

126 lattice

4-st RC Sl 2 sts to cn and hold to back, k2, k2 from cn.

4-st LC Sl 2 sts to cn and hold to front, k2, k2 from cn.

4-st RPC Sl 2 sts to cn and hold to back, k2, p2 from cn.

4-st LPC Sl 2 sts to cn and hold to front, p2, k2 from cn.

(multiple of 16 sts plus 2)

Row 1 (RS) K1, *4-st LC, p8, 4-st RC; rep from *, end k1.

Row 2 P1, *p4, k8, p4; rep from *, end p1.

Row 3 K1, *k2, 4-st LPC, p4, 4-st RPC, k2; rep from *, end k1.

Rows 4 and 10 P1, *p2, k2, p2, k4, p2, k2, p2; rep from *, end p1.

Row 5 K1, *k2, p2, 4-st LPC, 4-st RPC, p2, k2; rep from *, end k1.

Rows 6 and 8 P1, *p2, k4, p4, k4, p2; rep from *, end p1.

Row 7 K1, *k2, p4, 4-st RC, p4, k2; rep from *, end k1.

Row 9 K1, *k2, p2, 4-st RPC, 4-st LPC, p2, k2; rep from *, end k1.

Row 11 K1, *k2, 4-st RPC, p4, 4-st LPC, k2; rep from *, end k1.

Row 12 Rep row 2.

Rep rows 1–12.

127 pie crust

6-st RC Sl 3 sts to cn and hold to back, k3, k3 from cn.

6-st LC Sl 3 sts to cn and hold to front, k3, k3 from cn.

(multiple of 6 sts)

Row 1 and and all WS rows Purl.

Rows 2 and 6 Knit.

Row 4 K3, *6-st RC; rep from *, end k3.

Row 8 *6-st LC; rep from * to end.

Rep rows 1–8.

allover

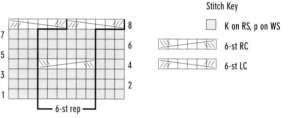

Stitch Key

☐ K on RS, p on WS

▨ 6-st RC

▨ 6-st LC

Stitch Key

☐ K on RS, p on WS

— P on RS, k on WS

▨ 4-st RC

▨ 4-st LC

▨ 4-st RPC

▨ 4-st LPC

126

127

128 bonbons

4-st RC Sl 2 sts to cn and hold to back, k2, k2 from cn.

(multiple of 22 sts plus 3)

Rows 1, 5, 9, 13, 17 and 21 (RS) P3, *K8, p3, k8, p3; rep from * to end.

Row 2 and all WS rows *K3, p8, k3, p8; rep from * to last 3 sts, k3.

Rows 3, 7 and 11 P3, *[4-st RC] twice, p3, k8, p3; rep from * to end.

Rows 15, 19 and 23 P3, *K8, p3, [4-st RC] twice, p3; rep from * to end.

Row 24 Rep row 2.

Rep rows 1–24.

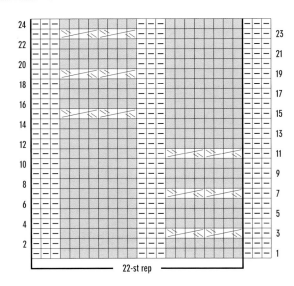

Stitch Key

- ☐ K on RS, p on WS
- — P on RS, k on WS
- ⧄ 4-st RC

129 holly berries

4-st RC Sl 2 sts to cn and hold to back, k2, k2 from cn.

4-st LC Sl 2 sts to cn and hold to front, k2, k2 from cn.

MB (Make Bobble) K into front, back, front, back and front of st, turn, p5, turn, k2tog, k3tog, pass k2tog st over k3tog st.

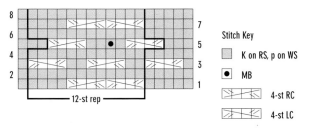

Stitch Key

- ☐ K on RS, p on WS
- • MB
- ⧄ 4-st RC
- ⧄ 4-st LC

130 blended chevron

(multiple of 12 sts plus 6)

Row 1 (RS) K5, *4-st LC, 4-st RC, k4; rep from *, end k1.

Row 2 and all WS rows Purl.

Row 3 K1, 4-st LC, *k2, 4-st RC, k2, 4-st LC; rep from *, end k1.

Row 5 K3, *4-st LC, k1, MB, k2, 4-st RC; rep from *, end k3.

Row 7 K5, *4-st LC, 4-st RC, k4; rep from *, end k1.

Row 8 Purl.

Rep rows 1–8.

6-st RC Sl 3 sts to cn and hold to back, k3, k3 from cn.

6-st LC Sl 3 sts to cn and hold to front, k3, k3 from cn.

(multiple of 36 plus 28)

Row 1 (RS) K2, 6-st RC, [k3, 6-st RC] 2 times, *k3, 6-st LC, [k3, 6-st RC] 3 times; rep from *, end k2.

Row 2 and all WS rows Purl.

Row 3 K8, 6-st RC, k3, 6-st RC, *[6-st LC, k3] twice, k3, 6-st RC, k3, 6-st RC; rep from *, end k5.

Row 5 K5, [6-st RC, k3] twice, *k3, 6-st LC, k3, 6-st LC, [6-st RC, k3] twice; rep from *, end k5.

Row 6 Purl.

Rep rows 1–6.

36-st rep

Stitch Key

■ K on RS, p on WS

⬛ 6-st RC

⬛ 6-st LC

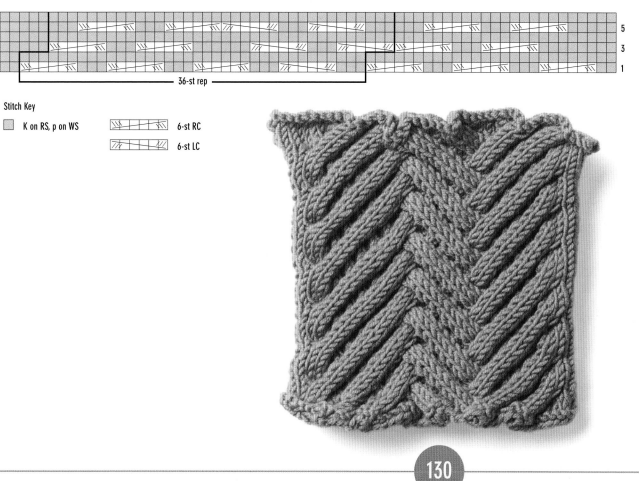

130

131 double alternating

4-st RC Sl 2 sts to cn and hold to back, k2, k2 from cn.

4-st LC Sl 2 sts to cn and hold to front, k2, k2 from cn.

8-st RC Sl 4 sts to cn and hold to back, k4, k4 from cn.

8-st LC Sl 4 sts to cn and hold to front, k4, k4 from cn.

(multiple of 34 sts plus 1)

Rows 1 and 17 (RS) *P1, 8-st RC, 8-st LC, p1, 8-st RC, 8-st LC; rep from *, end p1.

Row 2 and all WS rows K1, *p16, k1, p16, k1; rep from * to end.

Rows 3, 7, 11, 15, 19, 23, 27 and 31 *P1, k16, p1, k16; rep from *, end p1.

Rows 5, 9 and 13 *P1, 4-st RC, k12, p1, k12, 4-st LC; rep from *, end p1.

Rows 21, 25 and 29 *P1, k12, 4-st LC, p1, 4-st RC, k12; rep from *, end p1.

Row 32 Rep row 2.

Rep rows 1–32.

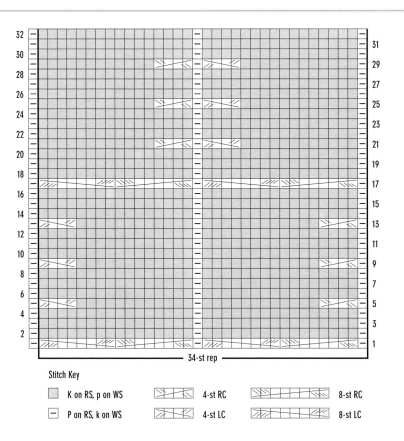

Stitch Key

- ⬛ K on RS, p on WS
- ⊟ P on RS, k on WS
- 4-st RC
- 4-st LC
- 8-st RC
- 8-st LC

34-st rep

132 steps

6-st RC Sl 3 sts to cn and hold to back, k3, k3 from cn.

(multiple of 12 sts plus 6)

Rows 1 and 3 (RS) *P6, k6; rep from *, end p6.

Rows 2, 4 and 6 K6, *p6, k6 ; rep from * to end.

Row 5 *P6, 6-st RC; rep from *, end p6.

Rows 7 and 9 *K6, p6; rep from *, end k6.

Rows 8 and 10 P6, *k6, p6; rep from * to end.

Row 11 *6-st RC, p6; rep from *, end 6-st RC.

Row 12 Rep row 8.

Rep rows 1–12.

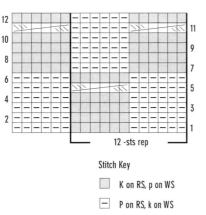

Stitch Key

▢ K on RS, p on WS

▬ P on RS, k on WS

6-st RC

133 tightly woven

4-st RC Sl 2 sts to cn and hold to back, k2, k2 from cn.

4-st LC Sl 2 sts to cn and hold to front, k2, k2 from cn.

(multiple of 4 sts)

Row 1 (RS) K2, *4-st RC; rep from *, end k2.

Row 2 Purl.

Row 3 *4-st LC; rep from * to end.

Row 4 Purl.

Rep rows 1–4.

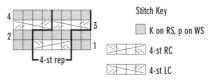

Stitch Key

▢ K on RS, p on WS

4-st RC

4-st LC

allover

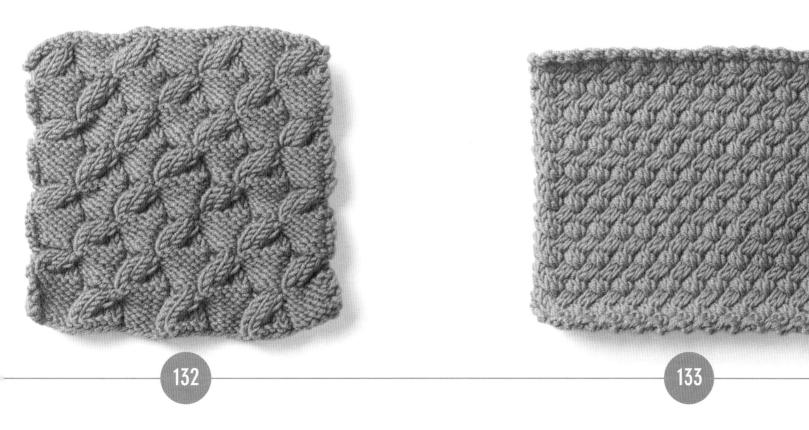

132

133

134 garter twists

13-st LPC Sl 6 sts to cn and hold to front, k6, p1; then k6 from cn.

(multiple of 28 sts plus 15)

Rows 1, 3, 5, 7, 9, 13, 15, 17, 19 and 21 (RS) *P1, k6; rep from *, end p1.

Row 2 and all WS rows Knit.

Row 11 *P1, 13-st LPC, [p1, k6] twice; rep from *, end 13-st LPC, p1.

Row 23 *[P1, k6] twice, p1, 13-st LPC, rep from *, end [p1, k6] twice, p1.

Row 24 Knit.

Rep rows 1–24.

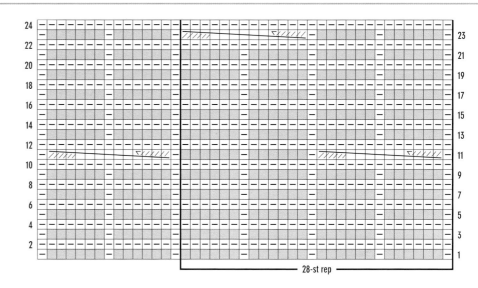

28-st rep

Stitch Key

K on RS, p on WS

— P on RS, k on WS

13-st LPC

6-st RC Sl 3 sts to cn and hold to back, k3, k3 from cn.

6-st LC Sl 3 sts to cn and hold to front, k3, k3 from cn.

(multiple of 12 sts)

Preparation Row (WS) *P3, k3; rep from * to end.

Rows 1, 5, 7, 11, 13, 17, 19 and 23 (RS) Knit.

Row 2 *P3, k3; rep from * to end.

Rows 3 and 15 *K6, 6-st LC; rep from * to end.

Rows 4, 6 and 8 *K3, p6, k3; rep from * to end.

Rows 9 and 21 *6-st RC, k6; rep from * to end.

Rows 10, 12 and 14 *K3, p3; rep from * to end.

Rows 16, 18 and 20 *P3, k6, p3; rep from * to end.

Rows 22 and 24 Rep row 2.

Rep rows 1–24.

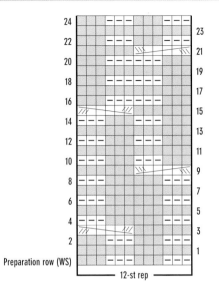

Preparation row (WS)

12-st rep

Stitch Key

☐ K on RS, p on WS

⊟ P on RS, k on WS

6-st RC

6-st LC

135

8-st LC Sl 4 sts to cn and hold to front, k4, k4 from cn.

6-st LPC Sl 4 st to cn and hold to front, p2, k4 from cn.

(multiple of 18 sts plus 26)

Rows 1, 3, 5, 15, 17, 19, 21, 23, 33, 35, 37, 39, 41, 51, 53 and 55 (RS) *P2, k4; rep from *, end p2.

Rows 2, 4, 6, 10, 14, 16, 18, 20, 22, 24, 28, 32, 34, 36, 38, 40, 42, 46, 50, 52 and 54 K2, *p4, k2; rep from * to end.

Rows 7 and 47 P2, 8-st LC, k2, *p2, k4, p2, 8-st LC, k2; rep from * to last 14 sts, end [p2, k4] twice, p2.

Rows 8 and 48 [K2, p4] twice, k2, *p10, k2, p4, k2; rep from * to last 12 sts, end p10, k2.

Rows 9 and 49 P2, k4, 6-st LPC, *[p2, k4] twice, 6-st LPC; rep from * to last 14 sts, end [p2, k4] twice, p2.

Rows 11 and 25 P2, k4, p2, 8-st LC, *k2, p2, k4, p2, 8-st LC; rep from * to last 10 sts, end k2, p2, k4, p2.

Rows 12 and 26 *K2, p4, k2, p10; rep from * to last 8 sts, end k2, p4, k2.

Rows 13 and 27 [P2, k4] twice, *6-st LPC, [p2, k4] twice; rep from * to last 14 sts, end 6-st LPC, p2, k4, p2.

Rows 29 and 43 [P2, k4] twice, *p2, 8-st LC, k2, p2, k4; rep from * to last 14 sts, end p2, 8-st LC, k2, p2.

Rows 30 and 44 K2, p10, k2, *p4, k2, p10, k2; rep from * to last 12 sts, end [p4, k2] twice.

Rows 31 and 45 [P2, k4] twice, *p2, k4, 6-st LPC, p2, k4; rep from * to last 14 sts, end p2, k4, 8-st LPC, p2.

Row 56 Rep row 2.

Rep rows 1–56.

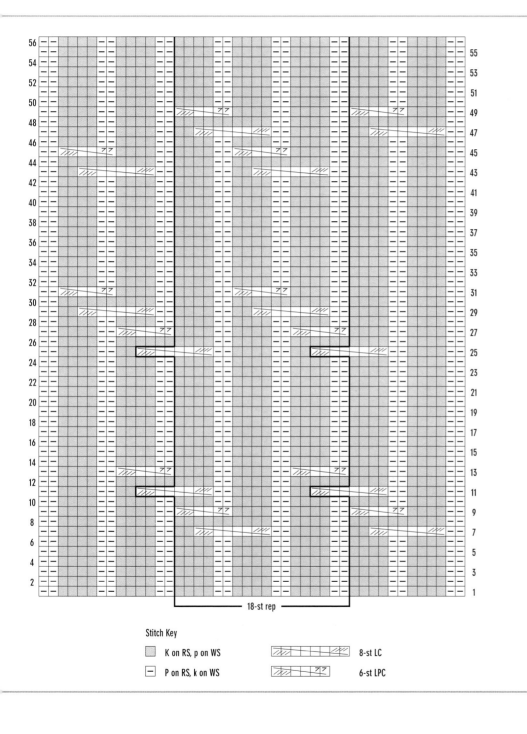

56 · 55
54 · 53
52 · 51
50 · 49
48 · 47
46 · 45
44 · 43
42 · 41
40 · 39
38 · 37
36 · 35
34 · 33
32 · 31
30 · 29
28 · 27
26 · 25
24 · 23
22 · 21
20 · 19
18 · 17
16 · 15
14 · 13
12 · 11
10 · 9
8 · 7
6 · 5
4 · 3
2 · 1

|— 18-st rep —|

Stitch Key

K on RS, p on WS   8-st LC

— P on RS, k on WS   6-st LPC

137 snails

8-st RPC Sl 4 sts to cn and hold to back, k4; p4 from cn.

8-st LPC Sl 4 sts to cn and hold to front, p4; k4 from cn.

(multiple of 24 sts)

Rows 1, 3, 5, 9, 11 and 13 (RS) K4, p4, k8, p4, k4.

Row 2 and all WS rows P4, k4, p8, k4, p4.

Row 7 8-st RPC, k8, 8-st LPC.

Row 15 K4, 8-st LPC, 8-st RPC, k4.

Row 16 Rep row 2.

Rep rows 1–16.

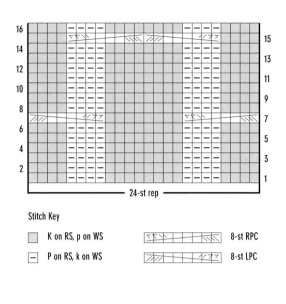

Stitch Key

- ▢ K on RS, p on WS
- ▭ P on RS, k on WS
- ⬛ 8-st RPC
- ⬛ 8-st LPC

138 penny candy

RT Passing in front of first st, k 2nd st then k first st and let both sts fall from needle.

LT Passing in back of first st, k 2nd st then k first st and let both sts fall from needle.

8-st RC Sl 4 sts from cn and hold to back, k4, k4 from cn.

8-st LC Sl 4 sts from cn and hold to front, k4, k4 from cn.

(multiple of 18 sts plus 1)

Rows 1, 3 and 7 (RS) *P1, k8, p1, RT, p4, LT; rep from *, end p1.

Rows 2, 4, 6 and 8 K1, *p2, k4, p2, k1, p8, k1; rep from * to end.

Row 5 *P1, 8-st LC, p1, RT, p4, LT; rep from *, end p1.

Rows 9, 11 and 15 *P1, RT, p4, LT, p1, k8; rep from *, end p1.

Rows 10, 12 and 14 K1, *p8, k1, p2, k4, p2, k1; rep from * to end.

Row 13 *P1, RT, p4, LT, p1, 8-st RC; rep from *, end p1.

Row 16 Rep row 10.

Rep rows 1–16.

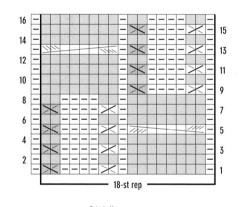

Stitch Key

- ▢ K on RS, p on WS
- ▭ P on RS, k on WS
- ⬛ RT
- ⬛ LT
- ⬛ 8-st RC
- ⬛ 8-st LC

8-st RGC (8-st right garter cable) Sl 4 sts to cn and hold to back, k4; [k1, wyif sl 2, k1] from cn.

8-st LGC (8-st left garter cable) Sl 4 sts to cn and hold to front, k1, wyif sl 2, k1; k4 from cn.

8-st RSC (8-st right slip cable) Sl 4 sts to cn and hold to back, k1, wyif sl 2, k1; k4 from cn.

8-st LSC (8-st left slip cable) Sl 4 sts to cn and hold to front, k4; [k1, wyif sl 2, k1] from cn. (multiple of 20 sts plus 2)

Rows 1, 3 and 5 *P2, k1, wyif sl 2, k5; rep from *, end p2.

Rows 2, 4 and 6 *K6, p4; rep from *, end k2.

Row 7 *P2, k1, wyif sl 2, k5, p2, 8-st LSC; rep from *, end p2.

Rows 8, 10, 12 and 14 K2, *p4, k10, p4; rep from *, end k2.

Rows 9, 11 and 13 *P2, k1, wyif sl 2, k5, p2, k5, wyif sl 2, k1; rep from *, end p2.

Row 15 * P2, 8-st RGC, p2, k5, wyif sl 2, k1; rep from *, end p2.

Rows 16, 18, 20 and 22 K2, *p4, k6; rep from * to end.

Rows 17, 19 and 21 *P2, k5, wyif sl 2, k1; rep from *, end p2.

Row 23 *P2, k5, wyif sl 2, k1, p2, 8-st LGC; rep from *; end, p2.

Rows 24, 26, 28 and 30 K2, *k4, p4, k2, p4, k6; rep from * to end.

Rows 25, 27 and 29 *P2, k5, wyif sl 2, k1, p2, k1, wyif sl 2, k5; rep from *, end p2.

Row 31 *P2, 8-st RSC, p2, k1, wyif sl 2, k5; rep from *, end p2.

Row 32 Rep row 2.

Rep rows 1–32.

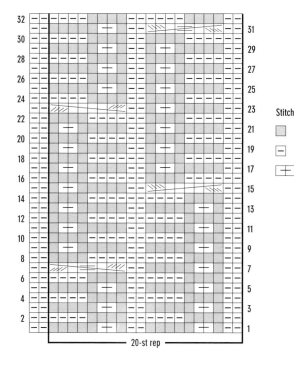

Stitch Key

▨	K on RS, p on WS
−	P on RS, k on WS
+	Slip 2 sts wyif

8-st RGC

8-st LGC

8-st RSC

8-st LSC

3-st RC Sl 1 st to cn and hold to back, k2, k1 from cn.

3-st LC Sl 2 sts to cn and hold to front, k1, k2 from cn.

3-st RPC Sl 1 st to cn and hold to back, k2, p1 from cn.

3-st LPC Sl 2 sts to cn and hold to front, p1, k2 from cn.

4-st LC Sl 2 sts to cn and hold to front, k2, k2 from cn.

(multiple of 26 sts plus 16)

Row 1 (RS) P2, *p1, k10, p6, k4, p5; rep from *, end p1, k10, p3.

Rows 2, 4 and 38 K3, p2, k6, p2, k1, *k5, p4, [k6, p2] twice, k1; rep from *, end k2.

Rows 3 and 39 P2, *p1, k10, p6, 4-st LC, p5; rep from *, end p1, k10, p3.

Row 5 P2, *p1, k10, p5, 3-st RC, 3-st LC, p4; rep from *, end p1, k10, p3.

Rows 6 and 36 K3, p2, k6, p2, k1, * k4, p2, k2, p2, k5, p2, k6, p2, k1; rep from *, end k2.

Row 7 P2, *p1, k10, p4, 3-st RC, k2, 3-st LC, p3; rep from *, end p1, k10, p3.

Rows 8 and 34 K3, p2, k6, p2, k1, *k3, p2, [k4, p2] twice, k6, p2, k1; rep from *, end k2.

Row 9 P2, *p1, k10, p3, 3-st RC, k4, 3-st LC, p2; rep from *, end p1, k10, p3.

Rows 10, 12, 30 and 32 K3, p2, k6, p2, k1, *k2, p2, k6, p2, k3, p2, k6, p2, k1; rep from *, end k2.

Rows 11 and 31 P2, *p1, k10, p3, k10, p2; rep from *, end p1, k10, p3.

Row 13 P2, *p1, 3-st LPC, k4, 3-st RPC, p3, k10, p2; rep from *, end p1, 3-st LPC, k4, 3-st RPC, p3.

Rows 14 and 28 [K4, p2] twice, k2, *k2, p2, k6, p2, [k4, p2] twice, k2; rep from *, end k2.

Row 15 P2, *p2, 3-st LPC, k2, 3-st RPC, p4, k10, p2; rep from *, end p2, 3-st LPC, k2, 3-st RPC, p4.

Rows 16 and 26 K5, p2, k2, p2, k3, *k2, p2, k6, p2, k5, p2, k2, p2, k3; rep from *, end k2.

Row 17 P2, *p3, 3-st LPC, 3-st RPC, p5, k10, p2; rep from *, end p3, 3-st LPC, 3-st RPC, p5.

Rows 18, 20, 22 and 24 K6, p4, k4, *k2, [p2, k6] twice, p4, k4; rep from *, end k2.

Rows 19 and 23 P2, *p4, 4-st LC, p6, k10, p2; rep from *, end p4, 4-st LC, p6.

Row 21 P2, *p4, k4, p6, k10, p2; rep from *, end p4, k4, p6.

Row 25 P2, *p3, 3-st RC, 3-st LC, p5, k10, p2; rep from *, end p3, 3-st RC, 3-st LC, p5.

Row 27 P2, *p2, 3-st RC, k2, 3-st LC, p4, k10, p2; rep from *, end p2, 3-st RC, k2, 3-st LC, p4.

Row 29 P2, *p1, 3-st RC, k4, 3-st LC, p3, k10, p2; rep from *, end p1, 3-st RC, k4, 3-st LC, p3.

Row 33 P2, *p1, k10, p3, 3-st LPC, k4, 3-st RPC, p2; rep from *, end p1, k10, p3.

Row 35 P2, *p1, k10, p4, 3-st LPC, k2, 3-st RPC, p3; rep from *, end p1, k10, p3.

Row 37 P2, *p1, k10, p5, 3-st LPC, 3-st RPC, p4; rep from *, end p1, k10, p3.

Row 40 K3, p2, k6, p2, k1, *k5, p4, [k6, p2] twice, k1; rep from *, end k2.

Rep rows 1–40.

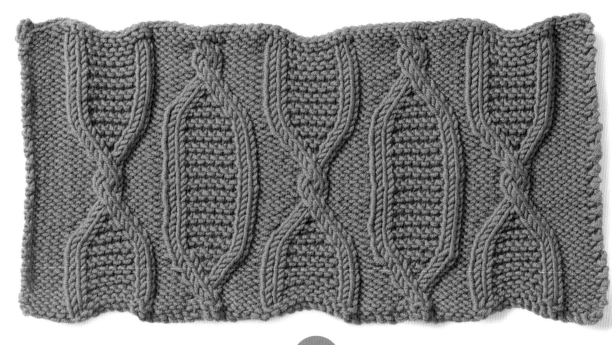

140

| 40 | | | | | | | | | | | | | | | | | | | | | | 39 |

26-st rep

Stitch Key

K on RS, p on WS   3-st RC   3-st RPC

P on RS, k on WS   3-st LC   3-st LPC

4-st LC

4-st RC Sl 2 sts to cn and hold to back, k2, k2 from cn.

4-st LC Sl 2 sts to cn and hold to front, k2, k2 from cn.

(multiple of 14 sts plus 10)

Rows 1 and 15 (RS) Knit.

Rows 2 and 16 Purl.

Row 3 P10, *k4, p10; rep from * to end.

Rows 4 and 14 *K10, p4; rep from *, end k10.

Row 5 P1, k8, p1, *4-st RC, p1, k8, p1; rep from * to end.

Rows 6 and 12 *K1, p8, k1, p4; rep from *, end k1, p8, k1.

Row 7 P1, k2, p4, k2, p1, *k4, p1, k2, p4, k2,

p1; rep from * to end.

Rows 8 and 10 *K1, p2, k4, p2, k1, p4; rep from *, end k1, p2, k4, p2, k1.

Row 9 P1, k2, p4, k2, p1, *4-st RC, p1, k2, p4, k2, p1; rep from * to end.

Row 11 P1, k8, p1, *k4, p1, k8, p1; rep from * to end.

Row 13 P10, *4-st RC, p10; rep from * to end.

Row 17 P3, k4, p3, *p7, k4, p3; rep from * to end.

Row 18 *K3, p4, k7; rep from *, end k3, p4, k3.

Row 19 K2, p1, 4-st LC, p1, k2, *k6, p1, 4-st LC, p1, k2; rep from * to end.

Rows 20 and 26 *P2, k1, p4, k1, p6; rep

from *, end p2, k1, p4, k1, p2.

Row 21 K2, p1, k4, p1, k2, *p4, k2, p1, k4, p1, k2; rep from * to end.

Rows 22 and 24 *P2, k1, p4, k1, p2, k4; rep from *, end p2, k1, p4, k1, p2.

Row 23 K2, p1, 4-st LC, p1, k2, *p4, k2, p1, 4-st LC, p1, k2; rep from * to end.

Row 25 K2, p1, k4, p1, k2, *k6, p1, k4, p1, k2; rep from * to end.

Row 27 P3, 4-st LC, p3, *p7, 4-st LC, p3; rep from * to end.

Row 28 Rep row 18.

Rep rows 1–28.

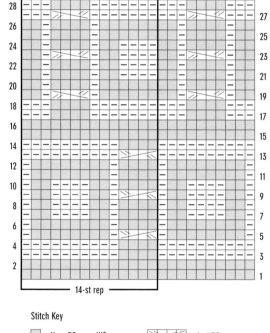

Stitch Key

□ K on RS, p on WS   4-st RC
— P on RS, k on WS   4-st LC

6-st RPC Sl 4 sts to cn and hold to back, k2, sl the 2 p sts from cn to LH needle and purl, then k2 from cn.

(multiple of 20 sts plus 10)

Rows 1, 5, 9, 13, 16, 20 and 24 *P2, k2; rep from *, end p2.

Rows 2, 6, 10, 14, 15, 19, 23 and 27 *K2, p2; rep from *, end k2.

Rows 3, 11, 17 and 25 *[P2, k2] twice; p4, [k2, p2] twice; rep from *, end [p2, k2] twice, p2.

Rows 4, 8, 12, 18, 22 and 26 [K2, p2] twice, k2, *[k2, p2] twice, k4, [p2, k2] twice; rep from * to end.

Row 7 *P2, 6-st RPC, p4, [k2, p2] twice; rep from *, end p2, 6-st RPC, p2.

Row 21 *[P2, k2] twice, p4, 6-st RPC, p2; rep from *, end [p2, k2] twice, p2.

Row 28 Rep row 24.

Rep rows 1–28.

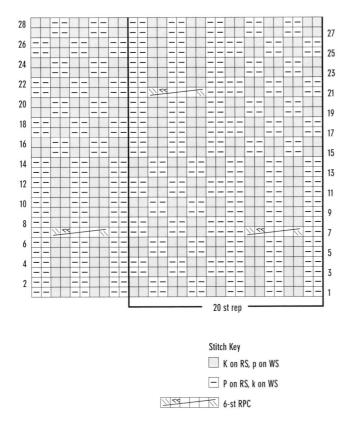

20 st rep

Stitch Key

☐ K on RS, p on WS

— P on RS, k on WS

6-st RPC

142

143 anchors and ropes

RT K2tog but do not drop sts from LH needle, k the first st again, drop both sts from needle.

3-st RPC Sl 1 st to cn and hold to back, k2, p1 from cn.

3-st LPC Sl 2 sts to cn and hold to front, p1, k2 from cn.

4-st RC Sl 2 sts to cn and hold to back, k2, k2 from cn.

4-st LC Sl 2 sts to cn and hold to front, k2, k2 from cn.

(multiple of 12 sts plus 14)

Row 1 (RS) *K2, p2; rep from *, end k2.

Row 2 P2, *k2, p2; rep from * to end.

Row 3 *RT, p2; rep from *, end RT.

Rows 4, 6, 8, 10, 12 and 14 K4, p6, *k2, p2, k2, p6; rep from *, end k4.

Row 5 P4, *4-st RC, [k2, p2] twice; rep from *, end 4-st RC, k2, p4.

Row 7 P4, *k2, 4-st LC, p2, RT, p2; rep from *, end k2, 4-st LC, p4.

Row 9 P4, *k6, p2, k2, p2; rep from *, end k6, p4.

Row 11 P4, *4-st RC, k2, p2, RT, p2; rep from *, end 4-st RC, k2, p4.

Row 13 P4, *k2, 4-st LC, p2, k2, p2; rep from *, end k2, 4-st LC, p4.

Row 15 P2, *p1, 3-st RPC, k2, 3-st LPC, p1, RT; rep from *, end p1, 3-st RPC, k2, 3-st LPC, p3.

Row 16 K3, *p2, k1; rep from *, end k2.

Row 17 P2, *3-st RPC, p1, RT, p1, 3-st LPC, k2; rep from *, end 3-st RPC, p1, RT, p1, 3-st LPC, p2.

Rows 18, 20, 22, 24, 26 and 28 P2, [k2, p2] twice, *p6, k2, p2, k2; rep from *, end p2, k2.

Row 19 P2, k2, *p2, k2, p2, 4-st RC, k2; rep from *, end [p2, k2] twice, p2.

Row 21 P2, k2, *p2, RT, p2, k2, 4-st LC; rep from *, end p2, RT, p2, k2, p2.

Row 23 P2, k2, *p2, k2, p2, k6; rep from *, end [p2, k2] twice, p2.

Row 25 P2, k2, *p2, RT, p2, 4-st RC, k2; rep from *, end p2, RT, p2, k2, p2.

Row 27 P2, k2, *[p2, k2] twice, 4-st LC; rep from *, end [p2, k2] twice, p2.

Row 29 P2, *3-st LPC, p1, RT, p1, 3-st RPC, k2; rep from *, end 3-st LPC, p1, RT, p1, 3-st RPC, p2.

Row 30 K3, *p2, k1; rep from *, end k2.

Row 31 P2, *p1, 3-st LPC, k2, 3-st RPC, p1, RT; rep from *, end p1, 3-st LPC, k2, 3-st RPC, p3.

Row 32 K4, p6, k2, *p2, k2, p6, k2; rep from *, end k2.

Rep rows 1–32.

Stitch Key

▢	K on RS, p on WS
−	P on RS, k on WS
⧗	RT
⧗	3-st RPC
⧗	3-st LPC
⧗	4-st RC
⧗	4-st LC

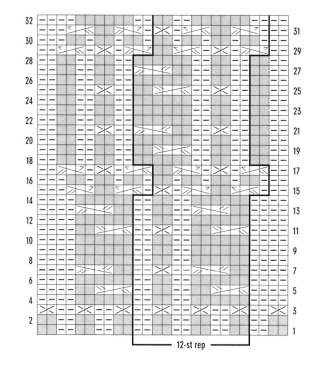

12-st rep

4-st RC Sl 2 sts to cn and hold to back, k2, k2 from cn.

4-st LC Sl 2 sts to cn and hold to front, k2, k2 from cn.

4-st RPC Sl 2 sts to cn and hold to back, k2, p2 from cn.

4-st LPC Sl 2 sts to cn and hold to front, p2, k2 from cn.

(multiple of 16 sts plus 8)

Rows 1 and 9 (RS) P2, *st RC, p4; rep from *, end 4-st RC, p2.

Rows 2 and 10 K2, p4, *k4, p4; rep from *, end k2.

Row 3 P2, k2, *4-st LPC, 4-st RPC; rep from *, end k2, p2.

Row 4 K2, p2, *k2, p4, k4, p4, k2; rep from *, end p2, k2.

Row 5 P2, k2, *p2, 4-st LC, p4, 4-st LC, p2; rep from *, end k2, p2.

Row 6 K2, p2, *k2, p4, k4, p4, k2; rep from *, end p2, k2.

Row 7 P2, k2, *4-st RPC, 4-st LPC; rep from *, end k2, p2.

Row 8 K2, p4, *k4, p4; rep from *, end k2.

Row 11 P2, *k4, p2, 4-st RPC, 4-st LPC, p2; rep from *, end k4, p2.

Rows 12 and 14 K2, p4, *k2, p2, k4, p2, k2, p4; rep from *, end k2.

Row 13 P2, *4-st RC, p2, k2, p4, k2, p2; rep from *, end 4-st RC, p2.

Row 15 P2, *k4, p2, 4-st LPC, 4-st RPC, p2; rep from *, end k4, p2.

Row 16 Rep row 2.

Rep rows 1–16.

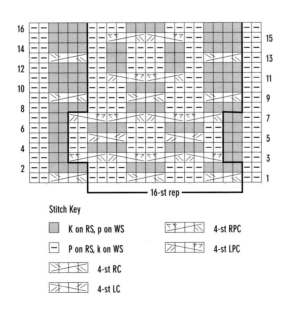

Stitch Key

- K on RS, p on WS
- − P on RS, k on WS
- 4-st RC
- 4-st LC
- 4-st RPC
- 4-st LPC

144

119

145 short cables and rib

8-st RC Sl 4 sts to cn and hold to back, k4, k4 from cn.

(multiple of 30 sts plus 20)

Row 1 (RS) [K1 tbl, p1] 3 times (twisted rib), *k8, [p1, k1 tbl] 3 times, p1 (twisted rib); rep from *, end k8, [p1, k1 tbl] 3 times (twisted rib).

Row 2 [P1, k1] 3 times (rib), p8, *[k1, p1] 3 times, k1 (rib), p8; rep from *, end [k1, p1] 3 times (rib).

Rows 3-6 Rep rows 1 and 2 twice.

Row 7 Twisted rib 6, *8-st RC, twisted rib 7, [k1 tbl, yo] 7 times, k1 tbl, twisted rib 7; rep from *, end 8-st RC, twisted rib 6.

Row 8 Rib 6, p8, *rib 29, p8; rep from *, end rib 6.

Row 9 Twisted rib 6, *k8, twisted rib 29; rep from *, end k8, twisted rib 6.

Rows 10-13 Rep rows 8 and 9 twice.

Row 14 Rep row 8.

Row 15 Twisted rib 6, *8-st RC, twisted rib 29; rep from *, end 8-st RC, twisted rib 6.

Rows 16-21 Rep rows 8 and 9 three times.

Row 22 Rep row 8.

Row 23 Twisted rib 6, *8-st RC, twisted rib 7, [SSK] 7 times, k1 tb1, twisted rib 7; rep from *, end 8-st RC, twisted rib 6.

Row 24 Rep row 2.

Rows 25-28 Rep rows 1 and 2 twice.

Row 29 Twisted rib 6, *[k1 tbl, yo] 7 times, k1 tbl, twisted rib 7, 8-st RC, twisted rib 7; rep from *, end [k1 tbl, yo] 7 times k1 tbl, twisted rib 6.

Row 30 Rib 21,*rib 7, p8, rib 22; rep from *, end rib 6.

Row 31 Twisted rib 6, *twisted rib 22, k8, twisted rib 7; rep from *, end twisted rib 21.

Rows 32-35 Rep rows 30 and 31 twice.

Row 36 Rep row 30.

Row 37 Twisted rib 6, *twisted rib 22, 8-st RC, twisted rib 7; rep from *, end twisted rib 21.

Rows 38-43 Rep rows 30 and 31 three times.

Row 44 Rep row 30.

Row 45 Twisted rib 6, *[SSK] 7 times, k1, twisted rib 7, 8-st RC, twisted rib 7; rep from *, end [SSK] 7 times, k1, twisted rib 6.

Row 46 Rep row 2.

Rep rows 3–46.

145

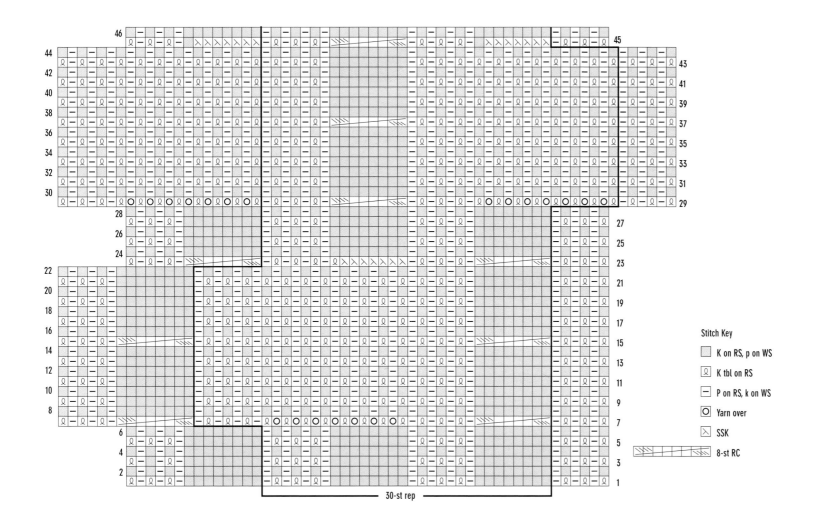

Stitch Key

☐ K on RS, p on WS

Ω K tbl on RS

— P on RS, k on WS

○ Yarn over

⟋ SSK

⟋⟋⟋⟋ 8-st RC

30-st rep

146 small cable and eyelet

4-st RC Sl 2 sts to cn and hold to back, k2, k2 from cn.

(multiple of 11 sts plus 4)

Rows 1 and 3 (WS) *K4, p2, k3, p2; rep from *, end k4.

Row 2 4-st RC, *p2, yo, ssk, k1, p2, 4-st RC; rep from * to end.

Row 4 K4, *p2, k1, k2tog, yo, p2, k4; rep from * to end.

Rep rows 1–4.

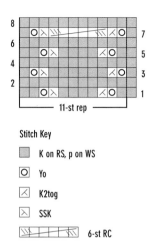

Stitch Key

▨ K on RS, p on WS	⊠ SSK
⊟ P on RS, k on WS	⊙ Yo
⊠ K2tog	▨▨ 4-st RC

147 large cable and eyelet

6-st RC Sl 3 sts to cn and hold to back, k3, k3 from cn.

(multiple of 11 sts plus 1)

Row 1 (RS) K1, *k1, yo, k2tog, k4, ssk, yo, k2; rep from * to end.

Row 2 and all WS rows Purl.

Row 3 K1, *yo, k2tog, k6, ssk, yo, k1; rep from * to end.

Row 5 K1, *k1, yo, k2tog, k4, ssk, yo, k2; rep from * to end.

Row 7 K1, *yo, k2tog, 6-st RC, ssk, yo, k1; rep from * to end.

Row 8 Purl.

Rep rows 1–8.

Stitch Key

▨ K on RS, p on WS	
⊙ Yo	
⊠ K2tog	
⊠ SSK	
▨▨ 6-st RC	

146

147

148 banded snakes

8-st RC Sl 4 sts to cn and hold to back, k4, k4 from cn.

8-st LC Sl 4 sts to cn and hold to front, k4, k4 from cn.

(multiple of 12 sts)

Row 1 (RS) *K8, p4; rep from * to end.

Row 2 *K4, p8; rep from * to end.

Rows 3, 7, 9, 13, 17 and 19 Knit.

Rows 4, 6, 8, 10, 14, 16 and 18 Purl.

Row 5 *K4, 8-st RC; rep from * to end.

Row 11 *P4, k8; rep from * to end.

Row 12 *P8, k4; rep from * to end.

Row 15 *8-st LC, k4; rep from * to end.

Row 20 Purl.

Rep rows 1–20.

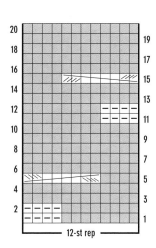

12-st rep

Stitch Key

K on RS, p on WS

— P on RS, k on WS

8-st RC

8-st LC

148

149 pumpkin cable rib

YS (Yo, Sl 1) Wyif, sl 1 purlwise, take yarn to back over top of needle.

RT With tip of RH needle, sl yo off LH needle knitwise, k next st, pass yo over k st.

LT Drop yo off LH needle and let it fall to back of work, insert RH needle between first and 2nd sts on LH needle and draw yo through to front, k next st, pass yo over k st.

9-st LC Sl 6 sts to cn and hold to front, k3, sl last 3 sts back to LH needle, hold cn with 3 k sts to back of work, p1, RT, p1, k3 from cn.

(multiple of 18 sts plus 5)

Preparation row (WS) K1, p3, k1, *YS, k1, p3, k1; rep from * to end.

Rows 1 and 9 *P1, k3, p1, RT; rep from *, end p1, k3, p1.

Row 2 and all WS rows K1, p3, k1, *YS, k1, p3, k1; rep from * to end.

Rows 3, 7 and 11 *P1, k3, p1, LT; rep from *, end p1, k3, p1.

Row 5 *P1, k3, p1, RT, p1, 9-st LC, p1, RT; rep from *, end p1, k3, p1.

Row 12 Rep row 2.

Rep rows 1–12.

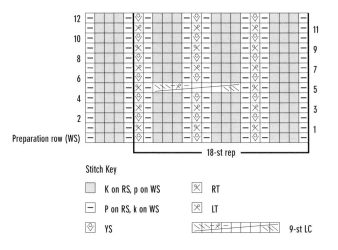

Stitch Key

▨ K on RS, p on WS	✘ RT
— P on RS, k on WS	✘ LT
♡ YS	〰✘〰 9-st LC

150 fisherman's twist

3-st RC Sl 2 sts to cn and hold to back, k1, k2 from cn.

K1b Knit next st in row below.

(multiple of 8 sts plus 2)

Rows 1, 3 and 5 (RS) Knit.

Row 2 and all WS rows K1, *p1, k1b; rep from *, end k1.

Row 7 K1, *k1, 3-st RC, k4; rep from *, end k1.

Rows 9 and 11 Knit.

Row 13 K1, *k5, 3-st RC; rep from *, end k1.

Rep rows 2–13.

Stitch Key

☐ K on RS, p on WS

– P on RS, k on WS

Ⓐ K1b

⬚⬚ 3-st RC

151 dropped stitch cable

6-st LPC (WS) Sl 3 to cn letting extra loops drop, hold to front of work, p3 letting extra loops drop; p3 from cn.

(multiple of 6 sts plus 2)

Rows 1 and 3 (RS) Knit.

Rows 2 and 4 Purl.

Row 5 K1, *k next st wrapping yarn twice around needle; rep from *, end k1.

Row 6 P1, *6-st LPC; rep from *, end p1.

Rep rows 1–6.

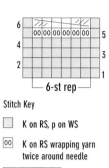

Stitch Key

☐ K on RS, p on WS

00 K on RS wrapping yarn twice around needle

⬚⬚⬚ 6-st LPC (WS)

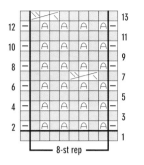

150

151

152 cable maze

6-st LC Sl 3 sts to cn and hold to front, k3, k3 from cn.
S2KP Sl 2 sts, k next st, pass 2 slipped sts over k1.
(multiple of 22 sts plus 2)
Row 1 (RS) K1, *k5, yo, k1, k3tog, k1, yo, k1, p2, k6, p2, k1; rep from *, end k1.
Row 2 and all WS rows K the knit sts and p the purl sts and yo's.
Row 3 K1, *k4, yo, k1, k3tog, k1, yo, k2, p2, k6, p2, k1; rep from *, end k1.
Row 5 K1, *k3, yo, k1, k3tog, k1, yo, k3, p2, k6, p2, k1; rep from *, end k1.
Row 7 K1, *k2, yo, k1, k3tog, k1, yo, k4, p2, 6-st LC, p2, k1; rep from *, end k1.

Row 9 K1, *k1, yo, k1, k3tog, k1, yo, k5, p2, k6, p2, k1; rep from *, end k1.
Row 11 K1, *yo, k1, k3tog, k1, yo, k6, p2, k6, p2, k1; rep from *, end k1.
Row 13 K1, *p2, k6, p2, k1, yo, k1, S2KP, k1, yo, k6; rep from *, end k1.
Row 15 K1, *p2, k6, p2, k2, yo, k1, S2KP, k1, yo, k5; rep from *, end k1.
Row 17 K1, *p2, k6, p2, k3, yo, k1, S2KP, k1, yo, k4; rep from *, end k1.
Row 19 K1, *p2, 6-st LC, p2, k4, yo, k1, S2KP, k1, yo, k3; rep from *, end k1.
Row 21 K1, *p2, k6, p2, k5, yo, k1, S2KP, k1, yo, k2; rep from *, end k1.
Row 23 K1, *p2, k6, p2, k6, yo, k1, S2KP, k1, yo, k1; rep from *, end k1.
Row 24 K the knit sts and p the purl sts and yo's.
Rep rows 1–24.

Stitch Key

- K on RS, p on WS
- P on RS, k on WS
- Yarn over
- K3tog
- SK2P
- 6-st LC

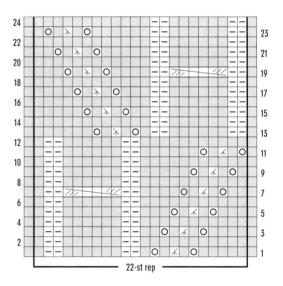

22-st rep

153 boxed twists and cable

allover

RT Skip first st and passing in front of st, k next st, k skipped st and let both sts fall from needle.

6-st RC Sl 3 sts to cn and hold to back, k3, k3 from cn.

(multiple of 18 sts plus 3)

Rows 1 and 11 (RS) K1, *k1 tbl, p8; rep from *, end k1 tbl, k1.

Rows 2 and 12 K1, sl 1 knitwise, *k8, sl 1 knitwise; rep from *, end k1.

Rows 3, 5 and 9 K1, *k1 tbl, p1, k6, p1, k1 tbl, p1, k1, [RT] twice, k1, p1; rep from *, end k1 tbl, k1.

Rows 4, 6, 8 and 10 K1, sl 1 knitwise, *k1, p6, k1, sl 1 knitwise; rep from *, end k1.

Row 7 K1, *k1 tbl, p1, 6-st RC, p1, k1 tbl, p1, k1, [RT] twice, k1, p1; rep from *, end k1 tbl, k1.

Rows 13, 15 and 19 K1, *k1 tbl, p1, k1, [RT] twice, k1, p1, k1 tbl, p1, k6, p1; rep from *, end k1 tbl, k1.

Rows 14, 16 and 18 K1, sl 1 knitwise, *k1, p6, k1, sl 1 knitwise; rep from *, end k1.

Row 17 K1, *k1 tbl, p1, k1, [RT] twice, k1, p1, k1 tbl, p1, 6-st RC, p1; rep from *, end k1 tbl, k1.

Row 20 Rep row 14.

Rep rows 1–20.

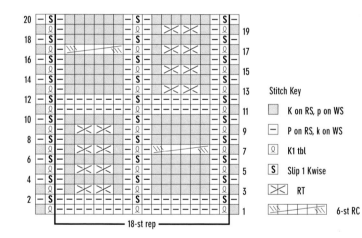

Stitch Key

- K on RS, p on WS
- ― P on RS, k on WS
- Ω K1 tbl
- S Slip 1 Kwise
- ⋈ RT
- 6-st RC

5-st RPC Sl 2 sts to cn and hold to back, k3; p1, k1 from cn.

5-st LPC Sl 3 sts to cn and hold to front, p1, k1; k3 from cn.

6-st RC Sl 3 sts to cn and hold to back, k3, k3 from cn.

(multiple of 14 sts plus 30)

Row 1 (RS) K1, *[p1, k1] twice, k6, [p1, k1] twice; rep from *, end k1.

Rows 2, 4 and 22 P1, *[k1, p1] twice, p6, [k1, p1] twice; rep from *, end p1.

Row 3 K1, *[p1, k1] twice, 6-st RC, [p1, k1] twice; rep from *, end k1.

Row 5 K1, *p1, k1, 5-st RPC, 5-st LPC, p1, k1; rep from *, end k1.

Rows 6 and 8 P1, *k1, p4, k1, p1, k1, p4, k1, p1; rep from *, end p1.

Row 7 K1, *p1, k4, p1, k1, p1, k4, p1, k1; rep from *, end k1.

Row 9 K1, *5-st RPC, [p1, k1] twice, 5-st LPC; rep from *, end k1.

Rows 10, 12, 14 and 16 P1, *p3, [k1, p1] 4 times, p3; rep from *, end p1.

Rows 11 and 15 K4, *[p1, k1] 4 times, 6-st RC; rep from * to last 12 sts, [p1, k1] 4 times, k4.

Row 13 K1, *k3, [p1, k1] 4 times, k3; rep from *, end k1.

Row 17 K1, *5-st LPC, [p1, k1] twice, 5-st RPC; rep from *, end k1.

Rows 18 and 20 P1, *k1, p4, [k1, p1] twice, p3, k1, p1; rep from *, end p1.

Row 19 K1, *p1, k4, [p1, k1] twice, k3, p1, k1; rep from *, end k1.

Row 21 K1, *p1, k1, 5-st LPC, 5-st RPC, p1, k1; rep from *, end k1.

Row 23 Rep row 3.

Row 24 Rep row 2.

Rep rows 1–24.

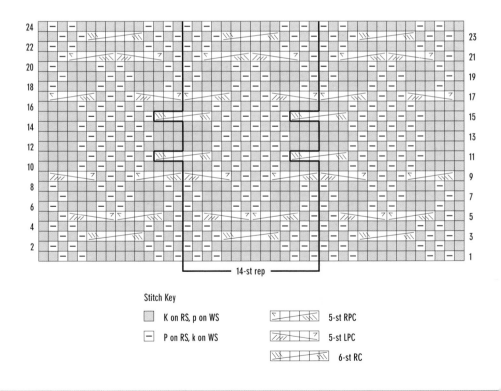

Stitch Key

K on RS, p on WS	5-st RPC
P on RS, k on WS	5-st LPC
	6-st RC

14-st rep

154

6-st RC Sl 3 sts to cn and hold to back, k3, k3 from cn.

SSK Sl 1, sl 1, knit these 2 slipped sts tog.

SK2P Sl 1, k2 tog, pass sl st over k2 tog.

(multiple of 22 sts plus 17)

Rows 1, 5 and 9 (RS) K6, yo, SSK, k1, k2tog, yo, *k17, yo, SSK, k1, k2tog, yo; rep from *, end k6.

Row 2 and all WS rows Purl.

Rows 3 and 11 K7, yo, SK2P, yo, k1, *k18, yo, SK2P, yo, k1; rep from *, end k6.

Row 7 6-st RC, k1, yo, SK2P, yo, k1, *6-st RC, k5, 6-st RC, k1, yo, SK2P, yo, k1; rep from *, end 6-st RC.

Rows 13, 17 and 21 K11, *k6, yo, SSK, k1, k2tog, yo, k11; rep from *, end k6.

Rows 15 and 23 6-st RC, k5, *6-st RC, k1, yo, SK2P, yo, k1, 6-st RC, k5; rep from *, end 6-st RC.

Row 19 K11, *k7, yo, SK2P, yo, k12; rep from *, end k6.

Row 24 Purl.

Rep rows 1–24.

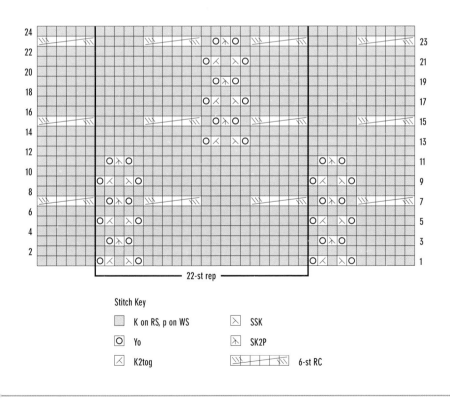

22-st rep

Stitch Key

▢	K on RS, p on WS	☒	SSK
⊙	Yo	⅄	SK2P
◺	K2tog	⟍⟍⟍⟋⟋⟋	6-st RC

155

3-st RPC Sl 2 sts to cn and hold to back, k1, p2 from cn.

3-st LPC Sl 1 st to cn and hold to front, p2, k1 from cn.

6-st RC Sl 3 sts to cn and hold to back, k3, k3 from cn.

6-st LC Sl 3 sts to cn and hold to front, k3, k3 from cn.

(multiple of 28 sts)

Rows 1 and 5 (RS) *P4, k6, p8, k6, p4; rep from * to end.

Rows 2, 4 and 6 *K4, p6, k8, p6, k4; rep from * to end.

Row 3 *P4, 6-st RC, p8, 6-st RC, p4; rep from * to end.

Row 7 *P2, 3-st RPC, k4, 3-st LPC, k4, 3-st RPC, k4, 3-st LPC, p2; rep from * to end.

Rows 8 and 34 *K2, p1, k2, p4, k2, p1, k4, p1, k2, p4, k2, p1, k2; rep from * to end.

Row 9 *3-st RPC, p2, k4, p2, 3-st LPC, 3-st RPC, p2, k4, p2, 3-st LPC; rep from * to end.

Rows 10 and 32 *P1, k4, p4, k4, p2, k4, p4, k4, p1; rep from * to end.

Row 11 *K1, p2, 3-st RPC, k2, 3-st LPC, p2, k2, p2, 3-st RPC, k2, 3-st LPC, p2, k1; rep from * to end.

Row 12 *P1, k2, p1, k2, p2, k2, p1, k2, p2, k2, p1, k2, p2, k2, p1, k2, p1; rep from * to end.

Row 13 *K1, 3-st RPC, p2, k2, p2, 3-st LPC, k2, 3-st RPC, p2, k2, p2, 3-st LPC, k1; rep from * to end.

Row 14 *[P2, k4] twice, p4, [k4, p2] twice; rep from * to end.

Row 15 *K2, p2, 3-st RPC, 3-st LPC, p2, k4, p2, 3-st RPC, 3-st LPC, p2, k2; rep from * to end.

Row 16 *P2, k2, p1, k4, p1, k2, p4, k2, p1, k4, p1, k2, p2; rep from * to end.

Row 17 *K2, 3-st RPC, p4, 3-st LPC, k4, 3-st RPC, p4, 3-st LPC, k2; rep from * to end.

Rows 18, 20, 22 and 24 *P3, k8, p6, k8, p3; rep from * to end.

Rows 19 and 23 *K3, p8, k6, p8, k3; rep from * to end.

Row 21 K3, *P8, 6-st LC; rep from *, end last rep k3.

Row 25 *K2, 3-st LPC, p4, 3-st RPC, k4, 3-st LPC, p4, 3-st RPC, k2; rep from * to end.

Row 26 *P2, k2, p1, k4, p1, k2, p4, k2, p1, k4, p1, k2, p2; rep from * to end.

Row 27 *K2, p2, 3-st LPC, 3-st RPC, p2, k4, p2, 3-st LPC, 3-st RPC, p2, k2; rep from * to end.

Row 28 *P2, k4, p2, k4, p4, k4, p2, k4, p2; rep from * to end.

Row 29 *K1, 3-st LPC, p2, k2, p2, 3-st RPC, k2, 3-st LPC, p2, k2, p2, 3-st RPC, k1; rep from * to end.

Row 30 *[P1, k2] twice, p2, k2, p1, k2, p2, k2, p1, k2, p2, k2, p1, k2, p1; rep from * to end.

Row 31 *K1, p2, 3-st LPC, k2, 3-st RPC, p2, k2, p2, 3-st LPC, k2, 3-st RPC, p2, k1; rep from * to end.

Row 33 *3-st LPC, p2, k4, p2, 3-st RPC, 3-st LPC, p2, k4, p2, 3-st RPC; rep from * to end.

Row 35 *P2, 3-st LPC, k4, 3-st RPC, p4, 3-st LPC, k4, 3-st RPC, p2; rep from * to end.

Row 36 Rep row 2.

Rep rows 1–36.

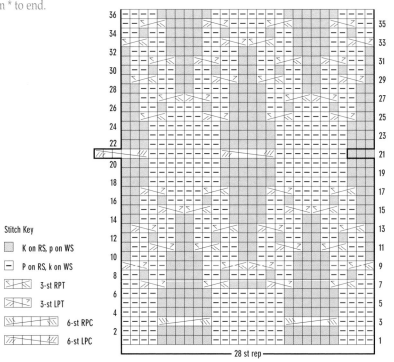

Stitch Key

K on RS, p on WS

— P on RS, k on WS

3-st RPT

3-st LPT

6-st RPC

6-st LPC

28 st rep

allover

24-st LC Sl 12 sts to cn and hold to front, [k2, p2] 3 times, work sts from cn as foll: [k2, p2] 3 times.

24-st RC Sl 12 sts to cn and hold to back, [k2, p2] 3 times, work sts from cn as foll: [k2, p2] 3 times.

(multiple of 48 sts)

Rows 1, 3, 5, 7, 11, 13, 15, 17, 19 and 23 *K2, p2; rep from * to end.

Row 2 and all WS rows *K2, p2; rep from * to end.

Row 9 *24-st LC, [k2, p2] 6 times; rep from * to end.

Row 21 *[K2, p2] 6 times, 24-st RC; rep from * to end.

Row 24 Rep row 2.

Rep rows 1–24.

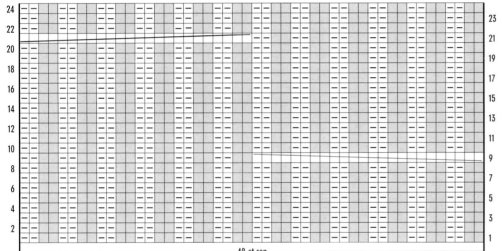

48-st rep

Stitch Key

- ▨ K on RS, p on WS
- ⊟ P on RS, k on WS

24-st RC

24-st LC

157

158 moss diamonds and bobbles

6-st LC Sl 3 sts to cn and hold to front, k3, k3 from cn.

6-st RPC Sl 3 sts to cn and hold to back, k3; p1, k1, p1 from cn.

6-st LPC Sl 3 sts to cn and hold to front, p1, k1, p1; k3 from cn.

MB K into front, back, front, back and front of st. Turn, p5, turn, p5, turn, p5, turn, k2tog, k1, SKP. Sl 3 sts back to LH needle, sl 2 tog knitwise, k1, pass 2 sl sts over k st.

(multiple of 27 sts plus 6)

Rows 1, 7, 11 and 13 *K6, p1, [k1 tbl, p2] 6 times, k1 tbl, p1; rep from *, end k6.

Rows 2, 4, 8, 10, 12 and 14 P6, *k1, [p1 tbl, k2] 6 times, p1 tbl, k1, p6; rep from * to end.

Rows 3 and 9 *6-st LC, p1, [k1 tbl, p2] 6 times, k1 tbl, p1; rep from *, end 6-st LC.

Row 5 *K6, p1, [k1 tbl, p2, MB, p2] 3 times, k1 tbl, p1; rep from *, end k6.

Row 6 P6, *k1, [p1 tbl, k2, p1, k2] 3 times, p1 tbl, k1, p6; rep from * to end.

Row 15 K3, *6-st LPC, p1, [k1 tbl, p2] 4 times, k1 tbl, p1, 6-st RPC; rep from *, end k3.

Rows 16 and 20 P1, k1, p1, *k1, p1, k1, p3, k1, [p1 tbl, k2] 4 times, p1 tbl, k1, p3, k1, p1, k1; rep from *, end p1, k1, p1.

Rows 17 and 41 K1, p1, k1, * p1, k1, p1, k3, p1, [k1 tbl, p2] 4 times, k1 tbl, p1, k3, p1, k1, p1; rep from *, end k1, p1, k1.

Rows 18 and 42 K1, p1, k1, *p1, k1, p4, k1, [p1 tbl, k2] 4 times, p1 tbl, k1, p4, k1, p1; rep from *, end p1, k1, p1.

Rows 19 and 43 P1, k1, p1, * k1, p1, k4, p1, [k1 tbl, p2] 4 times, k1 tbl, p1, k4, p1, k1; rep from *, end p1, k1, p1.

Row 21 K1, p1, k1, *p1, k1, p1, 6-st LPC, p1, [k1tbl, p2] twice, k1 tbl, p1, 6-st RPC, p1, k1, p1; rep from *, end k1, p1, k1.

Rows 22 and 38 K1, p1, k1, *[p1, k1] 3 times, p3, k1, [p1 tbl, k2] twice, p1 tbl, k1, p3, [k1, p1] 3 times; rep from *, end k1, p1, k1.

Rows 23 and 35 P1, k1, p1, *[k1, p1] 3 times, k3, p1, [k1 tbl, p2] twice, k1 tbl, p1, k3, [p1, k1] 3 times; rep from *, end p1, k1, p1.

Rows 24 and 36 P1, k1, p1, *[k1, p1] 3 times, p3, k1, [p1 tbl, k2] twice, p1 tbl, k1, p3, [p1, k1] 3 times; rep from *, end p1, k1, p1.

Rows 25 and 37 K1, p1, k1, *[p1, k1] 3 times, k3, p1, [k1 tbl, p2] twice, k1 tbl, p1, k3, [k1, p1] 3 times; rep from *, end k1, p1, k1.

Rows 26 and 34 K1, p1, k1, *[p1, k1] 3 times, p3, k1, [p1 tbl, k2] twice, p1 tbl, k1, p3, [k1, p1] 3 times; rep from *, end k1, p1, k1.

Row 27 P1, k1, p1, *[k1, p1] 3 times, 6-st LPC, p1, k1 tbl, p1, 6-st RPC, [p1, k1] 3 times; rep from *, end p1, k1, p1.

Row 28 P1, k1, p1, *[k1, p1] 4 times, k1, p3, k1, p1 tbl, k1, p3, [k1, p1] 4 times, k1; rep from *, end p1, k1, p1.

Row 29 K1, p1, k1, *[p1, k1] 5 times, k2, p1, MB, p1, k3, [p1, k1] 4 times, p1; rep from *, end k1, p1, k1.

Row 30 K1, p1, k1, *[p1, k1] 4 times, p4, k1, p1, k1, p4, [k1, p1] 4 times; rep from * end k1, p1, k1.

Row 31 P1, k1, p1, *[k1, p1] 4 times, k4, p1, k1 tbl, p1, k4, [p1, k1] 4 times; rep from *, end p1, k1, p1.

Row 32 P1, k1, p1, *[k1, p1] 5 times, p2, k1, p1 tbl, k1, p3, [k1, p1] 4 times, k1; rep from *, end p1, k1, p1.

Row 33 K1, p1, k1, *[p1, k1] 3 times, 6-st RPC, p1, k1 tbl, p1, 6-st LPC, [k1, p1] 3 times; rep from *, end k1, p1, k1.

Row 39 P1, k1, p1, *k1, p1, k1, 6-st RPC, p1, [k1 tbl, p2] twice, k1 tbl, p1, 6-st LPC, k1, p1, k1; rep from *, end p1, k1, p1.

Row 40 P1, k1, p1, *k1, p1, k1, p3, k1, [p1 tbl, k2] 4 times, p1 tbl, k1, p3, k1, p1, k1; rep from *, end p1, k1, p1.

Row 44 P1, k1, p1, *k1, p1, k1, p3, k1, [p1 tbl, k2] 4 times, p1 tbl, k1, p3, k1, p1, k1; rep from *, end p1, k1, p1.

Row 45 K3, *6-st RPC, p1, [k1 tbl, p2] 4 times, k1 tbl, p1, 6-st LPC; rep from *, end k3.

Row 46 P3, *p3, k1, [p1 tbl, k2] 6 times, p1tbl, k1, p3; rep from *, end p3.

Row 47 K3, *k3, p1, [k1 tbl, p2] 6 times, k1tbl, p1, k3; rep from * end k3.

Row 48 Rep row 46.

Rep rows 1–48.

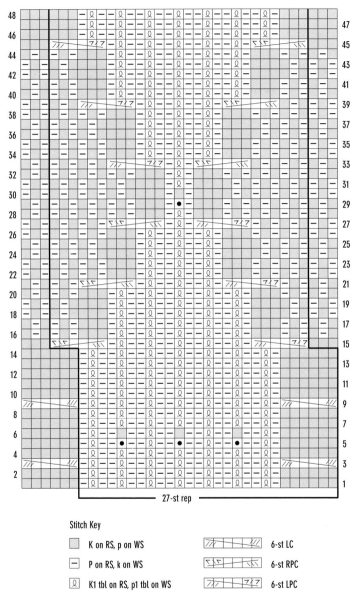

Stitch Key

- ☐ K on RS, p on WS
- — P on RS, k on WS
- Ω K1 tbl on RS, p1 tbl on WS
- • MB
- 6-st LC
- 6-st RPC
- 6-st LPC

159 pie crust diamonds

RT Skip first st, and passing in front of st, k next st, k skipped st and let both sts fall from needle.

RC Sl 5 sts to cn and hold in back, k4, sl last st from cn to LH needle and purl it, k4 from cn.

LC Sl 5 sts to cn and hold in front, k4, sl last st from cn to LH needle and purl it, k4 from cn.

RTTC Sl 5 sts to cn and hold in back, p1, RT, p1, sl last st from cn to LH needle and purl it, [p1, RT, p1] from cn.

LTTC Sl 5 sts to cn and hold in front, p1, RT, p1, sl last st from cn to LH needle and purl it, [p1, RT, p1] from cn.

RT4C Sl 5 sts to cn and hold in back, p1, RT, p1, sl last st from cn to LH needle and purl it, k4 from cn.

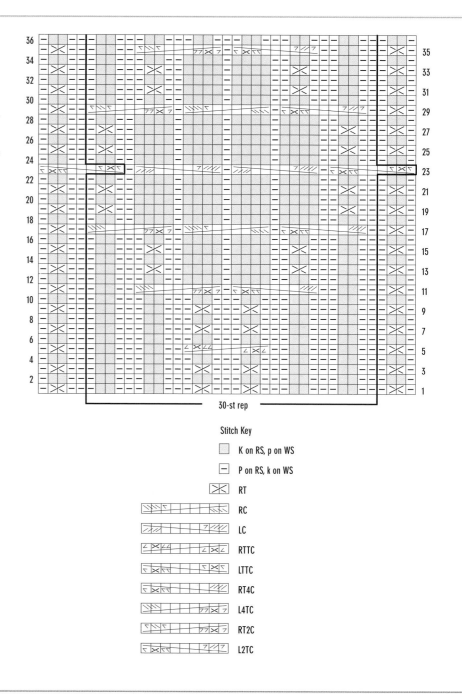

30-st rep

Stitch Key

☐	K on RS, p on WS
−	P on RS, k on WS
⧖	RT
	RC
	LC
	RTTC
	LTTC
	RT4C
	L4TC
	RT2C
	L2TC

159

134

allover

L4TC Sl 5 sts to cn and hold in front, k4, sl last st from cn to LH needle and purl it, [p1, RT, p1] from cn.

RT2C Sl 5 sts to cn and hold in back, p1, RT, p1, sl last st from cn to LH needle and purl it, [p1, k2, p1] from cn.

L2TC Sl 5 sts to cn and hold to front, p1, k2, p1, sl last st from cn to LH needle and purl it, [p1, RT, p1] from cn.

(multiple of 30 sts plus 9)

Rows 1, 3, 7 and 9 (RS) P1, RT, p1, *p2, [k2, p3] twice, RT, p3, RT, [p3, k2] twice, p1; rep from *, end p2, RT, p1.

Rows 2, 4, 6, 8 and 10 K1, p2, k2, *k1, [p2, k3] 5 times, p2, k2; rep from *, end k1, p2, k1.

Row 5 P1, RT, p1, *p2, k2, p3, k2, p2, RTTC, p2, k2, p3, k2, p1; rep from *, end p2, RT, p1.

Row 11 P1, RT, p1, *p2, k2, p2, RT4C, p1, L4TC, p2, k2, p1; rep from *, end p2, RT, p1.

Rows 12, 14 and 16 K1, p2, k2, *k1, p2, k3, p2, k2, p4, k1, p4, k2, p2, k3, p2, k2; rep from *, end k1, p2, k1.

Rows 13 and 15 P1, RT, p1, *p2, k2, p3, RT, p2, k4, p1, k4, p2, RT, p3, k2, p1; rep from *, end p2, RT, p1.

Row 17 P1, RT, p1, *p1, RT4C, p1, RC, p1, L4TC; rep from *, end p2, RT, p1.

Rows 18, 20, 22, 24, 26 and 28 K1, p2, k2, *k1, p2, k2, [p4, k1] 4 times, k1, p2, k2; rep from *, end k1, p2, k1.

Rows 19, 21, 25 and 27 P1, RT, p1, *p2, RT, p2, [k4, p1] 4 times, p1, RT, p1; rep from *, end p2, RT, p1.

Row 23 *LTTC, p1, LC, p1, LC, p1; rep from *, end LTTC.

Row 29 P1, RT, p1, *p1, L2TC, p1, RC, p1, RT2C; rep from *, end p2, RT, p1.

Rows 30, 32 and 34 K1, p2, k2, *k1, p2, k3, p2, k2, p4, k1, p4, k2, p2, k3, p2, k2; rep from *, end k1, p2, k1.

Rows 31 and 33 P1, RT, p1, *p2, k2, p3, RT, p2, k4, p1, k4, p2, RT, p3, k2, p1; rep from *, end p2, RT, p1.

Row 35 P1, RT, p1, *p2, k2, p2, L2TC, p1, RT2C, p2, k2, p1; rep from *, end p2, RT, p1.

Row 36 K1, p2, k2, *k1, [p2, k3] five times, p2, k2; rep from *, end k1, p2, k1.

Rep rows 1–36.

8-st RC Sl 4 sts to cn and hold to back, k4, k4 from cn.

(multiple of 16 sts plus 4)

Rows 1, 3, 5, 7, 9 and 11 (RS) *K4, p2, k8, p2; rep from *, end k4.

Row 2 and all WS rows P4, *k2, p8, k2, p4; rep from * to end.

Row 13 *K4, p2, 8-st RC, p2; rep from *, end k4.

Row 14 Rep row 2.

Rep rows 1–14.

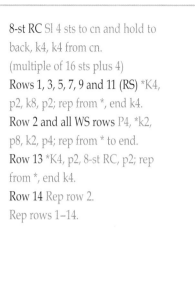

Stitch Key

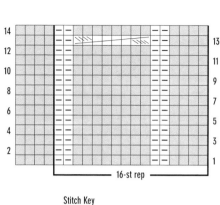

☐ K on RS, p on WS

– P on RS, k on WS

8-st RC

161 knotted diamonds

5-st RPC Sl 1 st to cn and hold to back, k4, p1 from cn.

5-st LPC Sl 4 sts to cn and hold to front, p1, k4 from cn.

8-st LC Sl 5 sts to cn and hold in front, k3, sl last 2 sts from cn to LH needle, move cn to back, p2, k3 from cn.

(multiple of 26 sts plus 14)

Row 1 (RS) P3, *8-st LC, p5; rep from *, end 8-st LC, p3.

Row 2 K3, p3, k1, *k1, p3, k5, p3, k2, p3, k5, p3, k1; rep from *, end k1, p3, k3.

Rows 3 and 47 P3, k3, p1, *p1, k3, p5, k8, p5, k3, p1; rep from *, end p1, k3, p3.

Rows 4 and 46 K3, p3, k1, *k1, p3, k5, p8, k5, p3, k1; rep from *, end k1, p3 k3.

Row 5 P3, k3, p1, *p1, k3, p4, 5-st RPC, 5-st LPC, p4, k3, p1; rep from *, end p1, k3, p3.

Rows 6 and 44 K3, p3, k1, *k1, p3, k4, p4, k2, p4, k4, p3, k1; rep from *, end k1, p3, k3.

Row 7 P3, k3, p1, *p1, k3, p3, 5-st RPC, p2, 5-st LPC, p3, k3, p1; rep from *, end p1, k3, p3.

Rows 8 and 42 K3, p3, k1, *k1, p3, k3, p4, k4, p4, k3, p3, k1; rep from *, end k1, p3, k3.

Row 9 P3, *8-st LC, p2, 5-st RPC, p4, 5-st LPC, p2; rep from *, end 8-st LC, p3.

Rows 10 and 40 K3, p3, k1, *k1, p3, k2, p4, k6, p4, k2, p3, k1; rep from *, end k1, p3, k3.

Row 11 P3, k3, p1, *p1, k3, p1, 5-st RPC, p6, 5-st LPC, p1, k3, p1; rep from *, end p1, k3, p3.

Rows 12 and 38 K3, p3, k1, *k1, p3, k1, p4, k8, p4, k1, p3, k1; rep from *, end k1, p3, k3.

Row 13 P3, k3, p1, *p1, k3, 5-st RPC, k3, p2, k3, 5-st LPC, k3, p1; rep from *, end p1, k3, p3.

Row 14 K3, p3, k1, *k1, p7, k1, p3, k2, p3, k1, p7, k1; rep from *, end p1, k3, p3.

Row 15 P2, k4, p1, *p3, 5-st RPC, p1, k3, p2, k3, p1, 5-st LPC, p3; rep from *, end p1, k4, p2.

Rows 16 and 34 P4, k3, *k3, p4, [k2, p3] twice, k2, p4, k3; rep from *, end k3, p4.

Row 17 5-st LPC, p2, *p2, 5-st RPC, p2, 8-st LC, p2, 5-st LPC, p2; rep from *, end p2, 5-st RPC.

Rows 18 and 32 K1, p4, k2, *k2, p4, k3, p3, k2, p3, k3, p4, k2; rep from *, end k2, p4, k1.

Row 19 P1, 5-st LPC, p1, *p1, 5-st RPC, p3, k3, p2, k3, p3, 5-st LPC, p1; rep from *, end p1, 5-st RPC, p1.

Rows 20 and 30 K2, p4, k1, *k1, p4, k4, p3, k2, p3, k4, p4, k1; rep from *, end k1, p4, k2.

Row 21 P2, 5-st LPC, *5-st RPC, p4, k3, p2, k3, p4, 5-st LPC; rep from *, end 5-st RPC, p2.

Rows 22 and 28 K3, p4, *p4, k5, p3, k2, p3, k5, p4; rep from *, end p4, k3.

Row 23 P3, k4, *k4, p5, k3, p2, k3, p5, k4; rep from *, end k4, p3.

Row 24 K3, p3, k1, *k1, p3, k5, p3, k2, p3, k5, p3, k1; rep from *, end k1, p3, k3.

Row 25 P3, *8-st LC, p5; rep from *, end 8-st LC, p3.

Row 26 K3, p3, k1, *k1, p3, k5, p3, k2, p3, k5, p3, k1; rep from *, end k1, p3, k3.

Row 27 P3, k4, *k4, p5, k3, p2, k3, p5, k4; rep from *, end k4, p3.

Row 29 P2, 5-st RPC, *5-st LPC, p4, k3, p2, k3, p4, 5-st RPC; rep from *, end 5-st LPC, p2.

Row 31 P1, 5-st RPC, p1, *p1, 5-st LPC, p3, k3, p2, k3, p3, 5-st RPC, p1; rep from *, end p1, 5-st LPC, p1.

Row 33 5-st RPC, p2, *p2, 5-st LPC, p2, 8-st LC, p2, 5-st RPC, p2; rep from *, end p2, 5-st LPC.

Row 35 P2, k4, p1, *p3, 5-st LPC, p1, k3, p2, k3, p1, 5-st RPC, p3; rep from *, end p1, k4, p2.

Row 36 K3, p3, k1, *k1, p7, k1, p3, k2, p3, k1, p7, k1; rep from *, end k1, p3, k3.

Row 37 P3, k3, p1, *p1, k3, 5-st LPC, k3, p2, k3, 5-st RPC, k3, p1; rep from *, end p1, k3, p3.

Row 39 P3, k3, p1, *p1, k3, p1, 5-st LPC, p6, 5-st RPC, p1, k3, p1; rep from *, end p1, k3, p3.

Row 41 P3, *8-st LC, p2, 5-st LPC, p4, 5-st RPC, p2; rep from *, end 8-st LC, p3.

Row 43 P3, k3, p1, *p1, k3, p3, 5-st LPC, p2, 5-st RPC, p3, k3, p1; rep from *, end p1, k3, p3.

Row 45 P3, k3, p1, *p1, k3, p4, 5-st LPC, 5-st RPC, p4, k3, p1; rep from *, end p1, k3, p3.

Row 48 Rep row 2.

Rep rows 1–48.

161

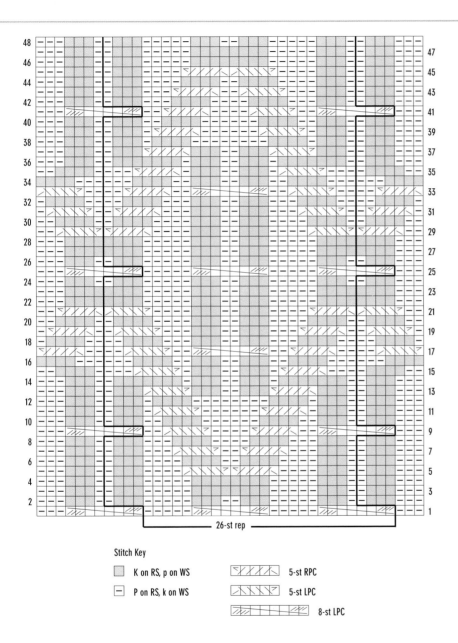

48 47
46 45
44 43
42 41
40 39
38 37
36 35
34 33
32 31
30 29
28 27
26 25
24 23
22 21
20 19
18 17
16 15
14 13
12 11
10 9
8 7
6 5
4 3
2 1

├─ 26-st rep ─┤

Stitch Key

☐ K on RS, p on WS   5-st RPC

─ P on RS, k on WS   5-st LPC

                            8-st LPC

3-st RC Sl 1 st to cn and hold in back, k2, k1 from cn.

4-st RC Sl 2 sts to cn and hold in back, k2, k2 from cn.

3-st RPC Sl 1 st to cn and hold in back, k2, p1 from cn.

4-st RPC Sl 2 sts to cn and hold in back, p2, k2 from cn.

5-st RPC Sl 3 sts to cn and hold in back, k2, sl last st on cn to LH needle and p it, k2 from cn.

3-st LC Sl 2 sts to cn and hold in front, k1, k2 from cn.

4-st LC Sl 2 sts to cn and hold in front, k2, k2 from cn.

3-st LPC Sl 2 sts to cn and hold in front, p1, k2 from cn.

4-st LPC Sl 2 sts to cn and hold in front, p2, k2 from cn.

(multiple of 21 sts)

Preparation row (WS) *P2, k6, p2, k1, p2, k6, p2; rep from * to end.

Rows 1 and 9 (RS) K2, *p6, k2, p1, k2, p6, 4-st RC; rep from *, end last rep k2.

Rows 2, 4, 6, 8 and 10 *P2, k6, p2, k1, p2, k6, p2; rep from * to end.

Rows 3 and 7 *K2, p6, k2, p1, k2, p6, k2; rep from * to end.

Row 5 K2, *p6, 5-st RPC, p6, 4-st RC; rep from *, end last rep k2.

Row 11 *3-st LPC, p5, 5-st RPC, p5, 3-st RC; rep from * to end.

Rows 12, 26, 32, 46 *K1, p2, k5, p2, k1, p2, k5, p3; rep from * to end.

Row 13 *P1, 3-st LC, p4, k2, p1, k2, p4, 3-st RPC, k1; rep from * to end.

Rows 14, 24, 34, 44 *K1, p3, k4, p2, k1, p2, k4, p2, k1, p1; rep from * to end.

Row 15 *P1, k1, 3-st LPC, p4, k1, p1, k1, p4, 3-st RC, p1, k1; rep from * to end.

Row 16 *K1, p1, k1, p2, k4, p1, k1, p1, k4, p3, k1, p1; rep from * to end.

Row 17 *P1, k1, p1, 3-st LC, p3, k1, p1, k1, p3, 3-st RPC, k1, p1, k1; rep from * to end.

Rows 18 and 40 *[K1, p1] twice, p2, k9, p2, [k1, p1] twice; rep from * to end.

Row 19 *[P1, k1] twice, 4-st LC, p5, 4-st RC, [p1, k1] twice; rep from * to end.

Rows 20 and 38 *[K1, p1] twice, p4, k5, p4, [k1, p1] twice; rep from * to end.

Row 21 *P1, k1, p1, 3-st RPC, 3-st LPC, p3, 3-st RPC, 3-st LPC, k1, p1, k1; rep from * to end.

Row 22 *K1, p1, k1, p2, k2, p2, k3, p2, k2, p3, k1, p1; rep from * to end.

Row 23 *P1, k1, 3-st RPC, p2, 3-st LPC, p1, 3-st RPC, p2, 3-st LPC, p1, k1; rep from * to end.

Row 24 *K1, p3, k4, p2, k1, p2, k4, p2, k1, p1; rep from * to end.

Row 25 *P1, 3-st RPC, p4, 5-st RPC, p4, 3-st LPC, k1; rep from * to end.

Row 27 *3-st RPC, p5, k2, p1, k2, p5, 3-st LPC; rep from * to end.

Rows 28 and 30 *P2, k6, p2, k1, p2, k6, p2; rep from * to end.

Row 29 K2, *p6, k2, p1, k2, p6, 4-st RC; rep from *, end last rep k2.

Row 31 *3-st LPC, p5, k2, p1, k2, p5, 3-st RC; rep from *, end.

Row 33 *P1, 3-st LC, p4, 5-st RPC, p4, 3-st RPC, k1; rep from * to end.

Row 34 *K1, p3, k4, p2, k1, p2, k4, p2, k1, p1; rep from * to end.

Row 35 *P1, k1, 3-st LPC, p2, 3-st RPC, p1, 3-st LPC, p2, 3-st RC, p1, k1; rep from * to end.

Row 36 *K1, p1, k1, p2, k2, p2, k3, p2, k2, p3, k1, p1; rep from * to end.

Row 37 *P1, k1, p1, 3-st LC, 3-st RPC, p3, 3-st LPC, 3-st RPC, k1, p1, k1; rep from * to end.

Row 39 *[P1, k1] twice, 4-st RPC, p5, 4-st LPC, [p1, k1] twice; rep from * to end.

Row 41 *P1, k1, p1, 3-st RPC, p3, k1, p1, k1, p3, 3-st LPC, k1, p1, k1; rep from * to end.

Row 42 *K1, p1, k1, p2, k4, p1, k1, p1, k4, p3, k1, p1; rep from * to end.

Row 43 *P1, k1, 3-st RPC, p4, k1, p1, k1, p4, 3-st LPC, p1, k1; rep from * to end.

Row 45 *P1, 3-st RPC, p4, k2, p1, k2, p4, 3-st LPC, k1; rep from * to end.

Row 47 *3-st RPC, p5, 5-st RPC, p5, 3-st LPC; rep from * to end.

Row 48 *P2, k6, p2, k1, p2, k6, p2; rep from * to end.

Rep rows 1–48.

Stitch Key

☐ K on RS, p on WS	3-st RPC
─ P on RS, k on WS	3-st LPC
3-st RC	4-st R
3-st LC	4-st L

21-st rep

Preparation row (WS)

3-st RC Sl 1 st to cn and hold to back, k2, k1 from cn.

3-st LC Sl 2 sts to cn and hold to front, k1, k2 from cn.

3-st RPC Sl 1 st to cn and hold to back, k2, p1 from cn.

3-st LPC Sl 2 sts to cn and hold to front, p1, k2 from cn.

4-st RC Sl 2 sts to cn and hold to back, k2, k2 from cn.

4-st LC Sl 2 sts to cn and hold to front, k2, k2 from cn.

4-st RPC Sl 2 sts to cn and hold to back, k2, p2 from cn.

4-st LPC Sl 2 sts to cn and hold to front, p2, k2 from cn.

(multiple of 20 sts plus 6)

Row 1 (RS) K3, *4-st RC, k2, 4-st RPC, 4-st LPC, k2, 4-st LC; rep from *, end k3.

Rows 2 and 8 P3, *p8, k4, p8; rep from *, end p3.

Row 3 K1, *4-st RC, k3, 3-st RPC, p4, 3-st LPC, k3; rep from *, end 4-st RC, k1.

Rows 4 and 6 P5, *p5, k6, p9; rep from *, end p1.

Row 5 K1, *k9, p6, k5; rep from *, end k5.

Row 7 K1, *4-st RC, k3, 3-st LC, p4, 3-st RC, p3; rep from *, end 4-st RC, k1.

Row 9 K3, *4-st LC, k2, 4-st LC, 4-st RC, k2, 4-st RC; rep from *, end k3.

Rows 10, 12, 14, 24 and 26 Purl.

Row 11 K3, *k2, 4-st LC, k8, 4-st RC, k2; rep from *, end k3.

Row 13 K3, *k4, 4-st LC, k4, 4-st RC, k4; rep from *, end k3.

Row 15 K3, * 4-st-LPC, k2, 4-st LC, 4-st RC, k2, 4-st RPC; rep from *, end k3.

Rows 16 and 22 P3, *k2, p16, k2; rep from *, end p3.

Row 17 K3, *p2, 3-st LPC, k3, 4-st RC, k3, 3-st RPC, p2; rep from *, end k3.

Rows 18 and 20 P3, *k3, p14, k3; rep from *, end p3.

Row 19 K3, *p3, k14, p3; rep from *, end k3.

Row 21 K3, *p2, 3-st RC, k3, 4-st RC, k3, 3-st LC, p2; rep from *, end k3.

Row 23 K3, *4-st RC, k2, 4-st RC, 4-st LC, k2, 4-st LC; rep from *, end k3.

Row 25 K3, *k4, 4-st RC, k4, 4-st LC, k4; rep from *, end k3.

Row 27 K3, *k2, 4-st RC, k8, 4-st LC, k2; rep from *, end k3.

Row 28 Purl.

Rep rows 1–28.

Stitch Key

☐ K on RS, p on WS

— P on RS, k on WS

3-st RC

3-st LC

3-st RPC

3-st LPC

4-st RC

4-st LC

4-st RPC

4-st LPC

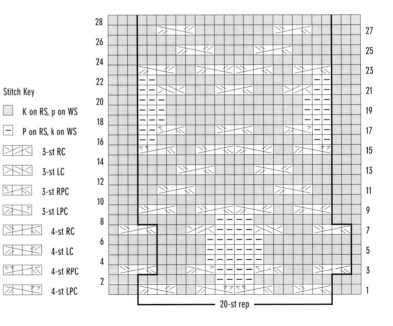

20-st rep

163

RT Sl 1 st to cn and hold to back, k1, k1 from cn.

LT Sl 1 st to cn and hold to front, k1, k1 from cn.

2-st RPT Sl 1 st to cn and hold to back, k1, p1 from cn.

2-st RPT (WS) Sl 1 st to cn and hold to back, k1, p st from cn.

2-st LPT Sl 1 st to cn and hold to front, p1, k1 from cn.

2-st LPT (WS) Sl 1 st to cn and hold to front, p1, k st from cn.

(multiple of 7 sts plus 2)

Row 1 (RS) P1, *p3, inc 1, p3; rep from *, end p1.

Row 2 K1, *k3, p2, k3; rep from *, end k1.

Row 3 P1, *p2, RT, LT, p2; rep from *, end p1.

Rows 4 and 10 K1, *k2, p4, k2; rep from *, end k1.

Row 5 P1, *p1, RT, p2, LT, p1; rep from *, end p1.

Rows 6 and 8 K1, *k1, p6, k1; rep from *, end k1.

Row 7 P1, *p1, k1 tbl, p4, k1 tbl, p1; rep from *, end p1.

Row 9 P1, *p1, 2-st LPT, p2, 2-st RPT, p1; rep from *, end p1.

Row 11 P1, *p2, 2-st LPT, 2-st RPT, p2; rep

from *, end p1.

Row 12 K1, *k3, p2, k3; rep from *, end k1.

Row 13 P1, *p3, LT, p3; rep from *, end p1.

Row 14 K1, *k2, 2-st LPT, 2-st RPT, k2; rep from *, end k1.

Row 15 P1, *p1, 2-st RPT, p2, 2-st LPT, p1; rep from *, end p1.

Rows 16 and 22 K1, *k1, p1, k4, p1, k1; rep from *, end k1.

Row 17 P1, *2-st RPT, p4, 2-st LPT; rep from *, end p1.

Rows 18 and 20 P1, *p1, k6, p1; rep from *, end p1.

Row 19 *RT, p6; rep from *, end RT.

Row 21 P1, *2-st LPT, p4, 2-st RPT; rep from *, end p1.

Row 23 P1, *p1, 2-st LPT, p2, 2-st RPT, p1;

rep from *, end p1.

Row 24 K1, *k2, 2-st RPT, 2-st LPT, k2; rep from *, end k1.

Row 25 Rep row 13.

Row 26 Rep row 2.

Row 27 Rep row 3.

Row 28 Rep row 4.

Row 29 Rep row 5.

Row 30 Rep row 6.

Row 31 Rep row 7.

Row 32 Rep row 8.

Row 33 Rep row 9.

Row 34 Rep row 4.

Row 35 Rep row 11.

Row 36 K1, *k3, p2tog, k3; rep from *, end k1.

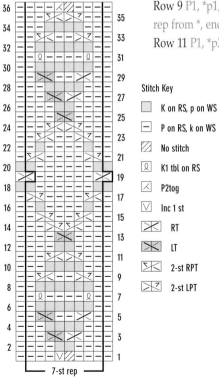

Stitch Key

☐ K on RS, p on WS

– P on RS, k on WS

▨ No stitch

Ω K1 tbl on RS

◺ P2tog

∨ Inc 1 st

⧓ RT

⧓ LT

⧓ 2-st RPT

⧓ 2-st LPT

SK2P (WS) Sl 1, k2 tog, pass sl st over k2tog.

2-st RC (WS) Sl 1 st to cn and hold to back, p1, p1 from cn.

2-st LC (WS) Sl 1 st to cn and hold to front, p1, p1 from cn.

2-st RPC Sl 1 st to cn and hold to back, k1, p1 from cn.

2-st LPC Sl 1 st to cn and hold to front, p1, k1 from cn.

3-st RPC Sl 1 st to cn and hold to back, k2, p1 from cn.

3-st LPC Sl 2 sts to cn and hold to front, p1, k2 from cn.

4-st RC Sl 2 sts to cn and hold to back, k2, k2 from cn.

4-st LC Sl 2 sts to cn and hold to front, k2, k2 from cn.

4-st RPC Sl 2 sts to cn and hold to back, k2, p2 from cn.

4-st LPC Sl 2 sts to cn and hold to front, p2, k2 from cn.

MB K in front, back and front of st, turn, p3, turn, s1 1-k2tog-psso.

(multiple of 15 sts)

Row 1 (RS) P2, k2, p3, *[p4, k2] twice, p3; rep from *, end p4, k2, p2.

Row 2 K2, p2, k4, *k3, [p2, k4] twice; rep from *, end k3, p2, k2.

Row 3 P2, 3-st LPC, p2, *MB, p2, 3-st RPC, p4, 3-st LPC, p2; rep from *, end MB, p2, 3-st RPC, p2.

Row 4 P2, k1, p2, k3, *k2, p2, k1, p4, k1, p2, k3; rep from *, end k2, p2, k1, p2.

Row 5 [3-st LPC] twice, p1, *p2, [3-st RPC] twice, [3-st LPC] twice, p1; rep from *, end p2, [3-st RPC] twice.

Row 6 [K1, p2] twice, k2, *[k1, p2] twice, k2, p2, k1, p2, k2; rep from *, end [k1, p2] twice, k1.

Row 7 P1, [3-st LPC] twice, *p1, [3-st RPC] twice, p2, [3-st LPC] twice; rep from *, end p1, [3-st RPC] twice, p1.

Row 8 K1, M1, k1, p2, k1, p1, SK2P, *p1, k1, p2, k1, M1, k2, M1, k1, p2, k1, p1, SK2P; rep from *, end p1, k1, p2, k1, M1, k1.

Row 9 P3, 3-st LPC, k1, *k2, 3-st RPC, p6, 3-st LPC, k1; rep from *, end k2, 3-st RPC, p3.

Row 10 K3, M1, k1, p2tog, p2, *p1, p2tog, k1, M1, k6, M1, k1, p2tog, p2; rep from *, end p1, p2tog, k1, M1, k3.

Rows 11 and 13 P5, k2, *k3, p10, k2; rep from *, end k3, p5.

Rows 12 and 14 K5, p3, *p2, k10, p3; rep from *, end p2, k5.

Rows 15 and 19 P5, k2, *k3, p1, [2-st LPC, 2-st RPC] twice, p1, k2; rep from *, end k3, p5.

Rows 16 and 20 K5, p3, *p2, k2, LC, k2, RC, k2, p3; rep from *, end p2, k5.

Rows 17 and 21 P5, k2, *k3, p1, [2-st RPC, 2-st LPC] twice, p1, k2; rep from *, end k3, p5.

Row 18 K5, p3, *p2, k1, p1, k2, LC, k2, p1, k1, p3; rep from *, end p2, k5.

Row 22 K5, p3, *p2, k1, p1, k2, p2, k2, p1, k1, p3; rep from *, end p2, k5.

Row 23 P5, k2, *k3, p1, k1, p6, k1, p1, k2; rep from *, end k3, p5.

Rows 24 and 26 K5, p3, *p2, k10, p3; rep from *, end p2, k5.

Row 25 P5, k2, *k3, p3, MB, p2, MB, p3, k2; rep from *, end k3, p5.

Row 27 Rep row 11.

Row 28 Rep row 12.

Row 29 P3, 4-st RC, *k1, 4-st LC, p6, 4-st RC; rep from *, end k1, 4-st LC, p3.

Row 30 K3, p5, *p4, k6, p5; rep from *, end p4, k3.

Row 31 P1, 4-st RPC, k2, *k3, 4-st LPC, p2, 4-st RPC, k2; rep from *, end k3, 4-st LPC, p1.

Row 32 K1, p2, k2, p3, *[p2, k2] 3 times, p3; rep from *, end p2, k2, p2, k1.

Row 33 3-st RPC, 4-st RC, *k1, 4-st LC, 3-st LPC, 3-st RPC, 4-st RC; rep from *, end k1, 4-st LC, 3-st LPC.

Row 34 P2, k1, p5, *[p4, k1] twice, p5; rep from *, end p4, k1, p2.

Row 35 K2, 3-st RPC, k2, *k3, 3-st LPC, 4-st LC, 3-st RPC, k2; rep from *, end k3, 3-st LPC, k2.

Rows 36 and 38 P4, k1, p3, *p2, k1, p8, k1, p3; rep from *, end p2, k1, p4.

Row 37 4-st RC, p1, k2, *k3, p1 [4-st RC] twice, p1, k2; rep from *, end k3, p1, 4-st RC.

Row 39 K2, 4-st LC, k1, *2-st LPC, 4-st RC, [4-st LC]twice, k1; rep from *, end 2-st LPC, 4-st RC, k2.

Row 40 P4, k1, p2, k1, *p2, k1, p8, k1, p2, k1; rep from *, end p2, k1, p4.

Row 41 4-st LPC, p1, 2-st RPC, *p1, 2-st LPC, p1, 4-st RPC, 4-st LPC, p1, 2-st RPC; rep from *, end p1, 2-st LPC, p1, 4-st RPC.

Row 42 K2, p2, k1, p1, k2, *k1, p1, k1, p2, k4, p2, k1, p1, k2; rep from *, end k1, p1, k1, p2, k2.

Row 43 P2, k2, 2-st RPC, p1, *p2, 2-st LPC, k2, p4, k2, 2-st RPC, p1; rep from *, end p2, 2-st LPC, k2, p2.

Row 44 K2, p3, k3, *k2, p3, k4, p3, k3; rep from *, end k2, p3, k2.

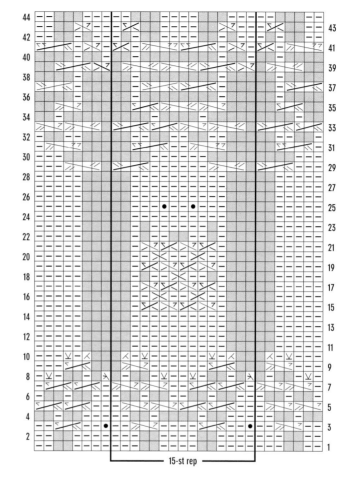

15-st rep

Stitch Key

▢	K on RS, p on WS	●	MB	◹◸	3-st RPC
−	P on RS, k on WS	✕	2-st RC	◿◺	3-st LPC
⋁	M1 on WS	✕	2-st LC	◹◸	4-st RC
⋋	P2tog on WS	✕	2-st RPC	◿◺	4-st LC
⋌	SK2P on WS	✕	2-st LPC	◹◸	4-st RPC
				◿◺	4-st LPC

143

4-st RC Sl 2 sts to cn and hold to back, k2, k2 from cn.

4-st LC Sl 2 sts to cn and hold to front, k2, k2 from cn.

4-st RPC Sl 2 sts to cn and hold to back, k2, p2 from cn.

4-st LPC Sl 2 sts to cn and hold to front, p2, k2 from cn.

(multiple of 16 sts plus 32)

Preparation row (WS) *[K4, p2] twice, k4; rep from * to end.

Row 1 (RS) *P4, 4-st LC, 4-st RC, p4; rep from * to end.

Row 2 *K4, p10, k2; rep from * to end.

Row 3 *P2, [4-st RC] twice, 4-st LC, p2; rep from * to end.

Rows 4 and 6 *K2, p12, k2; rep from * to end.

Row 5 *P2, k2, [4-st LC] twice, k2, p2; rep from * to end.

Row 7 *P2, 4-st LPC, 4-st RC, 4-st RPC, p2; rep from * to end.

Row 8 *K4, p8, k4; rep from * to end.

Row 9 *P4, 4-st RPC, 4-st LPC, p4; rep from * to end.

Row 10 *[K4, p2] twice, k4; rep from * to end.

Row 11 *P2, 4-st RPC, p4, 4-st LPC, p2; rep from *, end.

Row 12 *K2, p2, k8, p2, k2; rep from * to end.

Row 13 P12, 4-st LC, *4-st RC, p8, 4-st LC; rep from *, end 4-st RC, p12.

Row 14 K12, p4, *p4, k8, p4; rep from *, end p4, k12.

Row 15 P10, 4-st RC, *[4-st LC] twice, p4, 4-st RC; rep from *, end [4-st LC] twice, p10.

Row 16 K10, p8, *p4, k4, p8; rep from *, end p4, k10.

Row 17 P10, k2, 4-st RC, *4-st RC, k2, p4, k2, 4-st RC; rep from *, end 4-st RC, k2, p10.

Row 18 K10, p6, *p6, k4, p6; rep from *, end p6, k10.

Row 19 P10, 4-st LPC, *4-st LC, 4-st RPC, p4, 4-st LPC; rep from *, end 4-st LC, 4-st RPC, p10.

Row 20 K12, p6, *p2, k8, p6; rep from *, end p2, k12.

Row 21 P2, k2, p8, 4-st RPC, *4-st LPC, p8, 4-st RPC; rep from *, end 4-st LPC, p8, k2, p2.

Row 22 *K2, p2, k8, p2, k2; rep from * to end.

Row 23 *P2, 4-st LPC, p4, 4-st RPC, p2; rep from * to end.

Row 24 *[K4, p2] twice, k4; rep from * to end.

Rep rows 1–24.

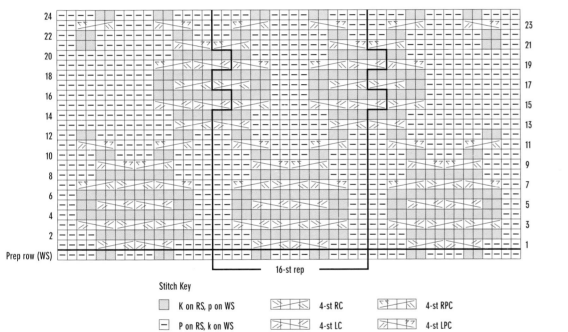

24
22
20
18
16
14
12
10
8
6
4
2

Prep row (WS)

23
21
19
17
15
13
11
9
7
5
3
1

16-st rep

Stitch Key

	K on RS, p on WS		4-st RC		4-st RPC
−	P on RS, k on WS		4-st LC		4-st LPC

167 open trellis

5-st RPC Sl 1 st to cn and hold to back, k4, p1 from cn.
5-st LPC Sl 4 sts to cn and hold to front, p1, k4 from cn.
8-st RC Sl 4 sts to cn and hold to back, k4, k4 from cn.
8-st LC Sl 4 sts to cn and hold to front, k4, k4 from cn.
10-st LC Sl 5 sts to cn and hold to front, k5, k5 from cn.
(multiple of 32 sts)
Rows 1 and 35 (WS) *K1, p4, k7,p8, k7, p4, k1; rep from * to end.
Row 2 *P1, 5-st LPC, p6, 8-st RC, p6, 5-st RPC, p1; rep from * to end.
Rows 3 and 33 *K2, p4, k6, p8, k6, p4, k2; rep from * to end.
Rows 4 and 20 *P2, 5-st LPC, p4, 5-st RPC, 5-st LPC, p4, 5-st RPC, p2; rep from * to end.

Rows 5, 15, 21 and 31 *K3, p4, k4, p4, k2, p4, k4, p4, k3; rep from * to end.
Rows 6 and 22 *P3, 5-st LPC, p2, 5-st RPC, p2, 5-st LPC, p2, 5-st RPC, p3; rep from * to end.
Rows 7, 13, 23 and 29 *[K4, p4, k2, p4] twice, k4; rep from * to end.
Rows 8 and 24 *[P4, 5-st LPC, 5-st RPC] twice, p4; rep from * to end.
Rows 9, 11, 25 and 27 *K5, p8, k6, p8, k5; rep from * to end.
Rows 10 and 26 *P5, 8-st RC, p6, 8-st RC, p5; rep from * to end.
Row 12 *P4, 5-st RPC, 5-st LPC, p4, 5-st RPC, 5-st LPC, p4; rep from * to end.
Rows 14 and 30 *P3, 5-st RPC, p2, 5-st LPC, p2, 5-st RPC, p2, 5-st LPC, p3; rep from * to end.
Rows 16 and 32 *P2, 5-st RPC, p4, 5-st LPC, 5-st RPC, p4, 5-st LPC, p2; rep from * to end.
Rows 17 and 19 *K2, p4, k6, p8, k6, p4, k2; rep from * to end.
Row 18 *P2, k4, p6, 8-st LC, p6, k4, p2; rep from * to end.
Row 28 *[P4, 5-st RPC, 5-st LPC] twice, p4; rep from * to end.
Row 34 *P1, 5-st RPC, p6, 8-st RC, p6, 5-st LPC, p1; rep from * to end.
Row 36 5-st RPC, *p7, k8, p7, 10-st LC; rep from *; end last rep 5-st LPC.
Row 37 *P4, k8, p8, k8, p4; rep from * to end.
Row 38 *5-st LPC, p7, k8, p7, 5-st RPC; rep from * to end.
Rep rows 1–38.

167

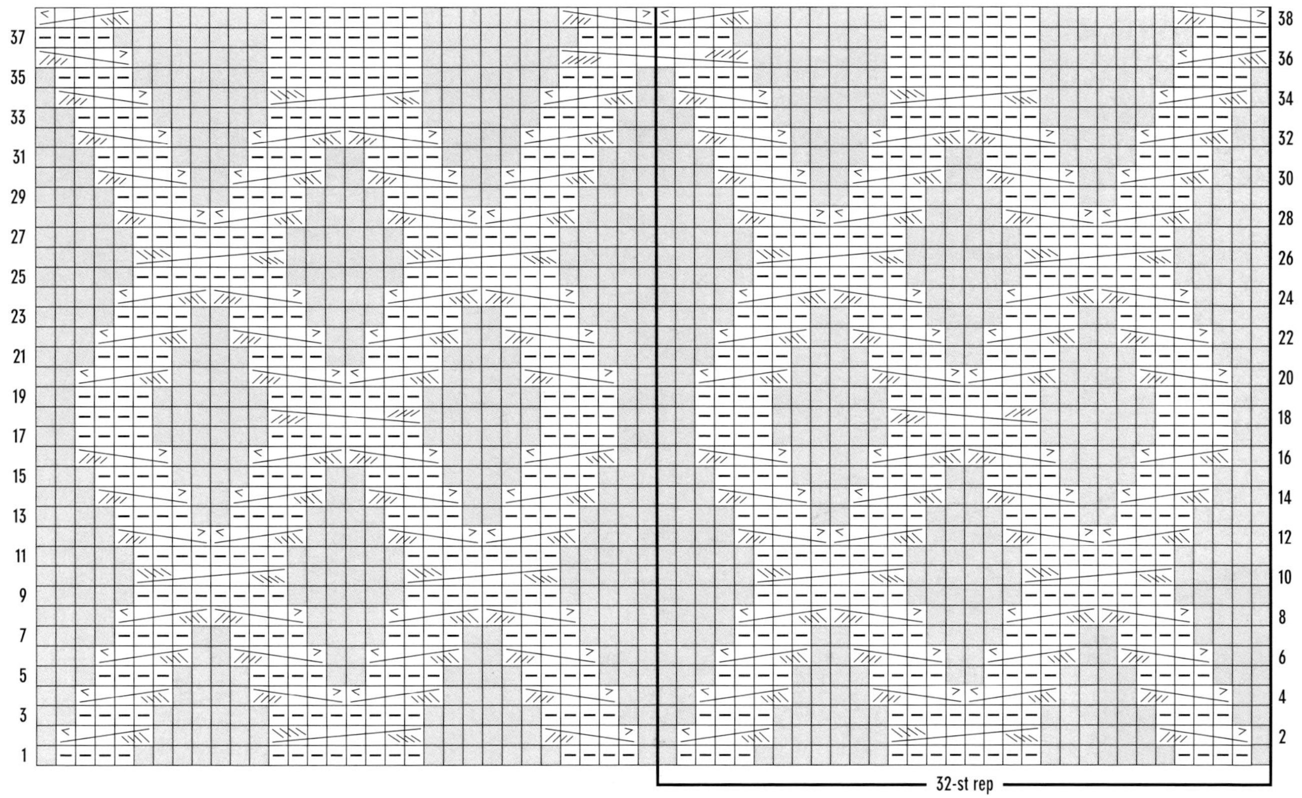

Stitch Key

— K on RS, p on WS	8-st RC
▨ P on RS, k on WS	8-st LC
◁ 5-st RPC	10-st LC
▷ 5-st LPC	

32-st rep

3-st RC Sl 1 st to cn and hold to back, k2, k1 from cn.

3-st LC Sl 2 sts to cn and hold to front, k1, k2 from cn.

4-st RC Sl 2 sts to cn and hold to back, k2, k2 from cn.

4-st LC Sl 2 sts to cn and hold to front, k2, k2 from cn.

4-st LPC Sl 2 sts to cn and hold to front, k1, p1; k2 from cn.

4-st RPC Sl 2 sts to cn and hold to back, k2; p1, k1 from cn.

(multiple of 10 sts plus 11)

Row 1 (RS) *P1, k1; rep from *, end p1.

Row 2 *K1, p1; rep from *, end k1.

Row 3 P1, k5, *p1, SKP, yo, k1, p1, k5; rep from *, end p1, SKP, yo, k1, p1.

Row 4 K1, [p1, k1] twice, * p5, [k1, p1] twice, k1; rep from *, end p5, k1.

Rows 5, 13 and 21 P1, 4-st RC, k1, *p1, SKP, yo, k1, p1, 4-st RC, k1; rep from *, end p1, SKP, yo, k1, p1.

Rows 6, 8, 10, 12, 14, 16, 18, 20 and 22 K1, [p1, k1] twice, * p5, [k1, p1] twice, k1; rep from *, end p5, k1.

Rows 7, 9, 11, 15, 17 and 19 P1, k5, *p1, SKP, yo, k1, p1, k5; rep from *, end p1, SKP, yo, k1, p1.

Row 23 P1, k2, 4-st LPC, *SKP, yo, k1, p1, k2, 4-st LPC; rep from *, end SKP, yo, k1, p1.

Row 24 K1, p1, k1, p2, *[p1, k1] 4 times, p2; rep from *, end [p1, k1] 3 times.

Row 25 P1, SKP, yo, k1, p1, 3-st LC, *k2, p1, SKP, yo, k1, p1, 3-st LC; rep from *, end k2, p1.

Rows 26, 28, 30, 32, 34, 36, 38, 40, 42 and 44 K1, p4, *[p1, k1] 3 times, p4; rep from *, end [p1, k1] 3 times.

Rows 27, 35 and 43 P1, SKP, yo, k1, p1, k1, *4-st LC, p1, SKP, yo, k1, p1, k1; rep from *, end 4-st LC, p1.

Rows 29, 31, 33, 37, 39 and 41 P1, SKP, yo, k1, p1, k1, *k4, p1, SKP, yo, k1, p1, k1; rep from *, end k4, p1.

Row 45 [P1, k1] twice, 4-st RPC, *k2, p1, SKP, yo, k1, 4-st RPC; rep from *, end k2, p1.

Row 46 K1, [p1, k1] twice, *p3, [k1, p1] 2 times, k1, p2; rep from *, end p3, k1, p1, k1.

Row 47 P1, k1, p1, 3-st RC, *p1, SKP, yo, [k1, p1] twice, 3-st RC; rep from *, end p1, SKP, yo, k1, p1.

Row 48 K1, [p1, k1] twice, *p5, [k1, p1] twice, k1; rep from *, end p5, k1.

Rep rows 5–48.

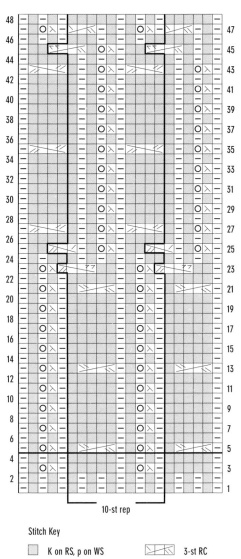

Stitch Key

▢ K on RS, p on WS	◰ 3-st RC
▬ P on RS, k on WS	◰ 3-st LC
ⵔ Yo	◰ 4-st RC
ⵥ SKP	◰ 4-st LC
	◰ 4-st RPC
	◰ 4-st LPC

6-st RC Sl 3 sts to cn and hold to back, k3, k3 from cn.

(multiple of 16 sts plus 8)

Rows 1, 5 and 7 (RS) [K1, p1] 4 times, *p1, k6, p1, [p1, k1] 4 times; rep from * to end.

Rows 2, 4 and 6 *[K1, p1] 4 times, k1, p6, k1; rep from *, end [p1, k1] 4 times.

Row 3 [K1, p1] 4 times, *p1, 6-st RC, p1, [p1, k1] 4 times; rep from * to end.

Row 8 Rep row 2.

Rep rows 1–8.

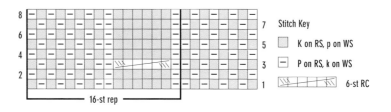

Stitch Key

▢	K on RS, p on WS
—	P on RS, k on WS
⟍⟍⟍	6-st RC

16-st rep

4-st RC Sl 2 sts to cn and hold to back, k2, k2 from cn.

4-st LC Sl 2 sts to cn and hold to front, k2, k2 from cn.

4-st RPC Sl 2 sts to cn and hold to back, k2, p2 from cn.

4-st LPC Sl 2 sts to cn and hold to front, p2, k2 from cn.

Double Inc K in back of st in row below, then in back of st on LH needle, with LH needle pick up left side strand of same st in row below and k1 tbl in this strand to make 3rd st.

SK2P Sl 1, k2 tog, pass sl st over k2 tog.

4-st dec SSK, k3tog, pass SSK over k3tog.

(multiple of 30 sts plus 8)

Row 1 (WS) K2, p2, *k6, p5, k6, p2, [k1 tbl, k1] twice, p1, [k1, k1 tbl] twice, p2; rep from *, end k4.

Row 2 P4, *k2, p4, double inc, p4, k2, p6, ssk, k1, k2tog, p6; rep from *, end k2, p2.

Row 3 K2, p2, *k6, p3, k6, p2, k4, p3, k4, p2; rep from *, end k4.

Row 4 P2, p2tog, k1, *k1, yo, p4, k1, double inc, k1, p4, yo, k2, p2tog, p4, SK2P, p4, p2tog, k1; rep from *, end k1, yo, p2.

Row 5 K2, k1 tbl, p1, *p1, k11, p2, k1 tbl, k4, p5, k4, k1 tbl, p1; rep from *, end p2, k2.

Row 6 P1, p2tog, k2, *yo, p5, k2, double inc, k2, p5, yo, k2, p2tog, p7, p2tog, k2; rep from *, end yo, p3.

Row 7 K3, k1 tbl, *p2, k9, p2, k1 tbl, k5, p7, k5, k1 tbl; rep from *, end p2, k2.

Row 8 P2, k2, *p6, k3, double inc, k3, p6, 4-st LC, p5, 4-st RC; rep from *, end p4.

Row 9 K4, *p4, k5, p4, k6, p9, k6; rep from *, end p2, k2.

Row 10 P2, k2, *p6, ssk, k5, k2tog, p6, k2, 4-st LPC, p1, 4-st RPC, k2; rep from *, end p4.

Row 11 K4, *p2, k2, p2, k1, p2, k2, p2, k6, p7, k6; rep from *, end p2, k2.

Row 12 P2, k2, *p6, ssk, k3, k2tog, p6, k2, [yo, p1] twice, 4-st dec, [p1, yo] twice, k2; rep from *, end p4.

Row 13 K4, *p2, [k1 tbl, k1] twice, p1, [k1, k1 tbl] twice, p2, k6, p5, k6; rep from *, end p2, k2.

Row 14 P2, k2, *p6, ssk, k1, k2tog, p6, k2, p4, double inc, p4, k2; rep from *, end p4.

Row 15 K4, *p2, k4, p3, k4, p2, k6, p3, k6; rep from *, end p2, k2.

Row 16 P2, yo, k1, *k1, p2tog, p4, SK2P, p4, p2tog, k2, yo, p4, k1, double inc, k1, p4, yo, k1; rep from *, end k1, p2tog, p2.

Row 17 K3, p1, *p1, k1tbl, k4, p5, k4, k1 tbl, p2, k11, p1; rep from *, end p1, k1 tbl, k2.

Row 18 P3, yo, *k2, p2tog, p7, p2tog, k2, yo, p5, k2, double inc, k2, p5, yo; rep from *, end k2, p2tog, p1.

Row 19 K2, p2, *k1tbl, k5, p7, k5, k1 tbl, p2, k9, p2; rep from *, end k1 tbl, k3.

Row 20 P4, *4-st LC, p5, 4-st RC, p6, k3, double inc, k3, p6; rep from *, end k2, p2.

Row 21 K2, p2, *k6, p9, k6, p4, k5, p4; rep from *, end k4.

Row 22 P4, *k2, 4-st LPC, p1, 4-st RPC, k2, p6, ssk, k5, k2tog, p6; rep from *, end k2, p2.

Row 23 K2, p2, *k6, p7, k6, p2, k2, p2, k1, p2, k2, p2; rep from *, end k4.

Row 24 P4, *k2, [yo, p1] twice, 4-st dec, [p1, yo] twice, k2, p6, ssk, k3, k2tog, p6; rep from *, end k2, p2.

Rep rows 1–24.

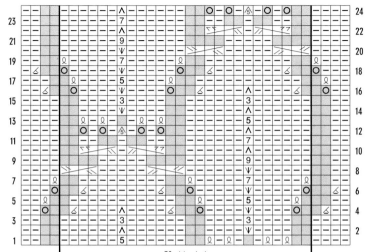

30-st to start

Stitch Key

▨ K on RS, p on WS	⬓⬓ 4-st RC
⊟ P on RS, k on WS	⬓⬓ 4-st LC
⑤ 5 sts all show in one square	⬓⬓ 4-st RPC
③ 3 sts all show in one square	⬓⬓ 4-st LPC
⑦ 7 sts all show in one square	Ⅴ Double inc in center st
⑨ 9 sts all show in one square	⑤ 4-st decrease
○ Yo	∧ Dec leaf sts
⬓ P2tog	
Ω K1 tb1	

171 sailors knot

5-st RPC Sl 2 sts to cn and hold to back, k3, p2 from cn.

5-st LPC Sl 2 sts to cn and hold to front, p2, k3 from cn.

6-st RC Sl 3 sts to cn and hold to back, k3, p2 from cn.

6-st LC Sl 3 sts to cn and hold to front, p2, k3 from cn.

8-st RPC Sl 5 sts to cn and hold to back, k3; k3, p2 from cn.

8-st LPC Sl 3 sts to cn and hold to front, p2, k3; k3 from cn.

(multiple of 28 sts plus 8)

Row 1 (RS) P4, *8-st RPC, p12, 8-st LPC; rep from *, end p4.

Row 2 K1, p3, *p6, k16, p6; rep from *, end p3, k1.

Row 3 P1, *6-st RC, 5-st LPC, p12, 5-st RPC; rep from *, end 6-st RC, p1.

Row 4 K1, p3, *p3, k2, p3, k12, p3, k2, p3; rep from *, end p3, k1.

Row 5 P1, k3, *k3, p2, 5-st LPC, p8, 5-st RPC, p2, k3; rep from *, end k3, p1.

Row 6 K1, p3, *p3, k4, p3, k8, p3, k4, p3; rep from *, end p3, k1.

Row 7 P1, k3, *k3, p4, 5-st LPC, p4, 5-st RPC, p4, k3; rep from *, end k3, p1.

Row 8 K1, p3, *p3, k6, p3, k4, p3, k6, p3; rep from *, end p3, k1.

Row 9 P1, *6-st RC, p6, 5-st LPC, 5-st RPC, p6; rep from *, end 6-st RC, p1.

Row 10 K1, p3, *p3, k8, p6, k8, p3; rep from *, end p3, k1.

Row 11 P4, *5-st LPC, p6, 6-st LC, p6, 5-st RPC; rep from *, end p4.

Row 12 K4, *k2, p3, k6, p6, k6, p3, k2; rep from *, end k4.

Row 13 P4, *p2, 5-st LPC, p4, k6, p4, 5-st RPC, p2; rep from *, end p4.

Row 14 K4, *k4, p3, k4, p6, k4, p3, k4; rep from *, end k4.

Row 15 P4, *p4, 5-st LPC, p2, k6, p2, 5-st RPC, p4; rep from *, end p4.

Row 16 K4, *k6, p3, k2, p6, k2, p3, k6; rep from *, end k4.

Row 17 P4, *p6, 5-st LPC, 6-st LC, 5-st RPC, p6; rep from *, end p4.

Row 18 K4, *k8, p12, k8; rep from *, end k4.

Row 19 P4, *p6, 8-st RPC, 8-st LPC, p6; rep from *, end p4.

Rows 20, 22 and 24 K4, *k6, p6, k4, p6, k6; rep from *, end k4.

Rows 21 and 23 P4, *p6, k6, p4, k6, p6; rep from *, end p4.

Row 25 P4, *p4, 8-st RPC, p4, 8-st LPC, p4; rep from *, end p4.

Rows 26, 28 and 30 K4, *k4, p6, k8, p6, k4; rep from *, end k4.

Rows 27 and 29 P4, *p4, k6, p8, k6, p4; rep from *, end p4.

Row 31 P4, *p2, 8-st RPC, p8, 8-st LPC, p2; rep from *, end p4.

Rows 32 and 34 K4, *k2, p6, k12, p6, k2; rep from *, end k4.

Rows 33 and 35 P4, *p2, k6, p12, k6, p2; rep from *, end p4.

Row 36 Rep row 32.

Rep rows 1–36.

171

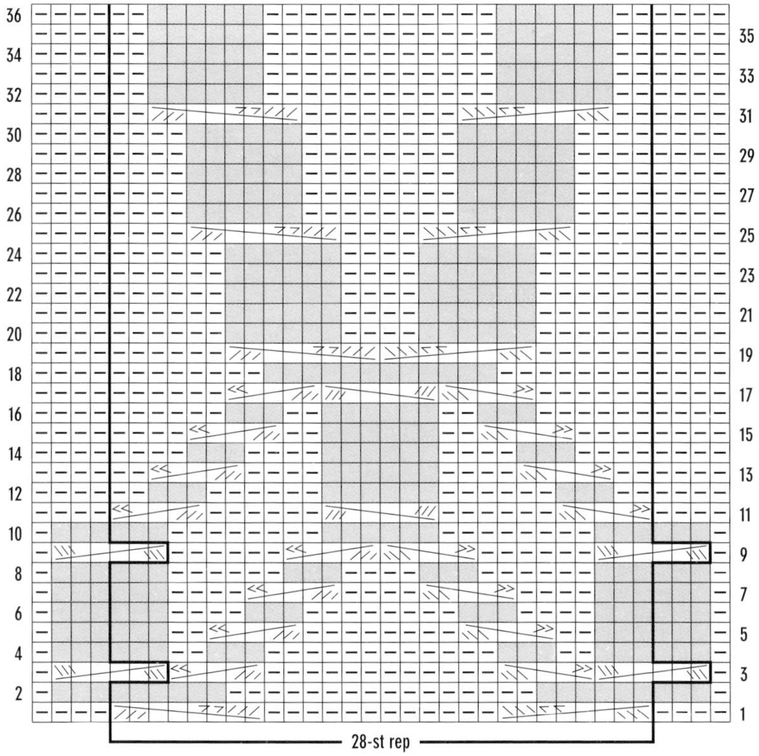

Stitch Key

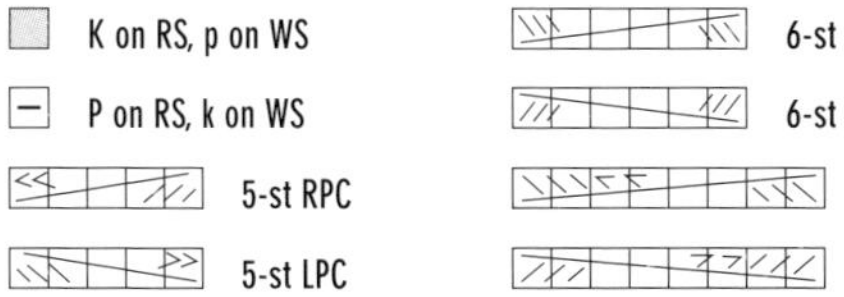

▢ K on RS, p on WS

— P on RS, k on WS

⬔ 5-st RPC

⬔ 5-st LPC

⬔ 6-st RC

⬔ 6-st LC

⬔ 8-st RPC

⬔ 8-st LPC

28-st rep

RT Pass in front of first st, k next st, then k first st.

5-st RTC Sl 3 sts to cn and hold to back, work RT over next 2 sts, p3 from cn.

(multiple of 24 sts plus 3)

Rows 1, 3 and 5 (RS) *P3, k3, RT; rep from *, end p3.

Rows 2, 4 and 6 K3, *p5, k3; rep from * to end.

Row 7 *P3, 5-st RTC; rep from *, end p3.

Rows 8, 10, 12 and 14 P3, *k3, p5; rep from * to end.

Rows 9, 11 and 13 *K3, RT, p3; rep from *, end k3.

Row 15 *5-st RTC, p3; rep from *, end k3.

Rows 16, 18, 20 and 22 K1, *p5, k3; rep from *, end p2.

Rows 17, 19 and 21 RT, *p3, k3, RT; rep from *, end p1.

Row 23 P2, *p3, 5-st RTC; rep from *, end p1.

Rows 24, 26, 28 and 30 P1, *k3, p5; rep from *, end k2.

Rows 25, 27 and 29 P2, *k3, RT, p3; rep from *, end k1.

Row 31 P2, *5-st RTC, p3; rep from *, end k1.

Rows 32, 34, 36 and 38 P1, *p3, k3, p2; rep from *, end p2.

Rows 33, 35 and 37 K2, *RT, p3, k3; rep from *, end k1.

Row 39 K4, p3, *5-st RTC, p3; rep from *, end k4.

Rows 40, 42, 44 and 46 K2, *p5, k3; rep from *, end k1.

Rows 41, 43 and 45 P1, *p3, k3, RT; rep from *, end p2.

Row 47 P1, *p3, 5-st RTC; rep from *, end p2.

Rows 48, 50, 52 and 54 P2, *k3, p5; rep from *, end p1.

Rows 49, 51 and 53 K1, *k3, RT, p3; rep from *, end k2.

Row 55 K1, *5-st RTC, p3; rep from *, end k2.

Rows 56, 58, 60 and 62 *P5, k3; rep from *, end p3.

Rows 57, 59, and 61 K1, RT, *p3, k3, RT; rep from * to end.

Row 63 P3, *p3, 5-st RTC; rep from * to end.

Row 64 *K3, p5; rep from *, end k3.

Rep rows 1–64.

172

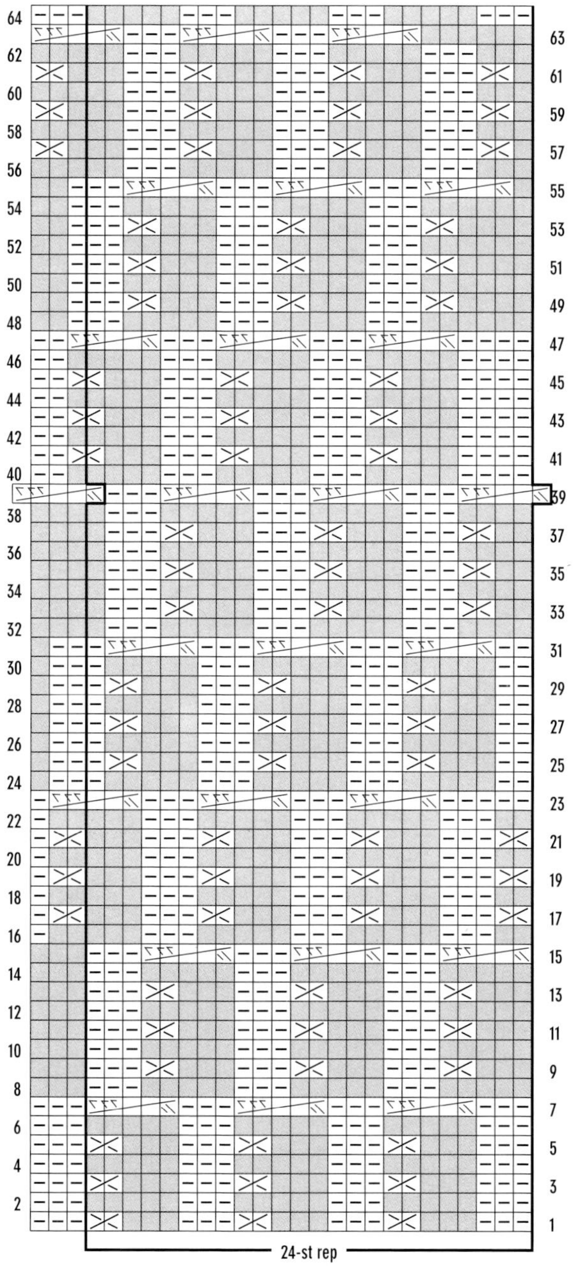

Row numbers (left side): 64, 62, 60, 58, 56, 54, 52, 50, 48, 46, 44, 42, 40, 38, 36, 34, 32, 30, 28, 26, 24, 22, 20, 18, 16, 14, 12, 10, 8, 6, 4, 2

Row numbers (right side): 63, 61, 59, 57, 55, 53, 51, 49, 47, 45, 43, 41, 39, 37, 35, 33, 31, 29, 27, 25, 23, 21, 19, 17, 15, 13, 11, 9, 7, 5, 3, 1

24-st rep

Stitch Key

K on RS, p on WS

P on RS, k on WS

RT

5-st RTC

7-st RC Sl 4 sts to cn and hold to back, k3, k4 from cn.

MB [K1, p1, k1, p1, k1] in next st, pass 4th, 3rd, 2nd and first sts separately over last st made.

(multiple of 30 sts plus 8)

Rows 1 and 3 (WS) K3, *k5, p7, k8, p7, k3; rep from *, end k5.

Row 2 P5, *MB, p2, 7-st RC, p2, MB, p5, 7-st RC, p5; rep from *, end p3.

Row 4 P5, *p3, k7, p6, k3tog, yo, k1, yo, k2tog, [yo, k1] twice, yo, k3tog tbl, p3; rep from *, end p3.

Rows 5 and 15 K3, *k3, p11, k6, p7, k3; rep from *, end k5.

Row 6 P5, *p3, k7, p5, [k2tog, yo] 3 times, k1 tbl, [yo, k2tog tbl] 3 times, p2; rep from *, end p3.

Rows 7 and 13 K3, *k2, p13, k5, p7, k3; rep from *, end k5.

Row 8 P5, *p3, k7, p3, k3tog, [yo, k2tog] twice, yo, k1 tbl, yo, k1, yo, k1 tbl, [yo, k2tog tbl] twice, yo, k3tog tbl; rep from *, end p3.

Row 9 K3, *p17, k3, p7, k3; rep from *, end k5.

Row 10 P5, *p3, 7-st RC, p1, MB, p2, [k2tog, yo] 3 times, k1 tbl, k1, k1 tbl, [yo, k2tog tbl] 3 times, p1; rep from *, end p1, MB, p1.

Row 11 K3, *k1, p15, k4, p7, k3; rep from *, end k5.

Row 12 P5, *p3, k7, p2, MB, p2, [k2tog, yo] twice, k1 tbl, k3, k1 tbl, [yo, k2tog tbl] twice, p2; rep from *, end MB, p2.

Row 14 P5, *p3, k7, p3, MB, p2, k2tog, yo, k1 tbl, k5, k1 tbl, yo, k2tog tbl, p2, MB; rep from *, end p3.

Row 16 P5, *p3, k7, p4, MB, p3, k7, p3, MB, p1; rep from *, end p3.

Rows 17 and 19 K5, *k3, p7, k8, p7, k5; rep from *, end k3.

Row 18 P3, *p5, 7-st RC, p5, MB, p2, 7-st RC, p2, MB; rep from *, end p5.

Row 20 P3, *p3, k3tog, yo, k1, yo, k2tog, yo, [k1, yo] twice, k3tog tbl, p6, k7, p3; rep from *, end p5.

Rows 21 and 31 K5, *k3, p7, k6, p11, k3; rep from *, end k3.

Row 22 P3, *p2, [k2tog, yo] 3 times, k1 tbl, [yo, k2tog tbl] 3 times, p5, k7, p3; rep from *, end p5.

Rows 23 and 29 K5, *k3, p7, k5, p13, k2; rep from *, end k3.

Row 24 P3, *k3tog, [yo, k2tog] twice, yo, k1 tbl, yo, k1, yo, k1 tbl, [yo, k2tog tbl] twice, yo, k3tog tbl, p3, k7, p3; rep from *, end p5.

Row 25 K5, *k3, p7, k3, p17; rep from *, end k3.

Row 26 P1, MB, p1, *p1, [k2tog, yo] 3 times, k1 tbl, k1, k1 tbl, [yo, k2tog tbl] 3 times, p2, MB, p1, 7-st RC, p3; rep from *, end p5.

Row 27 K5, *k3, p7, k4, p15, k1; rep from *, end k3.

Row 28 P2, MB, *p2, [k2tog, yo] twice, k1 tbl, k3, k1 tbl, [yo, k2tog tbl] twice, p2, MB, p2, k7, p3; rep from *, end p5.

Row 30 P3, *MB, p2, k2tog, yo, k1 tbl, k5, k1 tbl, yo, k2tog tbl, p2, MB, p3, k7, p3; rep from *, end p5.

Row 32 P3, *p1, MB, p3, k7, p3, MB, p4, k7, p3; rep from *, end p5.

Rep rows 1–32.

Stitch Key

−	P on RS, k on WS	◌	Yo
▯	K on RS, p on WS	╱	K2tog
7-st RC		╲	K2tog tbl
B	MB	╱₃	K3 tog
Ω	K1 tbl	╲₃	K3 tog tbl

2-st RPC Sl 1 st to cn and hold to back, k1, p1 from cn.

2-st LPC Sl 1 st to cn and hold to front, p1, k1 from cn.

3-st RPC Sl 2 sts to cn and hold to back, k1, p2 from cn.

3-st LPC Sl 1 st to cn and hold to front, p2, k1 from cn.

RT Skip first st, with RH needle in front, k the 2nd st, then k the skipped st.

LT Skip first st, with RH needle in back, k the 2nd st tbl, then k the skipped st.

(multiple of 32 sts plus 1)

Row 1 (RS) *[K1, p4] 3 times, k3, p4, [k1, p4] twice; rep from *, end k1.

Row 2 P1, *[k4, p1] 3 times, p2, [k4, p1] 3 times; rep from * to end.

Row 3 *K1, [p3, 2-st RPC] twice, p4, k3, p1, [p3, 2-st LPC] twice, p3; rep from *, end k1.

Row 4 P1, *k3, p1, k4, p1, k5, p3, k5, p1, k4, p1, k3, p1; rep from * to end.

Row 5 *K1, p2, 2-st RPC, p3, 2-st RPC, p4, RT, k1, LT, p4, 2-st LPC, p3, 2-st LPC, p2; rep from *, end k1.

Row 6 P1, *k2, p1, k4, p1, k5, p5, k5, p1, k4, p1, k2, p1; rep from * to end.

Row 7 *K1, p1, 2-st RPC, p2, 3-st RPC, p3, 3-st RPC, k3, 3-st LPC, p3, 3-st LPC, p2, 2-st LPC, p1; rep from *, end k1.

Row 8 P1, *k1, p1, k3, p1, k5, p1, k2, p3, k2, p1, k5, p1, k3, p1, k1, p1; rep from * to end.

Row 9 *K1, 2-st RPC, p1, 3-st RPC, p3, 3-st RPC, p1, 2-st RPC, k1, 2-st LPC, p1, 3-st LPC, p3, 3-st LPC, p1, 2-st LPC; rep from *, end k1.

Row 10 P1, *p1, k2, p1, k5, p1, k3, [p1, k1] twice, p1, k3, p1, k5, p1, k2, p2; rep from * to end.

Row 11 *K2, 3-st RPC, p3, 3-st RPC, p2, 2-st RPC, p1, k1, p1, 2-st LPC, p2, 3-st LPC, p3, 3-st LPC, k1; rep from *, end k1.

Row 12 P1, *p2, k5, p1, k4, [p1, k2] twice, p1, k4, p1, k5, p3; rep from * to end.

Row 13 *K1, 2-st RPC, p4, 2-st RPC, p3, 2-st RPC, p2, k1, p2, 2-st LPC, p3, 2-st LPC, p4, 2-st LPC; rep from *, end k1.

Row 14 P1, *p1, k5, p1, k4, [p1, k3] twice, p1, k4, p1, k5, p2; rep from * to end.

Row 15 *K2, p4, [2-st RPC, p3] twice, k1, [p3, 2-st LPC] twice, p4, k1; rep from *, end k1.

Rows 16 and 18 P1, *[p1, k4] 6 times, p2; rep from * to end.

Row 17 *K2, p4, [k1, p4] 5 times, k1; rep from *, end k1.

Row 19 *K2, p4, [2-st LPC, p3] twice, k1, [p3, 2-st RPC] twice, p4, k1; rep from *, end k1.

Row 20 P1, *p1, k5, p1, k4, [p1, k3] twice, p1, k4, p1, k5, p2; rep from * to end.

Row 21 *K1, LT, p4, 2-st LPC, p3, 2-st LPC, p2, k1, p2, 2-st RPC, p3, 2-st RPC, p4, RT; rep from *, end k1.

Row 22 P1, *p2, k5, p1, k4, [p1, k2] twice, p1, k4, p1, k5, p3; rep from * to end.

Row 23 *K2, 3-st LPC, p3, 3-st LPC, p2, 2-st LPC, p1, k1, p1, 2-st RPC, p2, 3-st RPC, p3, 3-st RPC, k1; rep from *, end k1.

Row 24 P1, *p1, k2, p1, k5, p1, k3, [p1, k1] twice, p1, k3, p1, k5, p1, k2, p2; rep from * to end.

Row 25 *K1, 2-st LPC, p1, 3-st LPC, p3, 3-st LPC, p1, 2-st LPC, k1, 2-st RPC, p1, 3-st RPC, p3, 3-st RPC, p1, 2-st RPC; rep from *, end k1.

Row 26 P1, * k1, p1, k3, p1, k5, p1, k2, p3, k2, p1, k5, p1, k3, p1, k1, p1; rep from * to end.

Row 27 *K1, p1, 2-st LPC, p2, 3-st LPC, p3, 3-st LPC, k3, 3-st RPC, p3, 3-st RPC, p2, 2-st RPC, p1; rep from *, end k1.

Row 28 P1, *k2, p1, k4, p1, k5, p5, k5, p1, k4, p1, k2, p1; rep from * to end.

Row 29 *K1, p2, 2-st LPC, p3, 2-st LPC, p4, 2-st LPC, k1, 2-st RPC, p4, 2-st RPC, p3, 2-st RPC, p2; rep from *, end k1.

Row 30 P1, *k3, p1, k4, p1, k5, p3, k5, p1, k4, p1, k3, p1; rep from * to end.

Row 31 *K1, [p3, 2-st LPC] twice, p4, k3, p4, [2-st RPC, p3] twice; rep from *, end k1.

Row 32 P1, *[k4, p1] 3 times, p2, [k4, p1] 3 times; rep from * to end.

Rep rows 1–32.

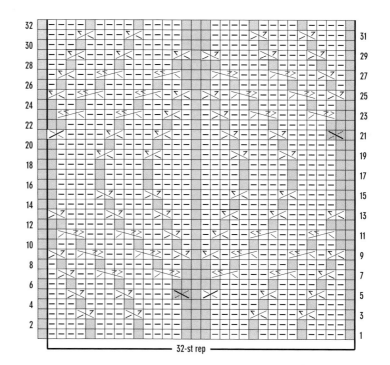

Stitch Key

▦	K on RS, p on WS	◹◸	2-st RPC
—	P on RS, k on WS	◺◿	2-st LPC
◹◸	RT	◹◸◸	3-st RPC
◸◹	LT	◺◺◿	3-st LPC

175 bubbles

3-st RPC Sl 1 st to cn and hold to back, k2, p1 from cn.

3-st LPC Sl 2 sts to cn and hold to front, p1, k2 from cn.

4-st RC Sl 2 sts to cn and hold to back, k2, k2 from cn.

4-st RPC Sl 2 sts to cn and hold to back, k2, p2 from cn.

4-st LPC Sl 2 sts to cn and hold to front, p2, k2 from cn.

(multiple of 20 sts plus 10)

Row 1 (RS) P3, k2, *k2, p3, k2, p6, k2, p3, k2; rep from *, end k2, p3.

Row 2 K3, p2, *p2, k3, p2, k6, p2, k3, p2; rep from *, end p2, k3.

Row 3 P3, *4-st RC, p3, 3-st LPC, p4, 3-st RPC, p3; rep from *, end 4-st RC, p3.

Row 4 K3, p2, *[p2, k4] 3 times, p2; rep from *, end p2, k3.

Row 5 P1, 4-st RPC, *4-st LPC, p2, 4-st LPC, 4-st RPC, p2, 4-st RPC; rep from *, end 4-st LPC, p1.

Rows 6 and 12 K1, p2, k2, *k2, p2, k4, p4, k4, p2, k2; rep from *, end k2, p2, k1.

Row 7 3-st RPC, p2, *p2, 3-st LPC, p3, 4-st RC, p3, 3-st RPC, p2; rep from *, p2, 3-st LPC.

Rows 8 and 10 P2, k3, *k3, p2, k3, p4, k3, p2, k3; rep from *, end k3, p2.

Row 9 K2, p3, *p3, k2, p3, k4, p3, k2, p3; rep from *, end p3, k2.

Row 11 3-st LPC, p2, *p2, 3-st RPC, p3, 4-st RC, p3, 3-st LPC, p2; rep from *, end p2, 3-st RPC.

Row 13 P1, 4-st LPC, *4-st RPC, p2, 4-st RPC, 4-st LPC, p2, 4-st LPC; rep from *, end 4-st RPC, p1.

Row 14 K3, p2, *[p2, k4] 3 times, p2; rep from *, end p2, k3.

Row 15 P3, *4-st RC, p3, 3-st RPC, p4, 3-st LPC, p3; rep from *, end 4-st RC, p3.

Row 16 K3, p2, *p2, k3, p2, k6, p2, k3, p2; rep from *, end p2, k3.

Rep rows 1–16.

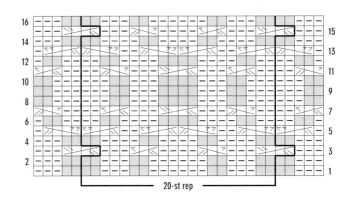

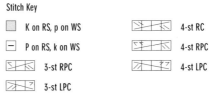

Stitch Key

- K on RS, p on WS
- P on RS, k on WS
- 3-st RPC
- 3-st LPC
- 4-st RC
- 4-st RPC
- 4-st LPC

20-st rep

175

176 crisscross

6-st RC Sl 3 sts to cn and hold to back, k3, k3 from cn.

6-st LC Sl 3 sts to cn and hold to front, k3, k3 from cn.

(multiple of 20 sts plus 8)

Row 1 (RS) P1, *[6-st LC, p4] twice; rep from *, end 6-st LC, p1.

Rows 2 and 4 K1, p3, *p3, k4, p6, k4, p3; rep from *, end p3, k1.

Row 3 P1, k3, *k3, p4, k6, p4, k3; rep from *, end k3, p1.

Rows 5, 7 and 11 P1, k1, p2, *p2, k6, p4, k6, p2; rep from *, end p2, k1, p1.

Rows 6, 8, 10 and 12 K1, p1, k2, *k2, p6, k4, p6, k2; rep from *, end k2, p1, k1.

Row 9 P1, k1, p2, *p2, 6-st RC, p4, 6-st RC, p2; rep from *, end p2, k1, p1.

Rows 13 and 15 P1, k3, *k3, p4, k6, p4, k3; rep from *, end k3, p1.

Rows 14 and 16 K1, p3, *p3, k4, p6, k4, p3; rep from *, end p3, k1.

Rep rows 1–16.

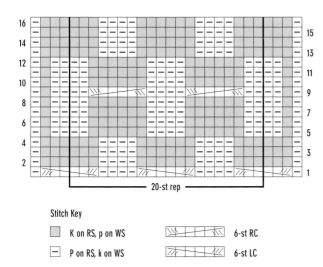

Stitch Key

☐ K on RS, p on WS

– P on RS, k on WS

⧄⧄⧄ 6-st RC

⧄⧄⧄ 6-st LC

176

8-st LC Sl 4 sts to cn and hold to front, k4, k4 from cn.

(multiple of 16 sts plus 10)

Rows 1, 3, 5, 7, 11, 13 and 15 (RS) K1, *[yo, p2tog] 4 times, k8; rep from * to last 9 sts, end [yo, p2tog] 4 times, k1.

Row 2 and all WS rows P1, *[yo, p2tog] 4 times, p8; rep from * to last 9 sts, end [yo, p2tog] 4 times, p1.

Row 9 K1, *[yo, p2tog] 4 times, 8-st LC; rep from * to last 9 sts, end [yo, p2tog] 4 times, k1.

Row 16 Rep row 2.

Rep rows 1–16.

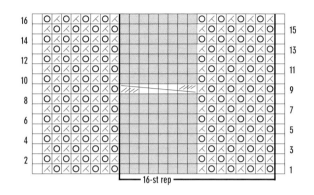

Stitch Key

K on RS, p on WS

O Yarn over

⧄ P2tog on WS

  8-st LC

combinations

6-st RC Sl 3 sts to cn and hold to back, k3, k3 from cn.

6-st LC Sl 3 sts to cn and hold to front, k3, k3 from cn.

Ladder Pattern

(worked over 14 sts)

Row 1 (RS) K1, p12, k1.

Row 2 P1, k12, p1.

Row 3 Knit.

Row 4 Purl.

Rep rows 1–4.

Right Cable (RC)

(worked over 6 sts)

Rows 1, 5 and 7 (RS) Knit.

Row 2 and all WS rows Purl.

Row 3 6-st RC.

Row 8 Purl.

Rep rows 1–8.

Left Cable (LC)

(worked over 6 sts)

Rows 1, 5 and 7 (RS) Knit.

Row 2 and all WS rows Purl.

Row 5 6-st LC

Row 8 Purl.

Rep rows 1–8.

(worked over 34 sts)

Row 1 (RS) P2, Right cable, p2, Ladder pat, p2, Left cable, p2.

Cont in pats as established.

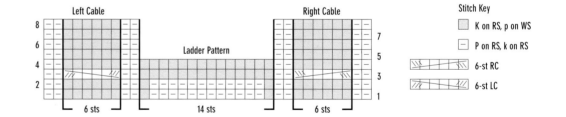

combinations

4-st RC Sl 2 sts to cn and hold to back, k2, k2 from cn.

4-st LC Sl 2 sts to cn and hold to front, k2, k2 from cn.

6-st RC Sl 3 sts to cn and hold to back, k3, k3 from cn.

6-st LC Sl 3 sts to cn and hold to front, k3, k3 from cn.

Right Cable Panel

(worked over 4 sts)

Row 1 (RS) Knit.

Row 2 Purl.

Row 3 4-st RC.

Row 4 Purl

Rep rows 1–4.

Left Cable Panel

(worked over 4 sts)

Row 1 (RS) Knit.

Row 2 Purl.

Row 3 4-st LC.

Row 4 Purl.

Rep rows 1–4.

Seed Cable Panel

(worked over 13 sts)

Rows 1, 3 and 15 (RS) K4, [p1, k1] twice, p1, k4.

Rows 2, 4 and 14 P3, [k1, p1] 3 times, k1, p3.

Row 5 6-st LC, k1, 6-st RC.

Rows 6, 8, 10 and 12 Purl.

Rows 7, 9 and 11 Knit.

Row 13 6-st RC, k1, 6-st LC.

Row 16 Rep row 2.

Rep rows 1–16.

(worked over 25 sts)

Row 1 (RS) P1, Right Cable Panel, p1, Seed Cable panel, p1, Left Cable Panel, p1.

Cont in pats as established.

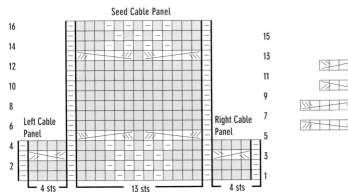

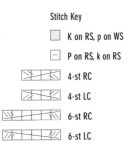

Stitch Key

☐ K on RS, p on WS

⊟ P on RS, k on RS

4-st RC

4-st LC

6-st RC

6-st LC

179

LT Skip 1 st, k 2nd st tbl, then k skipped st.

3-st LPC Sl 2 sts to cn and hold to front, p1, k2 from cn.

3-st RPC Sl 1 st to cn and hold to back, k2, p1 from cn.

6-st LC Sl 3 sts to cn and hold to front, k3, k3 from cn.

(worked over 48 sts)

Row 1 (RS) P1, LT, p1, k6, p6, 3-st RPC, k1, p1, k6, p1, k1, 3-st LPC, p6, k6, p1, LT, p1.

Row 2 K1, p2, k1, p6, k6, p3, k1, p8, k1, p3, k6, p6, k1, p2, k1.

Row 3 P1, LT, p1, 6-st LC, p5, 3-st RPC, p1, k1, p1, 6-st LC, p1, k1, p1, 3-st LPC, p5, 6-st LC, p1, LT, p1.

Row 4 K1, p2, k1, p6, k5, p2, k1, p1, k1, p8, k1, p1, k1, p2, k5, p6, k1, p2, k1.

Row 5 P1, LT, p1, k6, p4, 3-st RPC, [k1, p1] twice, k6, [p1, k1] twice, 3-st LPC, p4, k6, p1, LT, p1.

Row 6 K1, p2, k1, p6, k4, p3, k1, p1, k1, p8, k1, p1, k1, p3, k4, p6, k1, p2, k1.

Row 7 P1, LT, p1, k6, p3, 3-st RPC, p1, [k1, p1] twice, k6, [p1, k1] twice, p1, 3-st LPC, p3, k6, p1, LT, p1.

Row 8 K1, p2, k1, p6, k3, p2, k1, [p1, k1] twice, p8, k1, [p1, k1] twice, p2, k3, p6, k1, p2, k1.

Row 9 P1, LT, p1, 6-st LC, p2, 3-st RPC, [k1, p1] 3 times, 6-st LC, [p1, k1] 3 times, 3-st LPC, p2, 6-st LC, p1, LT, p1.

Row 10 K1, p2, k1, p6, k2, p3, k1, [p1, k1] twice, p8, k1, [p1, k1] twice, p3, k2, p6, k1, p2, k1.

Row 11 P1, LT, p1, k6, p1, 3-st RPC, p1, [k1, p1] 3 times, k6, p1, [k1, p1] 3 times, 3-st LPC, p1, k6, p1, LT, P1.

Row 12 K1, p2, k1, p6, k1, p2, k1, [p1, k1] 3 times, p8, k1, [p1, k1] 3 times, p2, k1, p6, k1, p2, k1.

Row 13 P1, LT, p1, k6, p1, 3-st LPC, p1, [k1, p1] 3 times, k6, p1, [k1, p1] 3 times, 3-st RPC, p1, k6, p1, LT, p1.

Row 14 K1, p2, k1, p6, k2, p3, k1, [p1, k1] twice, p8, k1, [p1, k1] twice, p3, k2, p6, k1, p2, k1.

Row 15 P1, LT, p1, 6-st LC, p2, 3-st LPC, [k1, p1] 3 times, 6-st LC, [p1, k1] 3 times, 3-st RPC, p2, 6-st LC, p1, LT, p1.

Row 16 K1, p2, k1, p6, k3, p2, k1, [p1, k1] twice, p8, k1, [p1, k1] twice, p2, k3, p6, k1, p2, k1.

Row 17 P1, LT, p1, k6, p3, 3-st LPC, p1, [k1, p1] twice, k6, p1, [k1, p1] twice, 3-st RPC, p3, k6, p1, LT, p1.

Row 18 K1, p2, k1, p6, k4, p3, k1, p1, k1, p8, k1, p1, k1, p3, k4, p6, k1, p2, k1.

Row 19 P1, LT, p1, k6, p4, 3-st LPC, [k1, p1] twice, k6, [p1, k1] twice, 3-st RPC, p4, k6, p1, LT, p1.

Row 20 K1, p2, k1, p6, k5, p2, k1, p1, k1, p8, k1, p1, k1, p2, k5, p6, k1, p2, k1.

Row 21 P1, LT, p1, 6-st LC, p5, 3-st LPC, p1, k1, p1, 6-st LC, p1, k1, p1, 3-st RPC, p5, 6-st LC, p1, LT, p1.

Row 22 K1, p2, k1, p6, k6, p3, k1, p8, k1, p3, k6, p6, k1, p2, k1.

Row 23 P1, LT, p1, k6, p6, 3-st LPC, k1, p1, k6, p1, k1, 3-st RPC, p6, k6, p1, LT, p1.

Row 24 K1, p2, k1, p6, k7, p2, k1, p8, k1, p2, k7, p6, k1, p2, k1.

Rep rows 1–24.

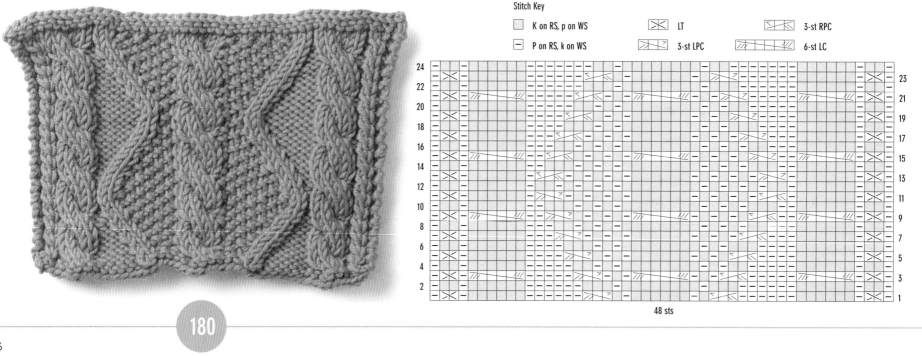

Stitch Key

◻ K on RS, p on WS ⊠ LT ⊠ 3-st RPC

⊟ P on RS, k on WS ⊠ 3-st LPC ⊠ 6-st LC

48 sts

MK (make knot) K7 sts in next st by k into front of st then [k into back and front of same st] 3 times, then pass 6th, 5th, 4th, 3rd, 2nd and first st separately over last st made.

LT With RH needle behind LH needle, skip 1 st and k 2nd st on LH needle tbl, then insert RH needle into back lps of both skipped st and 2nd st and k2tog tbl.

RT K2tog leaving sts on LH needle, then insert RH needle from front between 2 sts just knitted tog and k first st again, then sl both sts from needle tog.

3-st RPC Sl 1 st to cn and hold to back, k2, p1 from cn.

3-st LPC Sl 2 sts to cn and hold to front, p1, k2 from cn.

Braid Cable

(worked over 3 sts)

Row 1 (RS) RT, k1.

Row 2 Purl.

Row 3 K1, LT.

Row 4 Purl.

Rep rows 1–4.

Bobble Panel

(worked over 15 sts)

Row 1 (RS) P4, 3-st RPC, p1, 3-st LPC, p4.

Row 2 K4, p2, k1, p1, k1, p2, k4.

Row 3 P3, 3-st RPC, k1, p1, k1, 3-st LPC, p3.

Rows 4 and 10 K3, p3, k1, p1, k1, p3, k3.

Row 5 P2, 3-st RPC, [p1, k1] twice, p1, 3-st LPC, p2.

Rows 6 and 8 K2, p2, [k1, p1] 3 times, k1, p2, k2.

Row 7 P2, k3, [p1, k1] twice, p1, k3, p2.

Row 9 P2, 3-st LPC, [p1, k1] twice, p1, 3-st RPC, p2.

Row 11 P3, 3-st LPC, k1, p1, k1, 3-st RPC, p3.

Row 12 K4, p2, k1, p1, k1, p2, k4.

Row 13 P4, 3-st LPC, p1, 3-st RPC, p4.

Rows 14, 16 and 18 K5, p5, k5.

Rows 15 and 19 P5, k2, MK, k2, p5.

Row 17 P5, MK, k3, MK, p5.

Row 20 K5, p5, k5.

Rep rows 1–20.

(worked over 25 sts)

Preparation row (WS) K2, P3, k5, p5, k5, P3, k2.

Row 1 (RS) P2, Braid cable, Bobble panel, Braid cable, p2.

Cont in pats as established.

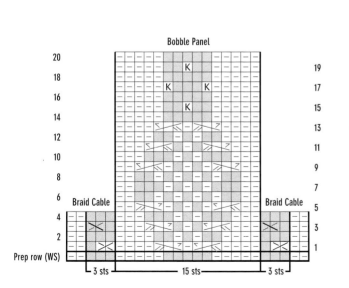

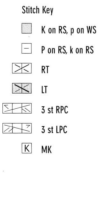

Stitch Key

	K on RS, p on WS
	P on RS, k on RS
	RT
	LT
	3 st RPC
	3 st LPC
K	MK

LT With RH needle behind LH needle, skip 1 st and k the 2nd st tbl, insert RH needle into the backs of both sts and k2tog tbl.

RT K2tog leaving sts on LH needle, insert RH needle between the 2 sts just k and k the first st again, sl both sts from needle tog.

3-st RPC Sl 1 st to cn and hold to back, k2, p1 from cn.

3-st LPC Sl 2 sts to cn and hold to front, p1, k2 from cn.

5-st LC Sl 3 sts to cn and hold to front, k2, k3 from cn.

6-st LC Sl 3 sts to cn and hold to front, k3, k3 from cn.

(worked over 51 sts)

Row 1 (RS) P2, 3-st LPC, p1, k2, p1, k6, [p1, k2] twice, [RT] twice, p1, [LT] twice, [k2, p1] twice, k6, p1, k2, p2, 3-st LPC, p1.

Row 2 K1, p2, k3, p2, k1, p6, [k1, p1, k1, p6] 3 times, [k1, p2] twice, k3.

Row 3 P3, 3-st LPC, k2, p1, k6, p1, k4, [RT] twice, p1, k1, p1, [LT] twice, k4, p1, k6, p1, k2, p3, 3-st LPC.

Row 4 P2, k4, p2, k1, p6, k1, p7, [k1, p1] twice, k1, p7, k1, p6, k1, p4, k4.

Row 5 P3, 3-st RPC, k2, p1, 6-st LC, p1, k3, [RT] twice, p1, [k1, p1] twice, [LT] twice, k3, p1, 6-st LC, p1, k2, p3, 3-st RPC.

Row 6 K1, p2, k3, p2, [k1, p6] twice, k1, p5, [k1, p6] twice, [k1, p2] twice, k3.

Row 7 P2, 3-st RPC, p1, k2, p1, k6, p1, k2, [RT] twice, p1, k5, p1, [LT] twice, k2, p1, k6, p1, k2, p2, 3-st RPC, p1.

Row 8 [K2, p2] twice, k1, p6, k1, p5, k1, p1, k1, p3, k1, p1, k1, p5, k1, p6, k1, [p2, k2] twice.

Row 9 P1, 3-st RPC, p2, k2, p1, k6, p1, k1, [RT] twice, p1, k7, p1, [LT] twice, k1, p1, k6, p1, k2, p1, 3-st RPC, p2.

Row 10 K3, [p2, k1] twice, p6, k1, p4, k1, p1, k1, p5, k1, p1, k1, p4, k1, p6, k1, p2, k3, p2, k1.

Row 11 3-st RPC, p3, k2, p1, k6, p1, [RT] twice, p1, k1, p1, 5-st LC, p1, k1, p1, [LT] twice, p1, k6, p1, k2, 3-st RPC, p3.

Row 12 K4, p4, k1, p6, k1, p5, k1, p7, k1, p5, k1, p6, k1, p2, k4, p2.

Row 13 3-st LPC, p3, k2, p1, k6, p1, [LT] twice, k1, p1, k7, p1, k1, [RT] twice, p1, k6, p1, k2, 3-st LPC, p3.

Row 14 K3, [p2, k1] twice, p6, k1, p4, k1, p1, k1, p5, k1, p1, k1, p4, k1, p6, k1, p2, k3, p2, k1.

Row 15 P1, 3-st LPC, p2, k2, p1, 6-st LC, p1, k1, [LT] twice, k1, p1, k5, p1, k1, [RT] twice, k1, p1, 6-st LC, p1, k2, p1, 3-st LPC, p2.

[k1, p6] twice, [k1, p2] twice, k3.

Row 16 [K2, p2] twice, k1, p6, k1, p5, k1, p1, k1, p3, k1, p1, k1, p5, k1, p6, k1, [p2, k2] twice.

Row 17 P2, 3-st LPC, p1, k2, p1, k6, p1, k2, [LT] twice, k1, p1, k3, p1, k1, [RT] twice, k2, p1, k6, p1, k2, p2, 3-st LPC, p1.

Row 18 K1, p2, k3, p2, [k1, p6] twice, [k1, p1] 3 times, [k1, p6] twice, [k1, p2] twice, k3.

Row 19 P3, 3-st LPC, k2, p1, k6, p1, k3, [LT] twice, [k1, p1] twice, k1, [RT] twice, k3, p1, k6, p1, k2, p3, 3-st LPC.

Row 20 P2, k4, p2, k1, p6, k1, p7, [k1, p1] twice, k1, p7, k1, p6, k1, p4, k4.

Row 21 P3, 3-st RPC, k2, p1, k6, p1, k4, [LT] twice, k1, p1, k1, [RT] twice, k4, p1, k6, p1, k2, p3, 3-st RPC.

Row 22 K1, p2, k3, p2, k1, p6, [k1, p1, k1, p6] 3 times, [k1, p2] twice, k3.

Row 23 P2, 3-st RPC, p1, k2, p1, k6, [p1, k2] twice, [LT] twice, k1, [RT] twice, [k2, p1] twice, k6, p1, k2, p2, 3-st RPC, p1.

Row 24 [K2, p2] twice, k1, p6, k1, [p1, k1] twice, [p5, k1] twice, [p1, k1] twice, p6, k1, [p2, k2] twice.

Rep rows 1–24.

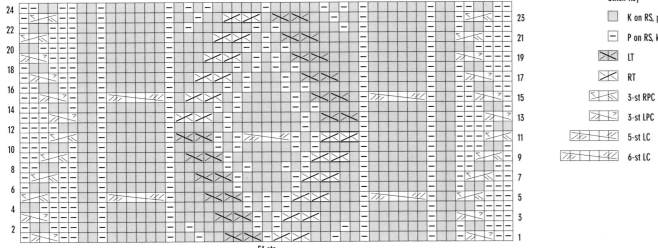

Stitch Key

▨	K on RS, p on WS
−	P on RS, k on WS
⊠	LT
⊠	RT
◁─▷	3-st RPC
◁─▷	3-st LPC
◁──▷	5-st LC
◁───▷	6-st LC

51 sts

3-st RPC Sl 1 st to cn and hold to back, k2, p1 from cn.

3-st LPC Sl 2 sts to cn and hold to front, p1, k2 from cn.

5-st RPC Sl 2 sts to cn and hold to back, sl next st to 2nd cn and hold to front, k2, sl st from front cn to RH needle, k2 from back cn.

6-st RC Sl 3 sts to cn and hold to back, k3, k3 from cn.

6-st LC Sl 3 sts to cn and hold to front, k3, k3 from cn.

Left Cable (LC)

(worked over 6 sts)

Rows 1 and 5 (RS) Knit.

Rows 2 and 4 Purl.

Row 3 6-st LC.

Row 6 Purl.

Rep rows 1–6.

Right Cable (RC)

(worked over 6 sts)

Rows 1 and 5 (RS) Knit.

Rows 2 and 4 Purl.

Row 3 6-st RC.

Row 6 Purl.

Rep rows 1–6.

Diamond Cable Panel

(worked over 21 sts)

Row 1 (RS) Sl 1, p7, 5-st RPC, p7, sl 1.

Rows 2 and 4 P1, k7, p5, k7, p1.

Rows 3 and 7 Sl 1, p7, k2, sl 1, k2, p7, sl 1.

Rows 5 and 9 Sl 1, p7, 5-st RPC, p7, sl 1.

Rows 6 and 8 P1, k7, p5, k7, p1.

Row 10 P1, k7, p2, k1, p2, k7, p1.

Row 11 Sl 1, p6, 3-st RPC, k1, 3-st LPC, p6, sl 1.

Row 12 P1, k6, p2, k1, p1, k1, p2, k6, p1.

Row 13 Sl 1, p5, 3-st RPC, k1, p1, k1, 3-st LPC, p5, sl 1.

Row 14 P1, k5, p2, k1, [p1, k1] twice, p2, k5, p1.

Row 15 Sl 1, p4, 3-st RPC, k1, [p1, k1] twice, 3-st LPC, p4, sl 1.

Row 16 P1, k4, p2, k1, [p1, k1] 3 times, p2, k4, p1.

Row 17 Sl 1, p3, 3-st RPC, k1, [p1, k1] 3 times, 3-st LPC, p3, sl 1.

Row 18 P1, k3, p2, k1, [p1, k1] 4 times, p2, k3, p1.

Row 19 Sl 1, p2, 3-st RPC, k1, [p1, k1] 4 times, 3-st LPC, p2, sl 1.

Row 20 P1, k2, p2, k1, [p1, k1] 5 times, p2, k2, p1.

Row 21 Sl 1, p2, k3, p1, [k1, p1] 4 times, k3, p2, sl 1.

Row 22 P1, k2, p3, k1, [p1, k1] 4 times, p3, k2, p1.

Row 23 Sl 1, p2, 3-st LPC, k1, [p1, k1] 4 times, 3-st RPC, p2, sl 1.

Row 24 P1, k3, p3, k1, [p1, k1] 3 times, p3, k3, p1.

Row 25 Sl 1, p3, 3-st LPC, k1, [p1, k1] 3 times, 3-st RPC, p3, sl 1.

Row 26 P1, k4, p3, k1, [p1, k1] twice, p3, k4, p1.

Row 27 Sl 1, p4, 3-st LPC, k1, [p1, k1] twice, 3-st RPC, p4, sl 1.

Row 28 P1, k5, p3, k1, p1, k1, p3, k5, p1.

Row 29 Sl 1, p5, 3-st LPC, k1, p1, k1, 3-st RPC, p5, sl 1.

Row 30 P1, k6, p3, k1, p3, k6, p1.

Row 31 Sl 1, p6, 3-st LPC, k1, 3-st RPC, p6, sl 1.

Row 32 P1, k7, p5, k7, p1.

Rep rows 1–32.

(worked over 41 sts)

Row 1 (RS) P2, Left cable, p2, Diamond cable panel, p2, Right cable, p2.

Cont in pats as established.

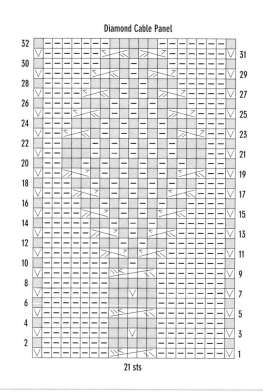

Diamond Cable Panel

21 sts

Left Cable

6 sts

Right Cable

6 sts

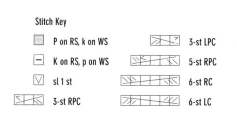

Stitch Key

- P on RS, k on WS
- − K on RS, p on WS
- ∨ sl 1 st
- 3-st RPC
- 3-st LPC
- 5-st RPC
- 6-st RC
- 6-st LC

combinations

4-st LC Sl 2 sts to cn and hold to front, k2, k2 from cn.

4-st RPC Sl 2 sts to cn and hold to back, k2, p2 from cn.

4-st LPC Sl 2 sts to cn and hold to front, p2, k2 from cn.

Tree of Life

(worked over 13 sts)

Row 1 (RS) P4, k2tog, yo twice, k1, yo twice, k2tog tbl, p4.

Row 2 K4, p1, [k1, p1] twice, k4.

Row 3 P3, k2tog, yo twice, p1, k1, p1, yo twice, k2tog tbl, p3.

Row 4 K3, p1, [k2, p1] twice, k3.

Row 5 P2, k2tog, yo twice, p2, k1, p2, yo twice, k2tog tbl, p2.

Row 6 K2, p1, [k3, p1] twice, k2.

Row 7 P1, k2tog, yo twice, p3, k1, p3, yo twice, k2tog tbl, p1.

Row 8 K1, p1, [k4, p1] twice, k1.

Row 9 K2tog, yo twice, p3, k3, p3, yo twice, k2tog tbl.

Row 10 P1, k4, p3, k4, p1.

Rep rows 1–10.

Lace Cable

(worked over 16 sts)

Row 1 (RS) K2, Yo twice, p2tog, P2, 4-st LC, P2, p2tog tbl, yo twice, k2.

Row 2 P2, p1 dropping extra yo, k3, p4, k3, p1 dropping extra yo, p2.

Row 3 K2, Yo twice, p2tog, 4-st RPC, 4-st LPC, p2tog tbl, yo twice, k2.

Rows 4, 6, 8, 10, 12, 14 and 16, P2, p1 dropping extra

yo, k1, p2, k4, p2, k1, p1 dropping extra yo, p2.

Rows 5, 7, 9, 11, 13 and 15 K2, yo twice, p2tog, k2, yo, p2tog, p2tog tbl, yo, k2, p2tog tbl, yo twice, k2.

Row 17 K2, Yo twice, p2tog, 4-st LPC, 4-st RPC, p2tog tbl, yo twice, k2.

Row 18 P2, p1 dropping extra yo, k3, p4, k3, k1 dropping extra yo, p2.

Rep rows 1–18.

(worked over 42 sts)

Preparation row (WS) K5, p3, k5, p3, k3, p4, k3, p3, k5, p3, k5.

Row 1 Tree of Life pat, k2, Lace cable, k2, Tree of Life pat.

Cont in pats as established.

Lace Cable

16 sts

Stitch Key

▢	K on RS, p on WS	◿	P2tog
▭	P on RS, k on WS	◺	P2tog tbl
00	Yo twice (or WS rows, always drop the extra)	⤬	4-st LC
O	Yo	⤬	4-st RPC
◢	K2tog	⤬	4-st LPC
◣	K2tog tbl		

Tree of Life

13 sts

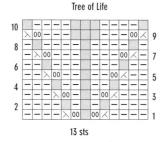

MB K1, p1, k1 into next st, turn, [p3, turn, k3, turn] twice; from RS, sl 2nd and 3rd st over first st—1 st rem.

2-st RPT Sl 1 st to cn and hold to back, k1tbl, p1 from cn.

2-st LPT Sl 1 st to cn and hold to front, p1, k1 tbl from cn.

2-st RT Sl 1 st to cn and hold to back, k1 tbl, k1t bl from cn.

2-st LT Sl 1 st to cn and hold to front, k1 tbl, k1 tbl from cn.

2-st LWPT Sl 1 st to cn and hold to front, p1 tbl, p1 tbl from cn.

6-st LC Sl 3 sts to cn and hold to front, k3, k3 from cn.

Rope Cable

(worked over 12 sts)

Rows 1 and 5 (RS) K1 tbl, p2, k6, p2, k1 tbl.

Rows 2 and 4 P1 tbl, k2, p6, k2, p1 tbl.

Row 3 K1 tbl, p2, 6-st LC, p2, k1 tbl.

Row 6 Rep row 2.

Rep rows 1–6.

Diamond Bobble Panel

(worked over 16 sts)

Row 1 (RS) P1, MB, p3, k1 tbl, p1, [k1 tbl] twice, p1, k1 tbl, p3, MB, p1.

Row 2 K5, p1 tbl, k1, [p1 tbl] twice, k1, p1 tbl, k5.

Row 3 P4, [2-st RPT] twice, [2-st LPT] twice, p4.

Row 4 K4, p1 tbl, k1, p1 tbl, k2, p1 tbl, k1, p1 tbl, k4.

Row 5 P3, [2-st RPT] twice, p2, [2-st LPT] twice, p3.

Row 6 K3, p1 tbl, k1, p1 tbl, k4, p1 tbl, k1, p1 tbl, k3.

Row 7 P2, 2-st RPT, 2-st RT, p4, 2-st LT, 2-st LPT, p2.

Row 8 K2, p1 tbl, k1, [p1 tbl] twice, k4, [p1 tbl] twice, k1, p1 tbl, k2.

Row 9 P1, [2-st RPT] twice, 2-st LPT, p2, 2-st RPT, [2-st LPT] twice, p1.

Row 10 [K1, p1 tbl] twice, [k2, p1 tbl] twice, k2, [p1 tbl, k1] twice.

Row 11 [2-st RPT] twice, p2, 2-st LPT, 2-st RPT, p2, [2-st LPT] twice.

Row 12 P1tbl, k1, p1 tbl, k4, 2-st LWPT, k4, p1 tbl, k1, p1 tbl.

Row 13 [2-st LPT] twice, p2, 2-st RPT, 2-st LPT, p2, [2-st RPT] twice.

Row 14 [K1, p1 tbl] twice, [k2, p1 tbl] twice, k2, [p1 tbl, k1] twice.

Row 15 P1, [2-st LPT] twice, 2-st RPT, p2, 2-st LPT, [2-st RPT] twice, p1.

Row 16 K2, p1 tbl, k1, [p1 tbl] twice, k4, [p1 tbl] twice, k1, p1 tbl, k2.

Row 17 P2, [2-st LPT] twice, p4, [2-st RPT] twice, p2.

Row 18 K3, p1 tbl, k1, p1 tbl, k4, p1 tbl, k1, p1 tbl, k3.

Row 19 P3, [2-st LPT] twice, p2, [2-st RPT] twice, p3.

Row 20 K4, p1 tbl, k1, p1 tbl, k2, p1 tbl, k1, p1 tbl, k4.

Row 21 P4, [2-st LPT] twice, [2-st RPT] twice, p4.

Row 22 K5, p1 tbl, k1, 2-st LWPT, k1, p1 tbl, k5.

Rep rows 1–22.

(worked over 40 sts)

Row 1 (RS) Rope cable, Diamond Bobble panel, Rope cable.

Cont in pats as established.

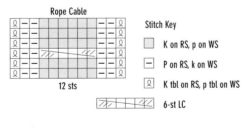

Rope Cable

Stitch Key

☐ K on RS, p on WS

— P on RS, k on WS

Ƣ K tbl on RS, p tbl on WS

6-st LC

12 sts

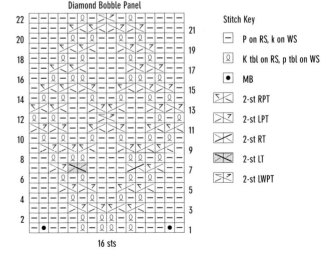

Diamond Bobble Panel

16 sts

Stitch Key

— P on RS, k on WS

Ƣ K tbl on RS, p tbl on WS

• MB

2-st RPT

2-st LPT

2-st RT

2-st LT

2-st LWPT

combinations

4-st RC Sl 2 sts to cn and hold to back, k2, k2 from cn.

4-st LC Sl 2 sts to cn and hold to front, k2, k2 from cn.

12-st LC Sl 6 sts to cn and hold to front, k6, k6 from cn.

Left Cable

(worked over 12 sts)

Rows 1, 3, 7 and 9 (RS) Knit.

Row 2 and all WS rows Purl.

Row 5 12-st LC.

Row 10 Purl.

Rep rows 1–10.

Diamond Panel

(worked over 16 sts)

Preparation row (WS) Purl.

Rows 1 and 5 (RS) [4-st RC] twice, [4-st LC] twice.

Row 2 and all WS rows Purl.

Rows 3 and 7 K2, 4-st RC, k4, 4-st LC, k2.

Rows 9 and 13 [4-st LC] twice, [4-st RC] twice.

Rows 11 and 15 K2, 4-st LC, k4, 4-st RC, k2.

Row 16 Purl.

Rep rows 1–16.

(worked over 40 sts)

Preparation row (WS) K2, p12, k2, p16, K2, p12, k2.

Row 1 (RS) K2, Left cable, k2, Diamond panel, k2, Left cable, k2.

Cont in pats as established.

Stitch Key

K on RS, p on WS

4-st RC

4-st LC

12-st LC

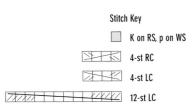

Left Cable

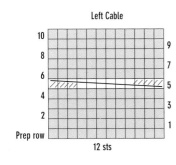

12 sts

Diamond Cable

16 sts

LT Pass in back of first st and k 2nd st tbl, then k first st and let both sts fall from needle.

RT Pass in front of first st and k 2nd st, then k first st and let both sts fall from needle.

4-st LC Sl 2 sts and hold in front, k2, k2 from cn.

4-st RC Sl 2 sts and hold in back, k2, k2 from cn.

5-st LPC/RT Sl 2 sts to cn and hold to front, p next 3 sts, work RT over 2 sts from cn.

5-st RPC/LT Sl 3 sts to cn and hold to back, LT over next 2 sts, p3 sts from cn.

5-st LPC/LT Sl 2 sts to cn and hold to front, p next 3 sts, work LT over 2 sts from cn.

5-st RPC/RT Sl 3 sts to cn and hold to back, RT over next 2 sts, p3 from cn.

Bobble Row 1 (RS) k1, p1, k1, p1, k1 loosely into space between last st worked and next st on LH needle.

Row 2 (WS) p5tog (the 5 made sts on previous row), pass the sl st over the 5tog st. (worked over 46 sts)

Preparation row (WS) K1, p2, k1, p8, k1, p2, k1, p1, k1, p2, k6, p2, k1, p1, k1, p2, k1, p8, k1, p2, k1.

Row 1 (RS) P1, k2, p1, 4-st LC, 4-st RC, p1, k2, p1, k1, p1, 5-st LPC/RT, 5-st RPC/LT, p1, k1, p1, k2, p1, 4-st LC, 4-st RC, p1, k2, p1.

Rows 2 and 4 K1, p2, k1, p8, k1, p2, k1, p1, k4, p4, k4, p1, k1, p2, k1, p8, k1, p2, k1.

Row 3 P1, k2, p1, k8, p1, k2, p1, k1, p4, RT, LT, p4, k1, p1, k2, p1, k8, p1, k2, p1.

Row 5 P1, k2, p1, 4-st LC, 4-st RC, p1, k2, p1, k1, p1, 5-st RPC/RT, 5-st LPC/LT, p1, k1, p1, k2, p1, 4-st LC, 4-st RC, p1, k2, p1.

Rows 6, 8, 12 and 16 K1, p2, k1, p8, k1, p2, k1, p1, k1, p2, k6, p2, k1, p1, k1, p2, k1, p8, k1, p2, k1.

Rows 7, 11, 15 and 19 P1, k2, p1, k8, p1, k2, p1, k1, p1, RT, p6, LT, p1, k1, p1, k2, p1, k8, p1, k2, p1.

Rows 9, 13 and 17 P1, k2, p1, 4-st LC, 4-st RC, p1, k2, p1, k1, p1, RT, p3, [k1, p1, k1, p1, k1 loosely into space between last st worked and next st on LH needle], p3, LT, p1, k1, p1, k2, p1, 4-st LC, 4-st RC, p1, k2, p1.

Rows 10, 14 and 18 K1, p2, k1, p8, k1, p2, k1, p1, k1, p2, k2, [sl 1 purlwise, p5tog (the 5 made sts on previous row), pass the sl st over the 5tog st], k3, p2, k1, p1, k1, p2, k1, p8, k1, p2, k1.

Row 20 K1, p2, k1, p8, k1, p2, k1, p1, k1, p2, k6, p2, k1, p1, k1, p2, k1, p8, k1, p2, k1.

Rep rows 1–20.

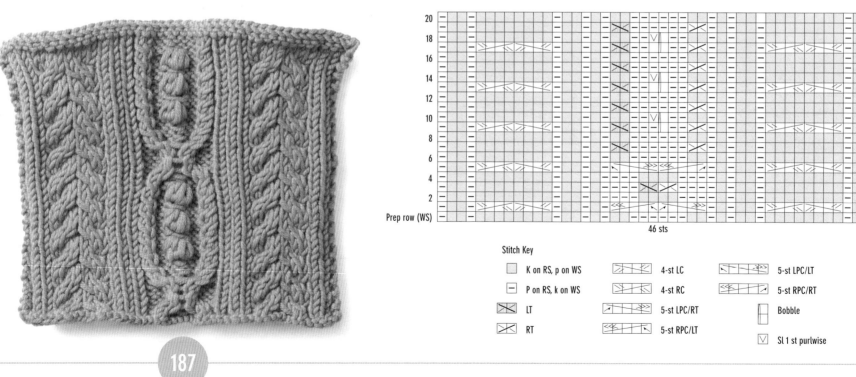

Stitch Key

☐	K on RS, p on WS
−	P on RS, k on WS
⬛	LT
⬛	RT
⟋⟍	4-st LC
⟍⟋	4-st RC
⟋⟍	5-st LPC/RT
⟍⟋	5-st RPC/LT
⟋⟍	5-st LPC/LT
⟍⟋	5-st RPC/RT
▯	Bobble
∨	Sl 1 st purlwise

RPT Sk 1 st, wyib insert needle into 2nd st as to p and hold on needle, k the skipped st, drop both sts from LH needle.

LPT Sk 1 st, k the 2nd st from the back and hold on needle, sl the skipped st as to p, drop both sts from LH needle.

4-st RC Sl 2 sts to cn and hold to back, k2, k2 from cn.

4-st LC Sl 2 sts to cn and hold to front, k2, k2 from cn.

Side Cable

(worked over 9 sts)

Row 1 (RS) Knit.

Row 2 Purl.

Row 3 4-st RC, k1, 4-st LC.

Row 4 Purl.

Rep rows 1–4.

Diamond panel

(worked over 14 sts)

Row 1 (RS) P5, RPT, LPT, p5.

Row 2 K5, p4, k5.

Row 3 P4, RPT, k1, p1, LPT, p4.

Row 4 K4, p2, k1, p3, k4.

Row 5 P3, RPT, [k1, p1] twice, LPT, p3.

Row 6 K3, p2, k1, p1, k1, p3, k3.

Row 7 P2, RPT, [k1, p1] 3 times, LPT, p2.

Row 8 K2, p2, k1, [p1, k1] twice, p3, k2.

Row 9 P1, RPT, [k1, p1] 4 times, LPT, p1.

Row 10 K1, p2, [k1, p1] 3 times, k1, p3, k1.

Row 11 RPT, [k1, p1] 5 times, LPT.

Row 12 P2, k1, [p1, k1] 4 times, p3.

Row 13 P1, LPT, [k1, p1] 4 times, RPT, p1.

Row 14 K1, p2, k1, [p1, k1] 3 times, p3, k1.

Row 15 P2, LPT, [k1, p1] 3 times, RPT, p2.

Row 16 K2, p2, k1, [p1, k1] twice, p3, k2.

Row 17 P3, LPT, [k1, p1] twice, RPT, p3.

Row 18 K3, p2, k1, p1, k1, p3, k3.

Row 19 P4, LPT, k1, p1, RPT, p4.

Row 20 K4, p2, k1, p3, k4.

Row 21 P5, LPT, RPT, p5.

Row 22 K5, p4, k5.

Rep rows 1–22.

(Worked over 46 sts)

Row 1 (RS) P2, k1, p1, k1, p2, Side cable, Diamond panel, Side cable, p2, k1, p1, k1, p2.

Cont in pats as established.

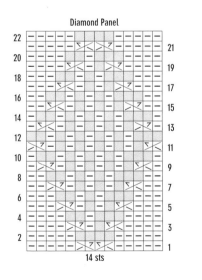

Diamond Panel / Side Cable / Stitch Key

MB K1, p1, k1 all into next st, turn, k3, turn, SK2P.

2-st RC Sl 1 st to cn and hold to back, k1, k1 from cn.

2-st LC Sl 1 st to cn and hold to front, k1, k1 from cn.

2-st RPC Sl 1 st to cn and hold to back, k1, p1 from cn.

2-st LPC Sl 1 st to cn and hold to front, p1, k1 from cn.

3-st RC Sl 1 st to cn and hold to back, k2, k1 from cn.

3-st LC Sl 2 sts to cn and hold to front, k1, k2 from cn.

6-st RC RS Rows Sl 3 sts to RH needle, lift 3 wrapped sts and drop 1 yo on each st making 3 long sts, keep on LH needle. Sl 3 sts from RH needle back to LH needle. Pass 3 long sts over 3 regular sts, keep all 6 sts on LH needle, k into back of 3 long sts, k3. WS rows P3 wrapping yarn twice around needle in each st, p3.

Left Eyelet

(worked over 3 sts)

Row 1 (RS) P1, yo, p2tog.

Row 2 P3.

Rep rows 1–2.

Right Eyelet

(worked over 3 sts)

Row 1 (RS) P2tog, yo, p1.

Row 2 P3.

Rep rows 1–2.

Wrapped Cable

(worked over 6 sts)

Rows 1 and 5 (RS) Knit.

Row 2 P3 wrapping yarn twice around needle in each st, p3.

Row 3 Sl 3 sts to RH needle, lift 3 wrapped sts and drop 1 yo on each st making 3 long sts, keep on LH needle. Sl 3 sts from RH needle back to LH needle. Pass 3 long sts over 3 regular sts, keep all 6 sts on LH needle, k into back of 3 long sts, k3.

Rows 4 and 6 Purl.

Rep rows 1–6.

Bobble Fan Stitch

(worked over 12 sts)

Row 1 (RS) P4, 2-st RC, 2-st LC, p4.

Row 2 K4, p4, k4.

Row 3 P3, 3-st RC, 3-st LC, p3.

Row 4 K3, p6, k3.

Row 5 P2, 2-st RPC, k4, 2-st LPC, p2.

Row 6 K2, p1, k1, p4, k1, p1, k2.

Row 7 P1, [2-st RPC] twice, k2, [2-st LPC] twice, p1.

Rows 8 and 10 K1, [p1, k1] twice, p2, [k1, p1] twice, k1.

Row 9 P1, [k1, p1] twice, k2, [k1, p1] twice, p1.

Row 11 P1, MB, p1, k1, p1, k2, p1, k1, p1, MB, p1.

Row 12 K3, p1, k1, p2, k1, p1, k3.

Row 13 P3, MB, 2-st RC, 2-st LC, MB, p3.

Row 14 K4, p4, k4.

Rep rows 1–14.

(worked over 40 sts)

Row 1 (RS) K1, Left eyelet, Wrapped cable, Right eyelet, k1, Bobble Fan pat, k1, Left eyelet, Wrapped cable, Right eyelet, k1.

Cont in pats as established.

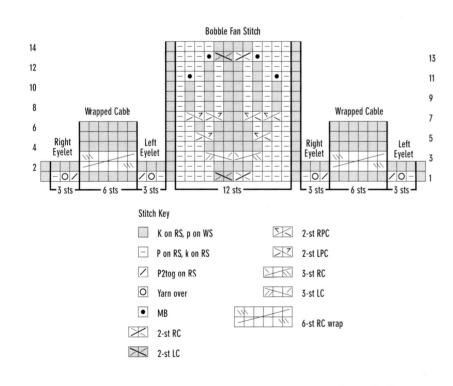

Bobble Fan Stitch

Wrapped Cable

Right Eyelet

Left Eyelet

14 12 10 8 6 4 2

13 11 9 7 5 3 1

3 sts — 6 sts — 3 sts — 12 sts — 3 sts — 6 sts — 3 sts

Stitch Key

- ☐ K on RS, p on WS
- − P on RS, k on RS
- ╱ P2tog on RS
- ○ Yarn over
- • MB
- 2-st RC
- 2-st LC
- 2-st RPC
- 2-st LPC
- 3-st RC
- 3-st LC
- 6-st RC wrap

189

combinations

WC (wrapped cable) Sl next 6 sts to cn, wrap the yarn 3 times around all the sts on the cn (pulling sts tog slightly), k6 sts from cn.

Left Cable (LC)
(worked over 6 sts)
Rows 1, 3, 5, 7 and 9 (RS) K2, p2, k2.
Row 2 and all WS rows P2, k2, p2.
Row 11 WC.
Row 12 P2, k2, p2.
Rep rows 1–12.

Right Cable (RC)
(worked over 6 sts)
Rows 1, 3, 7, 9 and 11 (RS) K2, p2, k2.
Row 2 and all WS rows P2, k2, p2.
Row 5 WC.
Row 12 P2, k2, p2.
Rep rows 1–12.

Fan Stitch
(worked over 15 sts, inc to 25 sts, dec to 15 sts)
Row 1 (RS) K2, [k1, yo] 10 times, k3.
Row 2 K2, p2tog tbl, p17, p2tog, k2.

Row 3 K2, k2tog, k15, SKP, k2.
Row 4 K2, p2tog tbl, p13, p2tog, k2.
Row 5 K2, k2tog, k11, SKP , k2.
Row 6 K2, p2tog tbl, p9, p2tog, k2.
Rep rows 1–6.
(worked over 43 sts)
Row 1 (RS) P1, RC, p1, LC, fan stitch, LC, p1, RC, p1.
Cont in pats as established.

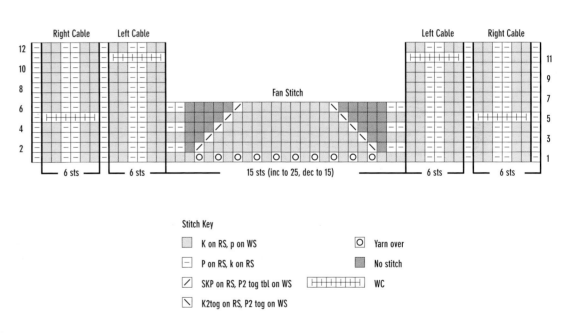

Stitch Key

▢	K on RS, p on WS	⊙	Yarn over
–	P on RS, k on RS	▨	No stitch
╱	SKP on RS, P2 tog tbl on WS	WC grid	WC
╲	K2tog on RS, P2 tog on WS		

MB K into (front, back, front, back, front) of st, turn; p5, turn; k2tog, k1, k2tog, turn; sl 1-p2tog-psso, sl st to RH needle.

LT Skip first st and passing behind the st, k 2nd st tbl, k skipped st through front loop, let both sts fall from LH needle.

3-st RPC Sl 1 st to cn and hold in back, k2, then p1 from cn.

3-st LPC Sl 2 sts to cn and hold in front, p1, k2 from cn.

4-st RC Sl 2 sts to cn and hold in back, k2, k2 from cn.

5-st LC Sl 2 sts to cn and hold in front, k3, k2; from cn.

5-st PLC Sl 2 sts to cn and hold in front, p1, k2, k2 from cn.

5-st LPC Sl 3 sts to cn and hold in front, k2; p1, k2 from cn.

Side Panel
(worked over 10 sts)

Row 1 (RS) LT, p1, 4-st RC p1, LT.
Row 2 P2, k1, p4, k1, p2.
Row 3 LT, p1, k4, p1, LT.
Row 4 Rep row 2.
Rep rows 1–4 for side panel.

Diamond Panel
(worked over 19 sts)

Row 1 (RS) P7, 5-st LC, p7.
Row 2 K7, p2, k1, p2, k7.
Row 3 P6, 3-st RPC, k1, 3-st LPC, p6.
Row 4 K6, p3, k1, p3, k6.
Row 5 P5, 3-st RPC, p1, k1, p1, 3-st LPC, p5.

Row 6 K5, p2, [k1, p1] twice, k1, p2, k5.
Row 7 P4, 3-st RPC, [k1, p1] twice, k1, 3-st LPC, p4.
Row 8 K4, p2, [p1, k1] 3 times, p3, k4.
Row 9 P3, 3-st RPC, [p1, k1] 3 times, p1, 3-st LPC, p3.
Row 10 K3, p2, [k1, p1] 4 times, k1, p2, k3.
Row 11 P2, 3-st RPC, [k1, p1] twice, MB, [p1, k1] twice, 3-st LPC, p2.
Row 12 K2, p2, [p1, k1] 5 times, p3, k2.
Row 13 P2, 3-st LPC, [k1, p1] 4 times, k1, 3-st RPC, p2.
Row 14 K3, p2, [k1, p1] 4 times, k1, p2, k3.
Row 15 P3, 3-st LPC, [p1, k1] 3 times, p1, 3-st RPC, p3.
Row 16 K4, p2, [p1, k1] 3 times, p3, k4.

Row 17 P4, 3-st LPC, [k1, p1] twice, k1, 3-st RPC, p4.
Row 18 K5, p2, [k1, p1] twice, k1, p2, k5.
Row 19 P5, 3-st LPC, p1, k1, p1, 3-st RPC, p5.
Row 20 K6, p3, k1, p3, k6.
Row 21 P6, 3-st LPC, k1, 3-st RPC, p6.
Row 22 K7, p2, k1, p2, k7.
Row 23 P7, 5-st PLC, p7.
Row 24 K7, p5, k7.
Row 25 P7, 5-st PLC, p7.
Row 26 K7, p2, k1, p2, k7.
Rep rows 3–26.
(worked over 39 sts)

Row 1 (RS) Side panel, Diamond panel, Side panel.
Cont in pats as established.

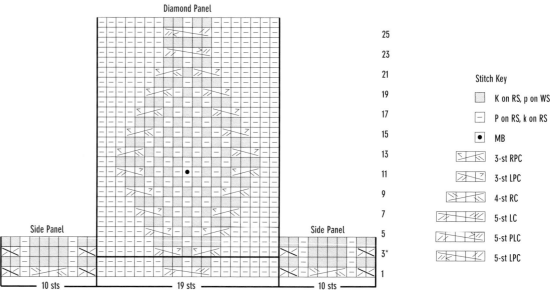

Diamond Panel

Stitch Key

☐ K on RS, p on WS

— P on RS, k on RS

● MB

3-st RPC

3-st LPC

4-st RC

5-st LC

5-st PLC

5-st LPC

Side Panel

10 sts — 19 sts — 10 sts

Inc 2 Into back loop of next st, p1, k1, p1.

4-st LPC Sl 3 sts to cn and hold to front, p1, k3 from cn.

5-st RPC Sl 2 sts to cn and hold to back, k3, p2 from cn.

5-st LC Sl 3 sts to cn and hold to front, k2, sl center st from cn to LH needle and purl it, k2 from cn.

6-st RC Sl 3 sts to cn and hold to back, k3, k3 from cn.

6-st LC Sl 3 sts to cn and hold to front, k3, k3 from cn.

Split Cable

(worked over 9 sts)

Rows 1, 3 and 5 (WS) P1, k1, p2, k1, p2, k1, p1.

Row 2 K1, p1, k2, p1, k2, p1, k1.

Row 4 K1, p1, 5-st LC, p1, k1.

Row 6 Rep row 2.

Rep rows 1–6.

Toggle Knot

(worked over 21 sts, inc to 25 sts, dec to 21 sts)

Row 1 (WS) K9, p3, k9.

Row 2 P4, inc 2, p4, k3, p9–23 sts.

Row 3 K9, p3, k4, p3, k4.

Row 4 P4, 4-st LPC, p3, k3, p9.

Row 5 K9, p3, k3, p3, k5.

Row 6 P5, 4-st LPC, p2, k3, p6, inc 2, p2–25 sts.

Row 7 K2, p3, k6, p3, k2, p3, k6.

Row 8 P6, 4-st LPC, p1, k3, p4, 5-st RPC, p2.

Row 9 [K4, p3] twice, k1, p3, k7.

Row 10 P7, 4-st LPC, k3, p2, 5-st RPC, p4.

Row 11 K6, p3, k2, p6, k8.

Row 12 P8, 6-st RC, 5-st RPC, p6.

Rows 13, 15 and 17 K8, p9, k8.

Row 14 P8, k3, 6-st LC, p8.

Row 16 P8, 6-st RC, k3, p8.

Row 18 P6, 5-st RPC, 6-st LC, p8.

Row 19 K8, p6, k2, p3, k6.

Row 20 P4, 5-st RPC, p2, k3, 4-st LPC, p7.

Row 21 K7, p3, k1, p3, k4, p3, k4.

Row 22 P2, 5-st RPC, p4, k3, p1, 4-st LPC, p6.

Row 23 K6, p3, k2, p3, k6, k3tog, k2 –23 sts.

Row 24 P9, k3, p2, 4-st LPC, p5.

Row 25 K5, p3, k3, p3, k9.

Row 26 P9, k3, p3, 4-st LPC, p4.

Row 27 K4, k3tog, k4, p3, k9–21 sts.

Row 28 P9, k3, p9.

Rep rows 1–28.

(worked over 39 sts)

Row 1 (WS) Split cable, Toggle Knot, Split cable.

Cont in pats as established.

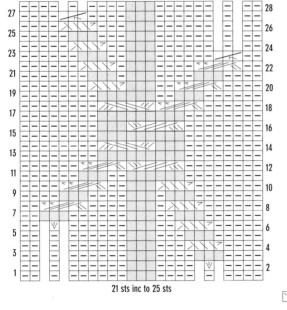

Toggle Knot

21 sts inc to 25 sts

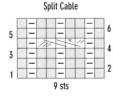

Split Cable

9 sts

Stitch Key

☐ K on RS, p on WS

— P on RS, k on WS

Ⅴ Inc 2 (p, k, p into back loop)

P3tog

4-st LPC

5-st RPC

5-st LC

6-st RC

6-st LC

(Swatch is worked with Double Seed Stitch background as charted. Replace with your choice of background stitch if desired.)

Inc 3 K into back and then front of st, insert LH needle behind work and into the vertical strand between the 2 sts just made and k1tbl in this strand.

Dec 5 Sl next 3 sts wyib, *pass 2nd st on RH needle over first (center) st, sl center st back to LH needle, pass 2nd st on LH needle over it*, sl center st back to RH needle and rep between *'s once more, pick up yarn and p center st.

4-st RC Sl 1 st to cn and hold to back, k3, k1 from cn.

4-st LC Sl 3 sts to cn and hold to front, k1, k3 from cn.

4-st RPC Sl 1 st to cn and hold to back, k3, p1 from cn.

4-st LPC Sl 3 sts to cn and hold to front, p1, k3 from cn.

5-st RPC Sl 2 sts to cn and hold to back, k3, p2 from cn.

5-st LPC Sl 3 sts to cn and hold to front, p2, k3 from cn.

5-st KC RC Sl 2 sts to cn and hold to back, k3; [k1, p1] from cn.

5-st KC LC Sl 3 sts to cn and hold to front, [k1, p1]; k3 from cn.

5-st PK RC Sl 2 sts to cn and hold to back, k3; [p1, k1] from cn.

5-st PK LC Sl 3 sts to cn and hold to front, [p1, k1]; k3 from cn.

6-st RC Sl 3 sts to cn and hold to back, k3, k3 from cn.

6-st LC Sl 3 sts to cn and hold to front, k3, k3 from cn.

Double Seed Stitch (DSS)
Row 1 (RS) *K1, p1; rep from * to end.
Row 2 K the knit sts and p the purl sts.
Row 3 *P1, k1; rep from * to end.
Row 4 Rep row 2.
Rep rows 1–4.
(worked over 38 sts on Double Seed st background)
Row 1 (RS) [K1, p1] 4 times, k3, p5, 6-st RC, p5, k3, [p1, k1] 4 times.
Row 2 [P1, k1] 4 times, p3, k5, p6, k5, p3, [k1, p1] 4 times.
Row 3 [P1, k1] 3 times, 5-st RPC, inc3, p4, k6, p4, inc3, 5-st LPC, [k1, p1] 3 times.
Row 4 [K1, p1] twice, k1, p4, k2, p3, k4, p6, k4, p3, k2, p4, [k1, p1] twice, k1.
Row 5 K1, [p1, k1] twice, 4-st RPC, p2, [inc1] 3 times, p4, 6-st RC, p4, [inc1] 3 times, p2, 4-st LPC, k1, [p1, k1] twice.

Row 6 [P1, k1] twice, p4, k3, [p6, k4] twice, p6, k3, p4, [k1, p1] twice.
Row 7 P1, k1, p1, 5-st RPC, p3, k3, 5-st LPC, p2, k6, p2, 5-st RPC, k3, p3, 5-st LPC, p1, k1, p1.
Row 8 K1, p1, k1, p3, k5, [p3, k2] twice, p6, [k2, p3] twice, k5, p3, k1, p1, k1.
Row 9 K1, p1, 4-st RPC, p5, [5-st LPC] twice, 6-st RC, [5-st RPC] twice, p5, 4-st LPC, p1, k1.
Row 10 P1, k1, p3, k6, p3, k2, p16, k2, p3, k6, p3, k1, p1.
Row 11 5-st RPC, p8, 5-st LPC, [6-st LC] twice, 5-st RPC, p8, 5-st LPC.
Rows 12 and 14 P3, k12, p18, k12, p3.
Row 13 K3, p12, [6-st RC] 3 times, p12, k3.
Row 15 5-st PK LC, p8, 5-st RPC, [6-st LC] twice, 5-st LPC, p8, 5-st KC RC.
Row 16 K1, p4, k8, p3, k2, p12, k2, p3, k8, p4, k1.
Row 17 K1, p1, 4-st LC, p5, [5-st RPC] twice,

6-st RC, [5-st LPC] twice, p5, 4-st RC, p1, k1.

Row 18 P1, k1, p4, k5, [p3, k2] twice, p6, [k2, p3] twice, k5, p4, k1, p1.

Row 19 P1, k1, p1, 5-st KC LC, p3, k3, 5-st RPC, p2, k6, p2, 5-st LPC, k3, p3, 5-st KC RC, p1, k1, p1.

Row 20 K1, [p1, k1] twice, p3, k3, p2, p2tog, p2, k4, p6, k4, p2, p2tog, p2, k3, p3, k1, [p1, k1] twice.

Row 21 K1, [p1, k1] twice, 4-st LPC, p2, dec5, p4, 6-st RC, p4, dec5, p2, 4-st RPC, k1, [p1, k1] twice.

Row 22 [P1, k1] 3 times, p3, k7, p6, k7, p3, [k1, p1] 3 times.

Row 23 [P1, k1] 3 times, 5-st PK LC, p5, k6, p5, 5-st KC RC, [k1, p1] 3 times.

Row 24 K1, [p1, k1] 3 times, p4, k5, p6, k5, p4, k1, [p1, k1] 3 times.

Rep rows 1–24.

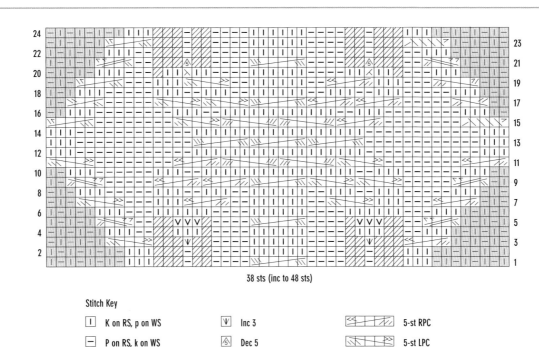

38 sts (inc to 48 sts)

Stitch Key

	K on RS, p on WS
—	P on RS, k on WS
	Double seed st (or background st)
	No stitch
	P2tog on WS
V	Inc 1

V	Inc 3
	Dec 5
	4-st RC
	4-st LC
	4-st RPC
	4-st LPC

	5-st RPC
	5-st LPC
	5-st KC RC
	5-st KC LC
	5-st PK RC
	5-st PK LC
	6-st RC
	6-st LC

4-st LC Sl 2 sts to cn and hold to front, k2, k2 from cn.

4-st RC Sl 2 sts to cn and hold to back, k2, k2 from cn.

9-st LC Sl 5 sts to cn and hold to front, k4, then sl the p st from cn to needle and p1; k4 from cn.

12-st LC Sl 8 sts to cn and hold to front, k4, then sl last 4 sts from cn to LH needle and k4, then k rem 4 sts from cn.

12-st RC Sl 8 sts to cn and hold to back, k4, then sl last 4 sts from cn to LH needle and k4, then k rem 4 sts from cn. (worked over 67 sts, inc to 75, dec to 67)

Row 1 (RS) P5, k4, [p2, k4] 4 times, p1, [k4, p2] 4 times, k4, p5.

Row 2 and all WS rows K the knit sts and p the purl sts.

Row 3 P5, 4-st LC, [p2, 4-st LC, p2, k4] twice, p1 [k4, p2, 4-st RC, p2] twice, 4-st RC, p5.

Row 5 P5, k4, [p2, k4] 4 times, p1, [k4, p2] 4 times, k4, p5.

Row 7 P5, [4-st LC, p2] twice, k4, p2, 4-st LC, p2, 9-st LC, p2, 4-st RC, p2, k4, [p2, 4-st RC] twice, p5.

Row 9 P5, [k4, p2] twice, *M1, [k4, p2] twice, k4, M1*, p1; rep between

*'s once, [p2, k4] twice, p5 –71 sts.

Row 11 P5, 4-st LC, p2, 4-st LC, p3, M1, k4, p2tog, 4-st LC, p2tog, k4, M1, p3, M1, k4, p2tog, 4-st RC, p2tog, k4, M1, p3, 4-st RC, p2, 4-st RC, p5.

Row 13 P5, k4, p2, k4, p4, M1, *k3, ssk, k4, k2tog, k3, M1*, p5; rep between *'s once, p4, k4, p2, k4, p5.

Row 15 P5, 4-st LC, p2, 4-st LC, p5, M1, k4, 4-st LC, k4, M1, p7, M1, k4, 4-st RC, k4, M1, p5, 4-st RC, p2, 4-st RC, p5—75 sts.

Row 17 P5, k4, p2, k4, p6, 12-st RC,

p9, 12-st LC, p6, k4, p2, k4, p5.

Row 19 P5, 4-st LC, p2, 4-st LC, p4, p2tog, k4, 4-st LC, k4, p2tog, p5, p2tog, k4, 4-st RC, k4, p2tog, p4, 4-st RC, p2, 4-st RC, p5 —71 sts.

Row 21 P5, k4, p2, k4, p3, *p2tog, [k4, M1] twice, k4, p2tog, p3; rep between *'s once, k4, p2, k4, p5.

Row 23 P5, [4-st LC, p2] twice, p2tog, k4, M1, p1, 4-st LC, p1, M1, k4, p2tog, p1, p2tog, k4, M1, p1, 4-st RC, p1, M1, k4, p2tog, [p2, 4-st RC] twice, p5.

Row 25 P5, k4, p2, k4, p1, p2tog,

[k4, p2] twice, k4, p3tog; rep between *'s once, p2tog, p1, k4, p2, k4, p567 sts.

Row 27 P5, [4-st LC, p2] twice, k4, p2, 4-st LC, p2, 9-st LC, p2, 4-st RC, p2, k4, [p2, 4-st RC] twice, p5.

Row 28 K the knit sts and p the purl sts.

Rep rows 1–28.

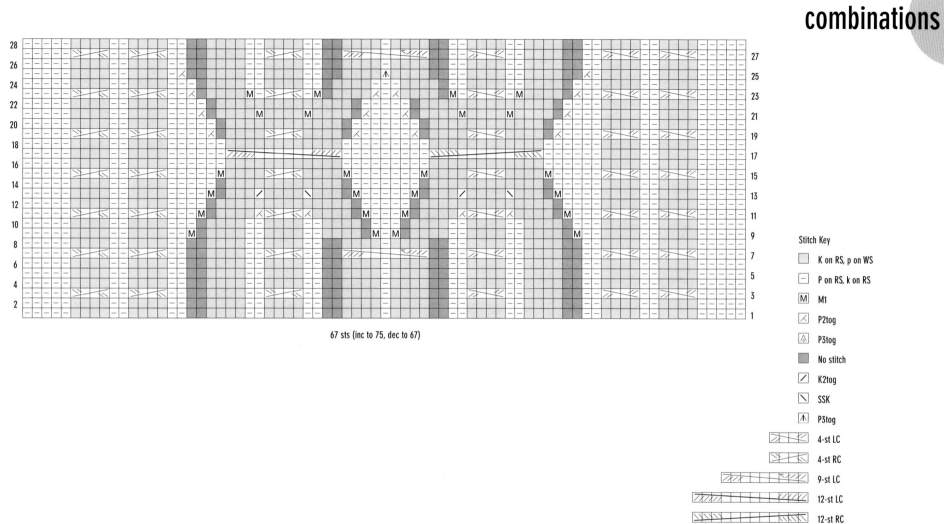

67 sts (inc to 75, dec to 67)

Stitch Key

☐	K on RS, p on WS
–	P on RS, k on RS
M	M1
⟋	P2tog
◹	P3tog
◼	No stitch
╱	K2tog
╲	SSK
⋀	P3tog
▱▱	4-st LC
▱▱	4-st RC
▱▱▱	9-st LC
▱▱▱▱	12-st LC
▱▱▱▱	12-st RC

3-st RPC Sl 1 st to cn and hold to back, k2, p1 from cn.

3-st LPC Sl 2 sts to cn and hold to front, p1, k2 from cn.

4-st RPC Sl 2 sts to cn and hold to back, k2, p2 from cn.

4-st LPC Sl 2 sts to cn and hold to front, p2, k2 from cn.

4-st RC Sl 2 sts to cn and hold to back, k2, k2 from cn.

4-st LC Sl 2 sts to cn and hold to front, k2, k2 from cn.

(worked over 55 sts)

Preparation row (WS) [K4, p4] twice, k5, p13, k5, [p4, k4] twice.

Row 1 [P4, 4-st RC] twice, p5, k13, p5, [4-st RC, p4] twice.

Row 2 [K4, p4] twice, k5, p13, k5, [p4, k4] twice.

Row 3 [P4, 4-st RC] twice, p5, 4-st LC, k2, p1, k2, 4-st RC, p5, [4-st RC, p4] twice.

Row 4 [K4, p4] twice, k5, p6, k1, p6, k5, [p4, k4] twice.

Row 5 P3, 3-st RPC, 4-st LPC, 4-st RPC, 3-st LPC, p4, k2, 4-st LC, p1, 4-st RC, k2, p4, 3-st RPC, 4-st LPC, 4-st RPC, 3-st LPC, p3.

Row 6 K3, p2, k3, p4, k3, p2, k4, p6, k1, p6, k4, p2, k3, p4, k3, p2, k3.

Row 7 P2, 3-st RPC, p3, 4-st RC, p3, 3-st LPC, p3, 4-st LC, k2, p1, k2, 4-st RC, p3, 3-st RPC, p3, 4-st RC, p3, 3-st LPC, p2.

Row 8 K2, p2, k4, p4, k4, p2, k3, p6, k1, p6, k3, p2, k4, p4, k4, p2, k2.

Row 9 P2, k2, p2, 4-st RPC, 4-st LPC, p2, k2, p3, k2, 4-st LC, p1, 4-st RC, k2, p3, k2, p2, 4-st RPC, 4-st LPC, p2, k2, p2.

Rows 10 and 12 [K2, p2] twice, k4, p2, k2, p2, k3, p6, k1, p6, k3, p2, k2, p2, k4, [p2, k2] twice.

Row 11 [P2, k2] twice, p4, k2, p2, k2, p3, 4-st LC, k2, p1, k2, 4-st RC, p3, k2, p2, k2, p4, [k2, p2] twice.

Row 13 P2, k2, p2, 4-st LPC, 4-st RPC, p2, k2, p3, k2, 4-st LC, p1, 4-st RC, k2, p3, k2, p2, 4-st LPC, 4-st RPC, p2, k2, p2.

Row 14 K2, p2, k4, p4, k4, p2, k3, p6, k1, p6, k3, p2, k4, p4, k4, p2, k2.

Row 15 P2, 3-st LPC, p3, 4-st RC, p3, 3-st RPC, p3, 4-st LC, k2, p1, k2, 4-st RC, p3, 3-st LPC, p3, 4-st RC, p3, 3-st RPC, p2.

Row 16 K3, p2, k3, p4, k3, p2, k4, p6, k1, p6, k4, p2, k3, p4, k3, p2, k3.

Row 17 P3, 3-st LPC, 4-st RPC, 4-st LPC, 3-st RPC, p4, k2, 4-st LC, p1, 4-st RC, k2, p4, 3-st LPC, 4-st RPC, 4-st LPC, 3-st RPC, p3.

Row 18 [K4, p4] twice, k5, p6, k1, p6, k5, [p4, k4] twice.

Rows 19, 23 and 27 [P4, 4-st RC] twice, p5, k2, p2, k5, p2, k2, p5, [4-st RC, p4] twice.

Rows 20, 22, 24 and 26 [K4, p4] twice, k5, p2, k2, p5, k2, p2, k5, [p4, k4] twice.

Rows 21 and 25 [P4, 4-st RC] twice, p5, k2, p9, k2, p5, [4-st RC, p4] twice.

Row 28 [K4, p4] twice, k5, p2, k2, p5, k2, p2, k5, [p4, k4] twice.

Rep rows 1–28.

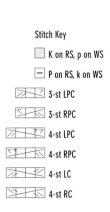

Stitch Key

■ K on RS, p on WS

− P on RS, k on WS

3-st LPC

3-st RPC

4-st LPC

4-st RPC

4-st LC

4-st RC

28 27
26 25
24 23
22 21
20 19
18 17
16 15
14 13
12 11
10 9
8   7
6   5
4   3
2   1

Prep row (WS)

55 sts

5-st RPC Sl 2 sts to cn and hold to back, k3, p2 from cn.

5-st LPC Sl 3 sts to cn and hold to front, p2, k3 from cn.

6-st RC Sl 3 sts to cn and hold to back, k3, k3 from cn.

6-st LC Sl 3 sts to cn and hold to front, k3, k3 from cn.

8-st RPC Sl 2 sts to cn and hold to back, k6, p2 from cn.

8-st LPC Sl 6 sts to cn and hold to front, p2, k6 from cn.

(worked over 62 sts)

Row 1 (RS) K6, p8, 6-st LC, p8, k6, p8, 6-st LC, p8, k6.

Row 2 and all WS rows K the knit sts and p the purl sts.

Row 3 K6, p6, 5-st RPC, 5-st LPC, p6, k6, p6, 5-st RPC, 5-st LPC, p6, k6.

Row 5 6-st RC, p4, 5-st RPC, p4, 5-st LPC, p4, 6-st RC, p4, 5-st RPC, p4, 5-st LPC, p4, 6-st RC.

Row 7 K6, p2, 5-st RPC, p8, 5-st LPC, p2, k6, p2, 5-st RPC, p8, 5-st LPC, p2, k6.

Row 9 K6, 5-st RPC, p12, 5-st LPC, k6, 5-st RPC, p12, 5-st LPC, k6.

Row 11 6-st RC, 5-st LPC, p12, 5-st RPC, 6-st RC, 5-st LPC, p12, 5-st RPC, 6-st RC.

Row 13 K6, p2, 5-st LPC, p8, 5-st RPC, p2, k6, p2, 5-st LPC, p8, 5-st RPC, p2, k6.

Row 15 K6, p4, 5-st LPC, p4, 5-st RPC, p4, k6, p4, 5-st LPC, p4, 5-st RPC, p4, k6.

Row 17 6-st RC, p6, 5-st LPC, 5-st RPC, p6, 6-st RC, p6, 5-st LPC, 5-st RPC, p6, 6-st RC.

Row 19 P3, 5-st LPC, p6, 6-st LC, p6, 5-st RPC, 5-st LPC, p6, 6-st LC, p6, 5-st RPC, p3.

Row 21 P5, 5-st LPC, p4, k6, p4, 5-st RPC, p4, 5-st LPC, p4, k6, p4, 5-st RPC, p5.

Row 23 P7, 5-st LPC, p2, k6, p2, 5-st RPC, p8, 5-st LPC, p2, k6, p2, 5-st RPC, p7.

Row 25 P9, 5-st LPC, 6-st LC, 5-st RPC, p12, 5-st LPC, 6-st LC, 5-st RPC, p9.

Row 27 P9, 8-st RPC, 8-st LPC, p12, 8-st RPC, 8-st LPC, p9.

Rows 29 and 31 P9, k6, p4, k6, p12, k6, p4, k6, p9.

Row 33 P7, 8-st RPC, p4, 8-st LPC, p8, 8-st RPC, p4, 8-st LPC, p7.

Rows 35 and 37 P7, [k6, p8] 3 times, k6, p7.

Row 39 P5, 8-st RPC, p8, 8-st LPC, p4, 8-st RPC, p8, 8-st LPC, p5.

Rows 41 and 43 P5, k6, p12, k6, p4, k6, p12, k6, p5.

Row 45 P3, [8-st RPC, p12, 8-st LPC] twice, p3.

Row 47 6-st RC, 5-st LPC, p12, 5-st RPC, 6-st RC, 5-st LPC, p12, 5-st RPC, 6-st RC.

Row 49 K6, p2, 5-st LPC, p8, 5-st RPC, p2, k6, p2, 5-st LPC, p8, 5-st RPC, p2, k6.

Row 51 K6, p4, 5-st LPC, p4, 5-st RPC, p4, k6, p4, 5-st LPC, p4, 5-st RPC, p4, k6.

Row 53 6-st RC, p6, 5-st LPC, 5-st RPC, p6, 6-st RC, p6, 5-st LPC, 5-st RPC, p6, 6-st RC.

Row 55 P3, 5-st LPC, p6, 6-st LC, p6, 5-st RPC, 5-st LPC, p6, 6-st LC, p6, 5-st RPC, p3.

Row 57 P5, 5-st LPC, p4, k6, p4, 5-st RPC, p4, 5-st LPC, p4, k6, p4, 5-st RPC, p5.

Row 59 P7, 5-st LPC, p2, k6, p2, 5-st RPC, p8, 5-st LPC, p2, k6, p2, 5-st RPC, p7.

Row 61 P9, 5-st LPC, 6-st LC, 5-st RPC, p12,

196

5-st LPC, 6-st LC, 5-st RPC, p9.

Row 63 P9, 5-st RPC, k6, 5-st LPC, p12, 5-st RPC, k6, 5-st LPC, p9.

Row 65 P7, 5-st RPC, p2, k6, p2, 5-st LPC, p8, 5-st RPC, p2, k6, p2, 5-st LPC, p7.

Row 67 P5, 5-st RPC, p4, 6-st LC, p4, 5-st LPC, p4, 5-st RPC, p4, 6-st LC, p4, 5-st LPC, p5.

Row 69 P3, 5-st RPC, p6, k6, p6, 5-st LPC, 5-st RPC, p6, k6, p6, 5-st LPC, p3.

Row 71 6-st RC, [p8, k6, p8, 6-st RC] twice.

Row 72 K the knit sts and p the purl sts.

Rep rows 1–72.

Stitch Key

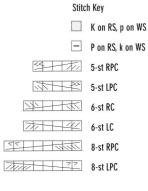

☐ K on RS, p on WS

— P on RS, k on WS

5-st RPC

5-st LPC

6-st RC

6-st LC

8-st RPC

8-st LPC

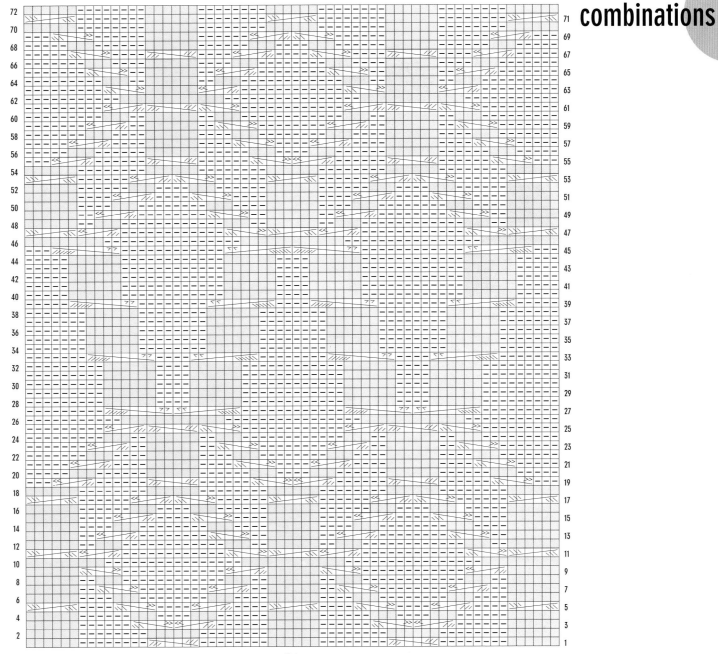

62 sts

4-st RC Sl 2 sts to cn and hold to back, k2, k2 from cn.

4-st LC Sl 2 sts to cn and hold to front, k2, k2 from cn.

8-st RC Sl 4 sts to cn and hold to back, k4, k4 from cn.

8-st LC Sl 4 sts to cn and hold to front, k4, k4 from cn.

Eyelet Cable

(worked over 8 sts)

Rows 1, 3 and 5 (RS) P2, ssk, yo, k2, p2.

Row 2 and all WS rows K2, p4, k2.

Row 7 P2, 4-st RC, p2.

Rows 9, 11 and 13 P2, k2, yo, k2tog, p2.

Row 15 P2, 4-st LC, p2.

Row 16 K2, p4, k2.

Rep rows 1–16.

Center Cable Panel

(worked over 20 sts)

Row 1 (RS) K2, p2, k12, p2, k2.

Rows 2, 4, 6, 8, 10, 12 and 14 P2, k2, p12, k2, p2.

Rows 3 and 11 K2, p2, 8-st RC, k4, p2, k2.

Rows 5, 9 and 13 K2, p2, k12, p2, k2.

Row 7 K2, p2, k4, 8-st LC, p2, k2.

Rows 15, 17, 19, 21 and 23 K2, p2, k3, yo, ssk, k4, yo, ssk, k1, p2, k2.

Rows 16, 18, 20, and 22 P2, k2, p3, yo, p2tog, p4, yo, p2tog, p1, k2, p2.

Row 24, P2, k2, p12, k2, p2.

Rep rows 1–24.

(worked over 36 sts)

Row 1 (RS) Eyelet cable, Cable panel, Eyelet cable.

Cont in pats as established.

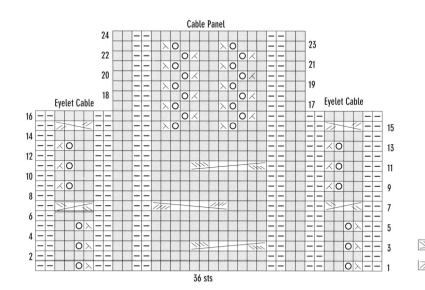

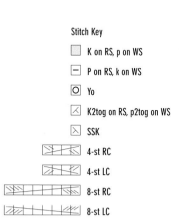

Stitch Key

◻ K on RS, p on WS

▭ P on RS, k on WS

⊙ Yo

╱ K2tog on RS, p2tog on WS

╲ SSK

4-st RC

4-st LC

8-st RC

8-st LC

2-st RC Sl 1 st to cn and hold in back, k1, k1 from cn.

2-st LC Sl 1 st to cn and hold in front, k1, k1 from cn.

2-st RPC Sl 1 st to cn and hold in back, k1, p1 from cn.

2-st LPC Sl 1 st to cn and hold in front, p1, k1 from cn.

Edge Pattern

(worked over 6 sts)

Row 1 (WS) P1, k1, p2, k1, p1.

Row 2 K1, p4, k1.

Rep rows 1–2.

Vine Panel

(worked over 24 sts)

Row 1 (WS) K5, p1, [k5, p2] twice, k4.

Row 2 P4, 2-st LC, p5, 2-st RC, p4, 2-st RPC, p5.

Row 3 K6, p1, k4, p2, k5, p2, k4.

Row 4 P3, 2-st RC, 2-st LC, p4, k2, p3, 2-st RPC, p6.

Row 5 K7, p1, k3, p2, k4, p4, k3.

Row 6 P2, 2-st RC, k2, 2-st LC, p3, 2-st RC, p2, 2-st RPC, p7.

Row 7 K8, p1, k2, p2, k3, p6, k2.

Row 8 P2, 2-st LPC, k2, 2-st RPC, p3, k2, p1, 2-st RPC, p8.

Row 9 K9, p1, k1, p2, k4, p4, k3.

Row 10 P3, 2-st LPC, 2-st RPC, p4, 2-st RC, 2-st RPC, p9.

Row 11 K10, p3, k5, p2, k4.

Row 12 P4, 2-st LPC, p5, k1, 2-st RPC, p10.

Row 13 K4, [p2, k5] twice, p1, k5.

Row 14 P5, 2-st LPC, p4, 2-st RC, p5, 2-st RC, p4.

Row 15 K4, p2, k5, p2, k4, p1, k6.

Row 16 P6, 2-st LPC, p3, k2, p4, 2-st RC, 2-st LC, p3.

Row 17 K3, p4, k4, p2, k3, p1, k7.

Row 18 P7, 2-st LPC, p2, 2-st RC, p3, 2-st RC, k2, 2-st LC, p2.

Row 19 K2, p6, k3, p2, k2, p1, k8.

Row 20 P8, 2-st LPC, p1, k2, p3, 2-st LPC, k2, 2-st RPC, p2.

Row 21 K3, p4, k4, p2, k1, p1, k9.

Row 22 P9, 2-st LPC, 2-st RC, p4, 2-st LPC, 2-st RPC, p3.

Row 23 K4, p2, k5, p3, k10.

Row 24 P10, 2-st LPC, k1, p5, 2-st RPC, p4.

Rep rows 1–24.

(worked over 36 sts)

Row 1 (WS) Edge pat, Vine panel, Edge pat.

Cont in pats as established.

Edge Pattern

6 sts

Vine Panel

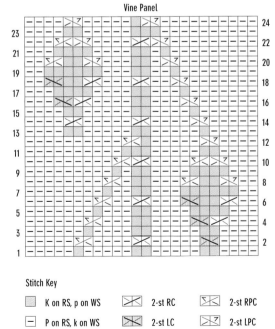

Stitch Key

- ▢ K on RS, p on WS
- ▭ P on RS, k on WS
- ⨝ 2-st RC
- ⨝ 2-st LC
- ⨝ 2-st RPC
- ⨝ 2-st LPC

198

5-st MB [K1, p1] twice, k1 into next st, [turn, p5, turn, k5] twice, slip 2nd, 3rd, 4th and 5th st over first.

MB Insert RH needle into next 2 sts as if to k2tog, [k1, p1] twice, k1 in these 2 sts, [turn, p5, turn, k5] twice, slip 3rd, 4th and 5th sts over first and 2nd st.

3-st RPC Sl 1 st to cn and hold to back, k2, p1 from cn.

3-st LPC Sl 2 sts to cn and hold to front, p1, k2 from cn.

4-st RC Sl 2 sts to cn and hold to back, k2, k2 from cn.

4-st RPC Sl 1 st to cn and hold to back, k3, p1 from cn.

4-st LPC Sl 3 sts to cn and hold to front, p1, k3 from cn.

7-st LPC Sl 4 sts to cn and hold to front, k3, then p1, k3 from cn.

Cable Twist
(worked over 20 sts)

Row 1 (RS) P2, k2, p4, 4-st RC, p4, k2, p2.

Row 2 and all WS rows K the knit sts and p the purl sts.

Row 3 P2, k2, p4, k4, p4, k2, p2.

Row 5 P2, k2, p4, 4-st RC, p4, k2, p2.

Row 7 P2, [3-st LPC, p2, 3-st RPC] twice, p2.

Row 9 P3, 3-st LPC, 3-st RPC, p2, 3-st LPC, 3-st RPC, p3.

Rows 11 and 15 P4, [4-st RC, p4] twice.

Row 13 P4, k4, p1, MB, p1, k4, p4.

Row 17 P3, 3-st RPC, 3-st LPC, p2, 3-st RPC, 3-st LPC, p3.

Row 19 P2, 3-st RPC, p2, 3-st LPC, 3-st RPC, p2, 3-st LPC, p2.

Row 20 K the knit sts and p the purl sts.

Rep rows 1–20.

Center Cable
(worked over 17 sts)

Row 1 (RS) P5, 7-st LPC, p5.

Row 2 and all WS rows K the knit sts and p the purl sts.

Row 3 P4, 4-st RPC, p1, 4-st LPC, p4.

Row 5 P3, 4-st RPC, p3, 4-st LPC, p3.

Row 7 P2, 4-st RPC, p5, 4-st LPC, p2.

Rows 9 and 13 P2, k3, p7, k3, p2.

Row 11 P2, k3, p3, 5-st MB, p3, k3, p2.

Row 15 P2, 4-st LPC, p5, 4-st RPC, p2.

Row 17 P3, 4-st LPC, p3, 4-st RPC, p3.

Row 19 P4, 4-st LPC, p1, 4-st RPC, p4.

Row 20 K the knit sts and p the purl sts.

Rep rows 1–20.

(worked over 57 sts)

Row 1 (RS) Cable twist, Center cable, Cable twist.

Cont in pats as established.

Stitch Key

☐ K on RS, p on WS	3-st RPC	4-st RPC
− P on RS, k on WS	3-st LPC	4-st LPC
• 5-st MB	4-st RC	7-st LPC
◆ MB		

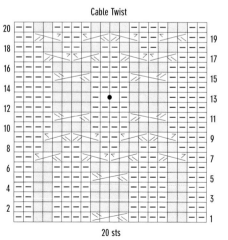

Cable Twist

20 sts

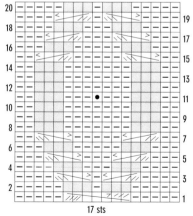

Center Cable

17 sts

combinations

8-st RC Sl 4 sts to cn and hold to back, k4, k4 from cn.

8-st LC Sl 4 sts to cn and hold to front, k4, k4 from cn.

12-st LC Sl 6 sts to cn and hold to front, k6, k6 from cn.

Left Cable

(worked over 12 sts)

Rows 1, 3, 7 and 9 (RS) Knit.

Row 2 and all WS rows Purl.

Row 5 12-st LC.

Row 10 Purl.

Rep rows 1–10.

Braid Panel

(multiple of 8 sts plus 12)

Row 1 (RS) *8-st LC; rep from *, end k4.

Rows 2, 4 and 6 Purl.

Rows 3 and 7 Knit.

Row 5 K4, *8-st RC; rep from * to end.

Row 8 Purl.

Rep rows 1–8.

(worked over 60 sts)

Preparation row (WS) K2, p12, k2, p28, k2, p12, k2.

Row 1 (RS) K2, Left cable, k2, Braid panel, k2, Left cable, k2.

Cont in pats as established.

Left Cable

```
10 |                | 
8  |                | 9
6  |                | 7
   |     ///////    | 5
4  |                | 3
2  |                | 1
        12 sts
```

Braid Panel

8-st rep

```
8  |                | 
6  |     ///////    | 7
4  |                | 5
2  |                | 3
   |     ///////    | 1
```

Stitch Key

☐ K on RS, p on WS

⬚⬚⬚ 8-st RC

⬚⬚⬚ 8-st LC

⬚⬚⬚ 12-st LC

2-st RPC Sl 1 st to cn and hold to back, k1, p1 from cn.

2-st LPC Sl 1 st to cn and hold to front, p1, k1 from cn.

4-st LC Sl 2 sts to cn and hold to front, k2, k2 from cn.

8-st LC Sl 4 sts to cn and hold to front, k4, k4 from cn.

8-st Cable

(worked over 8 sts)

Rows 1, 3 and 5 (RS) Knit.

Rows 2, 4 and 6 Purl.

Row 7 8-st LC.

Row 8 Purl.

Rep rows 1–8.

Lace Panel

(worked over 16 sts)

Row 1 (RS) P4, k1, p1, k4, p2, k2, p2.

Row 2 K2, p2, k2, p4, k1, p1, k4.

Row 3 P3, 2-st RPC, p1, 4-st LC, p2, yo, ssk, p2.

Row 4 K2, p2, k2, p4, k2, p1, k3.

Row 5 P2, 2-st RPC, p2, k4, p2, k2tog, yo, p2.

Row 6 K2, p2, k2, p4, k3, p1, k2.

Row 7 P1, 2-st RPC, p3, 4-st LC, p2, yo, ssk, p2.

Row 8 K2, p2, k2, p4, k4, p1, k1.

Row 9 P1, 2-st LPC, p3, k4, p2, k2tog, yo, p2.

Row 10 K2, p2, k2, p4, k3, p1, k2.

Row 11 P2, 2-st LPC, p2, 4-st LC, p2, yo, ssk, p2.

Row 12 K2, p2, k2, p4, k2, p1, k3.

Row 13 P3, 2-st LPC, p1, k4, p2, k2tog, yo, p2.

Row 14 K2, p2, k2, p4, k1, p1, k4.

Row 15 P6, 4-st LC, p6.

Row 16 K6, p4, k6.

Row 17 P2, k2, p2, k4, p4, k1, p1.

Row 18 K1, p1, k4, p4, k2, p2, k2.

Row 19 P2, yo, ssk, p2, 4-st LC, p3, 2-st RPC, p1.

Row 20 K2, p1, k3, p4, k2, p2, k2.

Row 21 P2, k2tog, yo, p2, k4, p2, 2-st RPC, p2.

Row 22 K3, p1, k2, p4, k2, p2, k2.

Row 23 P2, yo, ssk, p2, 4-st LC, p1, 2-st RPC, p3.

Row 24 K4, p1, k1, p4, k2, p2, k2.

Row 25 P2, k2tog, yo, p2, k4, p1, 2-st LPC, p3.

Row 26 K3, p1, k2, p4, k2, p2, k2.

Row 27 P2, yo, ssk, p2, 4-st LC, p2, 2-st LPC, p2.

Row 28 K2, p1, k3, p4, k2, p2, k2.

Row 29 P2, k2tog, yo, p2, k4, p3, 2-st LPC, p1.

Row 30 K1, p1, k4, p4, k2, p2, k2.

Row 31 P6, 4-st LC, p6.

Row 32 K6, p4, k6.

Rep rows 1–32.

(worked over 36 sts)

Row 1 (RS) P2, 8-st Cable, Lace panel, 8-st cable, p2.

Cont in pats as established.

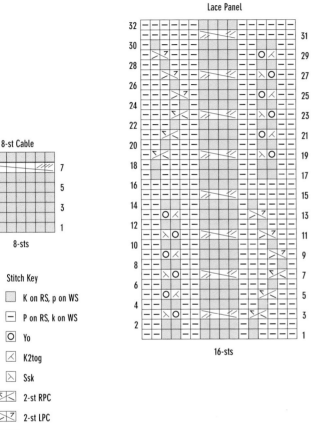

Lace Panel

8-st Cable

8-sts

Stitch Key

K on RS, p on WS

— P on RS, k on WS

O Yo

K2tog

Ssk

2-st RPC

2-st LPC

4-st LC

8-st LC

16-sts

4-st RC Sl 2 sts to cn and hold to back, k2, k2 from cn.

4-st LC Sl 2 sts to cn and hold to front, k2, k2 from cn.

6-st RC Sl 3 sts to cn and hold to back, k3, k3 from cn.

6-st LC Sl 3 sts to cn and hold to front, k3, k3 from cn.

Cable Twist

(worked over 6 sts)

Row 1 (RS) P1, k4, p1.

Row 2 and all WS rows K1, p4, k1.

Row 3 P1, 4-st RC, p1.

Row 5 P1, k4, p1.

Row 7 P1, 4-st LC, p1.

Row 8 K1, p4, k1.

Rep rows 1–8.

Center Cable

(worked over 20 sts)

Row 1 (RS) P7, k6, p7.

Row 2 K7, p6, k7.

Row 3 P4, k3, 6-st RC, k3, p4.

Rows 4, 6 and 8 K4, p12, k4.

Rows 5 and 7 P4, k12, p4.

Row 9 P1, k3, 6-st RC, 6-st LC, k3, p1.

Rows 10, 12 and 14 K1, p6, [k1, p1] twice, k1, p7, k1.

Rows 11 and 13 P1, k6, [p1, k1] twice, p1, k7, p1.

Row 15 P1, 6-st RC, [p1, k1] 3 times, 6-st LC, p1.

Rows 16, 18 and 20 K1, p4, [k1, p1] 5 times, k1, p3, k1.

Rows 17 and 19 P1, k4, [p1, k1] 5 times, p1, k3, p1.

Row 21 P1, 6-st LC, [p1, k1] 3 times, 6-st RC, p1.

Rows 22, 24 and 26 K1, p6, [k1, p1] twice, k1, p7, k1.

Rows 23 and 25 P1, k6, [p1, k1] twice, p1, k7, p1.

Row 27 P1, k3, 6-st LC, 6-st RC, k3, p1.

Rows 28, 30 and 32 K4, p12, k4.

Rows 29 and 31 P4, k12, p4.

Row 33 P7, 6-st RC, p7.

Row 34 K7, p6, k7.

Row 35 P7, k6, p7.

Row 36 K7, p6, k7.

Rep rows 1–36.

(worked over 32 sts)

Row 1 (RS) Cable twist, Center cable, Cable twist.

Cont in pats as established.

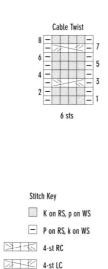

Cable Twist

6 sts

Stitch Key

☐ K on RS, p on WS

— P on RS, k on WS

4-st RC

4-st LC

6-st RC

6-st LC

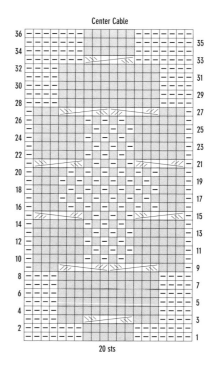

Center Cable

20 sts

approx – approximately

beg – begin; begins; beginning

cn – cable needle

cont – continue; continuing

dec – decrease; decreasing

dpn – double pointed needle

inc – increase; increasing

k – knit

k-b; k1-b – knit stitch in row below

k2tog – knit two together

k3tog – knit three together

LH – left-hand

lp; lps – loop; loops

m1 – make one

m1 p-st – make one purl stitch

p – purl

pat; pats – pattern; patterns

pm – place marker

psso – pass slip stitch over

p2tog – purl two together

p3tog – purl three together

rem – remain; remaining

rep – repeat

RH – right-hand

RS – right side

SKP – slip one, knit one, pass slip stitch over

SK2P – slip one, knit two together, pass slip stitch over

sl – slip

sm – slip marker

ssk – slip, slip, knit

st; sts – stitch; stitches

St st – stockinette stitch

tbl – through back loop

tog – together

WS – wrong side

wyib – with yarn in back

wyif – with yarn in front

yo – yarn over

yo twice; yo2 – yarn over two times

Yarn overs

1. Between two knit stitches

Bring the yarn from the back of the work to the front between the two needles. Knit the next stitch, bringing the yarn to the back over the right needle as shown.

2. Between two purl stitches

Leave the yarn at the front of the work. Bring the yarn to the back over the right needle and to the front again as shown. Purl the next stitch.

3. Between a knit and a purl stitch

Bring the yarn from the back to the front between the two needles, then to the back over the right needle and to the front again as shown. Purl the next stitch.

4. Between a purl and a knit stitch

Leave the yarn at the front of the work. Knit the next stitch, bringing the yarn to the back over the right needle as shown.

5. At the beginning of a knit row

Keep the yarn at the front of the work. Insert the right needle knitwise into the first stitch on the left needle. Bring the yarn over the right needle to the back and knit the next stitch, holding the yarn over with your thumb if necessary.

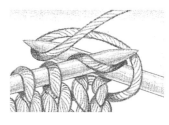

6. At the beginning of a purl row

To work a yarn over at the beginning of a purl row, keep the yarn at the back of the work. Insert the right needle purlwise into the first stitch on the left needle. Purl the stitch.

7. Multiple yarn overs

a. For multiple yarn overs (two or more), wrap the yarn around the needle as for a single yarn over, then wrap the yarn around the needle once more (or as many times as indicated). Work the next stitch on the left needle.

b. Alternate knitting and purling into the multiple yarn over on the subsequent row, always knitting the last stitch on a purl row and purling the last stitch on a knit row.

as foll Work the instructions that follow.

end last rep After completing a full repeat of a pattern and not enough stitches remain to complete another repeat, end the pattern repeat as directed.

hold to front (back) of work A term usually referring to stitches placed on a cable needle that are held to the front (or the back) of the work as it faces you.

k the knit sts and p the purl sts (as they face you) A phrase used when a pattern of knit and purl stitches has been established and will continue for a determined length (such as ribbing). Work the stitches as they face you: Knit the knit stitches and purl the purl stitches.

k the purl sts and p the knit sts: A phrase used when a pattern of knit and purl stitches will alternate on the following row or rows (such as in a seed stitch pattern). Work the stitches opposite of how they face you: Purl the knit stitches and knit the purl stitches.

knitwise (or as to knit) Insert the needle into the stitch as if you were going to knit it.

m1 Make one knit stitch as follows: Insert left needle from front to back under horizontal strand between stitch just worked and next stitch on left needle. Knit this strand through the back loop.

m1 p-st Make one purl stitch as follows: Insert left needle from front to back under horizontal strand between stitch just worked and next stitch on left needle. Purl this strand through the back loop.

multiple of . . . sts Used when working a pattern. The total number of stitches should be divisible by the number of stitches in one pattern repeat.

multiple of . . . sts plus . . . Used when working a pattern. The total number of stitches should be divisible by the number of stitches in one pattern repeat, plus the extra stitches (added only once).

next row (RS), or (WS) The row following the one just worked will be a right side (or wrong side) row.

place marker(s) Slide a stitch marker either onto the needle (where it is slipped every row) or attach it to a stitch, where it remains as a guide.

preparation row A row that sets up the stitch pattern but is not part of the pattern repeat.

purlwise Insert the needle into the stitch as if you were going to purl it.

rep from *, end . . . Repeat the instructions that begin at the asterisk as many times as you can work full repeats of the pattern, then end the row as directed.

rep from * to end Repeat the instructions that begin at the asterisk, ending the row with a full repeat of the pattern.

rep . . . times more Repeat a direction the designated number of times (not counting the first time you work it).

right side (or RS) Usually refers to the surface of the work that will face outside when the garment is worn.

row 2 and all WS (even-numbered) rows A term used when all the wrong-side or even-numbered rows are worked the same.

skp On RS, slip one stitch. Knit next stitch and pass slip stitch over knit stitch. On WS, slip next two stitches knitwise. Slip these two

stitches back to left needle without twisting them and purl them together through the back loops.

sk2p On RS, slip one stitch, knit two stitches together. Pass slipped stitch over two stitches knit together. On WS, slip two stitches to right needle as if knitting two together. Slip next stitch knitwise. Slip all stitches to left needle without twisting them. Purl these three stitches together through back loops.

slip marker To keep the stitch marker in the same position from one row to the next, transfer it from one needle to the other as you work each row.

ssk On RS, slip next two stitches knitwise. Insert tip of left needle into fronts of these two stitches and knit them together. On WS, slip one stitch, purl one stitch, then pass slip stitch over purl stitch.

stockinette stitch Knit every right-side row and purl every wrong-side row.

work to end Work the established pattern to the end of the row.

acknowledgments

Special thanks to:

The Knitters:

Lisa Buccellato

Jeannie Chin

Victoria Hilditch

Margarita Mejia

Charlotte Parry

Sandi Prosser

And also:

Maria Gerbino

Karen Greenwald

Claire Hilditch

Jenn Jarvis

Veronica Manno

Michelle Wiener

All yarn provided by Karabella Yarns

1201 Broadway

New York, NY 10001

Knitting needles on cover provided by Lantern Moon.

Lantern Moon knitting needles are currently available in 4 distinct wood varieties.

Made entirely by hand, they are the perfect tool for knitters. The design detail and handfinishing

makes these needles as wonderful to work with as they are beautiful. Visit Lantern Moon online at

www.lanternmoon.com.

notes

notes